Robert Donington, O.B.E., Hon. R.A.M., is
a musician and writer of international
distinction, now living in retirement but
active on another book.

MUSIC AND ITS INSTRUMENTS

MUSIC AND ITS INSTRUMENTS

ROBERT DONINGTON

METHUEN & CO. LTD

First published in 1982 by
Methuen & Co. Ltd
11 New Fetter Lane, London EC4P 4EE
Published in the USA by
Methuen & Co.
in association with Methuen, Inc.
733 Third Avenue, New York, NY 10017

Typeset by Scarborough Typesetting Services
and printed in Great Britain at the
University Press, Cambridge

British Library Cataloguing in Publication Data

Music and its instruments.
Donington, Robert
1. Musical instruments
I. Title
781.91   ML 460
ISBN 0 416 72270 9
ISBN 0 416 72280 6 Pbk

Library of Congress Cataloging in Publication Data

Donington, Robert.
Music and its instruments.
Bibliography: p.
Includes index.
1. Musical instruments.   I. Title.
ML460.D63 1982   781.91   82–8012
ISBN 0–416–72270–9   AACR2
ISBN 0–416–72280–6 (University paperback: pbk.)

CONTENTS

LIST OF PLATES

LIST OF TEXT FIGURES

Figs 1–5 and Fig. 13 are after Dayton C. Miller's *Sound Waves: Their*

Shape and Speed (1937) New York, The Macmillan Co. Figs 6–12 and 14–20 were specially prepared at the Department of Physics, University College, Cardiff, under the direction of Professor Charles A. Taylor, D.Sc., F.Inst.P.

PREFACE

Music is a subject of much importance to those whose lives are enriched by it, not only for enjoyable entertainment and relaxation, but for some deeper significance. What this significance may be is not on the face of it very obvious, since it does not contribute directly to survival as do the pleasures of eating and drinking, working, sleeping or mating, yet it has none of the appearance of being a mere casual pastime. On the contrary, music holds by common consent a power for inner reassurance and satisfaction which must stem from quite deep within the human spirit. Like life itself, music has a value which needs no accounting, being quite simply its own justification. Nevertheless, we have a very natural curiosity about the ways and means of this extraordinary bonus, given to almost everyone in some manner and degree, and to many people so keenly that they would count themselves very much the poorer without it.

Music results from operations which are material and lie within the customary methods of scientific investigation. It is possible to approach from that direction, asking how music works before asking why music works, and thus coming up on relatively solid ground to those boundaries of mind and matter where scientific method, though it is not irrelevant, is harder to apply. Many years ago I made an early attempt at this (*The Instruments of Music* (1949) Methuen, London), which had a long run and a moderate amount of success: partly, I think, because it was written so very much from a musician's point of view; and partly because it was checked for scientific accuracy by several colleagues, of whom the chief was that distinguished physicist and acoustician, Llewellyn S. Lloyd. When Lloyd at last expressed himself contented, I knew I should not fall down from mere inadvertent ignorance; and I dare say my own eagerness and pleasure conveyed themselves to readers having the same sort of curiosity, until in due course of time an exceptionally fertile sequence of acoustical advances put my already much-revised text beyond the reach

of any further up-dating. When Methuen asked me for another re-
vision, I offered them another book instead; and a very different book
it has turned out to be.

My first and very cordial thanks this time go to a most persistent and
constructive critic, Hugh Boyle, himself previously associated with
Llewellyn S. Lloyd and, more recently, both editing and continuing the
work of that great teacher; he has taken remarkable pains on my behalf.
On the highly technical and important subjects of electronic devices
and electronic music, I wish to express my thanks to Dr Peter Manning
of Durham University, with whom it has been a particular pleasure to
associate because he and I from quite different points of departure have
arrived at so much the same attitude toward the potentialities and
achievements of that exciting scene. We are both trying, as it seems to
us, to build the same kind of bridge from different ends. If you call the
two ends art and science you are, of course, grossly over-simplifying the
issue; but there is certainly some such meeting of the ways involved,
and I wish to pay tribute to Dr Manning's musicianly understanding
not less than to his technological support.

Professor Charles Taylor of University College, Cardiff, put himself
to yet more trouble, reading not only a part but the whole of my
finished text; and I have his kind permission to quote him as writing to
me that he found it 'quite absorbing', and that 'it was especially interesting to see how closely your attitudes as a musician and mine as a
scientist converged to common conclusions'. He added: 'in many
places you have a refreshingly different way of presenting scientific facts
which will certainly appeal to musicians. Some of these will sound a
little odd to scientists; but only if they are actually incorrectly based
have I mentioned them' – and I have done my best to correct them
before going to press. He, too, has my very grateful thanks. He and his
students also provided the wave traces and frequency analyses for Figs
6–12 and 14–20, which they prepared specially to illustrate exactly the
points of comparison which I wanted to make clear.

The slant of the book remains my own; but I hope it may point in a
direction where disciplines meet and new enquiries breed just as fast as
old ones are satisfied.

Robert Donington
Firle, E. Sussex

Spring, 1981

1 SOUND AND SENSE

EXPERIENCING MUSIC

What is happening to us when we are experiencing music? Something quite complicated on a variety of levels, but all of them connected with the fact of sound. It is this fact of sound itself which first requires description.

We can talk of sound existing out there. On a mechanical level, certain objective characteristics of our universe impinge on us, so that sound can be described in terms of physical events and mathematical calculations. But that does not complete a description of sound.

We can talk of sound entering our awareness. On a physiological level, our ears, our nerves and our brains process sound as subjective responses which vary with different people, though always within the mechanical possibilities of that physical universe of which we too are parts. And this, again, does not complete a description of sound.

We can talk of sound becoming sense. On a mental level, the psyche exerts an influence which includes not only rational but also irrational elements, as our entire human dilemma today makes evident; but then so also do the glorious irrationalities of art. Sound on a mental level can serve for speech and other forms of communication, including music. We can call music an experience of mind and body, a psycho-somatic experience, from which we should not wish to be deprived either of the mental or of the bodily sensations. It is true that we can sometimes enjoy music through the mind alone, but that is only in so far as we can recall having enjoyed it previously through the ears in the ordinary way. In short: to complete a description of sound we have to include everything that we are making of it through past and present associations and expectations, which in turn are linked with past and present feelings and intuitions. For sound is both outer stimulus and inner experience. Music, which we owe to sound, is acoustics, and music is meaning. We might put it that the physics and the physiology of music can be very elegantly measured, while the psychology of music cannot strictly be measured at all; but it is, of course, the object of the exercise.

WHAT DEFINES A MUSICAL EXPERIENCE?

For the purposes of this book, music may be defined as any sound having a musical intention. Whether that musical intention produces a musical response is a secondary though not an unimportant question. It is important whether the music is good or bad or to your liking or not to your liking; but that is a valuation or a choice rather than a definition. To have a musical intention merely implies having an urge to communicate by sonorous images. In the first instance, we may be communicating with ourselves, music being one way of focusing some of those imperious feelings and intuitions which are so apt to surge through us unsought and to demand expression as if of their own accord. In the second instance, we may be communicating either incidentally or deliberately with other people, which is possible because we are at bottom very similar and respond to similar images with similar emotions and associations. A full response to the more developed forms is of course only possible for the relatively gifted and experienced; but very few people who have hearing at all will miss the simpler messages.

Casual sounds have nothing of this human sort to communicate, except when we ourselves project meanings into them, as we may with the drippings of a tap or the rhythms of a railway train (or more systematically in *musique concrète*). Bird-song has something to communicate; but that is for the birds. Music is for human communication; and our chief novelty in this respect today has been in extending the range of sounds (including electronic sounds) which we make available to musical intention. Our experience of music has not been deepened as a consequence. But it has certainly been widened.

CURRENT EXTENSIONS OF MUSICAL EXPERIENCE

There have been other extensions of our musical experience in recent years, besides this remarkable extension in the kinds of sound regarded as acceptable for music. One has been an influx of Oriental and African material, particularly in rhythm and in various percussive instruments of rhythm. Another comes from the wide repertories of early music. These are so rightly preferred now in their own original sonorities that many of those sonorities are returning to current familiarity, and bringing back forgotten values from the past just as surely as electronic technology is evolving fresh values towards the future. No new principle is involved, since sound, however originated, behaves acoustically in the same basic ways. Nor have the traditional processes of music been invalidated; but they have not remained unaffected, since a good, more or less traditional composer will not be unaware of what is going on around him untraditionally.

Whether traditional or untraditional, my selection of material here will be guided by what is currently familiar. Sound and hearing generally will be my first concerns, and more particularly the underlying connections between our physiological and our psychological responses to the physical impact of sound. Then four great instrumental orders will be introduced: the traditional strings, wind and percussion, and the untraditional electronics. The traditional classifications are of course very approximate, but simple and well understood, whereas the more exact classifications available scientifically are not only complicated but (because of the intricate overlapping of actual instruments) cannot at best be wholly consistent, so that I have not thought it necessary to make use of them. The working methods of each order next lead up to our usual instruments arranged by families, grouped in their turn by their acoustic affinities. There is much else in the world which could as well have come in, but outlining our Western practices is task enough, and I have been more set on meeting the recent expansion of acoustic theory to allow, as we now must, for a greater contribution by subjective factors to our appreciation of objective sound.

The hearer and the heard cannot be separated; both physiologically and psychologically we affect that which we hear; the interface of mind and matter is that much mutual. Music is of the imagination, but the imagination is of the sound and the sound is of the instruments. That is why it is practicable to approach the meaning of the music by way of its acoustics, as this book attempts.

2 THE SOURCES OF SOUND

SOUND AS VIBRATION

The basic characteristic of our physical universe from which sound arises is that exceedingly pervasive embodiment of energy: vibration. Not all vibration is a source of sound, but only vibration within quite narrow limits out of the vast range occurring. Only through vibration, however, can sound arise. On a mechanical level, sound is vibration.

Now vibration can broadly be described as oscillation of which the repercussions rebound with a force equal to the force of impulse, subject to frictional or other loss of energy. The restoring force which causes the rebound is built up by departing from a point of equilibrium, which it overshoots on its return journey, thus again building itself up as a restoring force, which again overshoots. Hence there is an inherent regularity in the basic process of vibration; and its motion is symmetrical in so far as it is not disturbed by irregularities of resistance outside or inside the vibrating substance.

Such symmetrical motion can be described as pendular motion (since the pendulum is an obvious example of it), and one mathematical term for this is periodic (since the period within which its oscillations recur is, unless disturbed, the same in time, even when its extent in space diminishes with loss of energy); another term is harmonic, and another is sinusoidal. But when from any cause the oscillations do not repeat themselves symmetrically, the vibration can no longer be described as periodic or harmonic, but constitutes unperiodic or unharmonic vibration. Yet it may still be self-perpetuating, subject as usual to any incidental loss of energy. We shall find that both periodic and unperiodic vibration are significant for sound: periodic vibrations as the basic source of tone, and unperiodic vibrations as the basic source of noise.

The vibrations of sound are not different in principle from other vibrations, but only in being of a frequency which the ear can detect.

Even at their slowest, which is about twenty in a second, they are too fast for either the ear or the eye to follow separately, while at their fastest, which may barely reach in the most favourable circumstances to about 20,000 in a second, they are very much too fast. But they are not in any other respect a special kind of vibration. The balance wheel of a watch can easily be seen in periodic vibration, as the hairspring is compressed and relaxed in equal times and spaces, energy being maintained from the wound-up mainspring. A clock whose going is controlled by a pendulum will likewise show its visible displacement, which may be started by hand, and continued on either side of its centre of gravity by momentum; the energy required to overcome the loss by friction is again supplied by a wound-up spring or a falling weight (the spring must be wound or the weight raised again at needed intervals, or electric power imparted, since energy must come from somewhere and some friction is unavoidable under terrestrial conditions). The watch or the clock then goes quite evenly, and seems to go quite continuously, though it does in fact stop and start again at each reversal of its oscillation.

It is also possible to control a watch or a clock by the periodic oscillations of a very small electric current through the particles of a quartz crystal, vibrating so rapidly that a phenomenal degree of accuracy can be obtained. But rapid or slow, the principle of vibration remains the same. Subject to any distorting factors present in practice, vibration is in principle periodic. The period of repercussion or oscillation can be measured and described as vibration cycles per second (v.c.p.s.) or merely cycles per second (c.p.s.), now more commonly termed Hertz (Hz) after the distinguished physicist of that name (but this term is not so self-explanatory). The cycles are assumed to be double vibrations: i.e. in both directions from the point of equilibrium, out and back on one side, and out and back on the other side, when the next cycle begins.

Travelling sound vibrations are called sound waves; but they should not be compared too literally with waves in water. The up-and-down oscillations (often superimposed in very complicated patterns) of surface waves in water are indeed a visible instance of transverse vibration, such as occurs acoustically in vibrating strings. Air columns in wind instruments, and the atmosphere when transmitting sound, use longitudinal vibration, of which the oscillations are in-and-out: alternate compressions and rarefactions, i.e. pressure waves.

Vibration, then, is a pervasive characteristic of our physical universe; and sound is vibration within limits of frequency which are relatively narrow, but wide enough for the manifold complexities of the musician's craft. Vibration within these limits is audible, and thus comprises sound; vibration outside these limits is not audible, and thus does not comprise sound. It is in this sense that, on a mechanical level, we can describe sound as vibration.

FREQUENCY AND AMPLITUDE: PITCH

Frequency of vibration (the number of complete double cycles of repercussion alternating within a given time) is influenced primarily by the properties of the vibrating substance or structure and no more than secondarily by the manner of imparting the vibrations. Thus the frequency at which a pendulum will oscillate depends basically on its length, while the frequency at which a hairspring will oscillate depends basically upon its tension in relation to its length.

On the other hand, the distance traversed by the pendulum or spring during each cycle of its oscillation depends basically upon the energy imparted. Greater force imparts more energy and moves the pendulum or spring farther beyond the point of equilibrium before the build-up of a restoring force is sufficient to overcome its momentum and thus to stop and reverse its motion, again overshooting by a greater distance. This distance of maximum oscillation or displacement is called the amplitude, and basically it affects the frequency not at all. For as a moving pendulum or spring loses energy, so its swing grows narrower and slower until it finally comes to rest. But its rate of oscillation persists virtually unaltered to the last.

Frequency (which is a function of time) is the basic factor governing pitch in music. Amplitude (which is a function of energy) is the basic factor governing loudness. The greater the frequency, the higher the pitch; the greater the amplitude, the more the loudness. Both frequency and amplitude are quantities which can be measured scientifically. Both pitch and loudness are responses which occur subjectively in the ear-brain system, and cannot strictly be measured. The relationships are not exact although they may be approximately valid.

The speed of sound itself is a further basic factor, variable in different substances, but nearly (not quite) constant for a given substance. That essential substance on whose presence around us human life depends, air, is the most important medium by which sounds impinge upon us – in any ordinary circumstances, very nearly the only medium. The speed of sound in air is approximately twelve miles a minute, or just short of five seconds a mile: or say 345 metres a second.

The speed varies somewhat at different temperatures, with appreciable consequences for music; and it also varies somewhat for different pitches and intensities within the use of music, though fortunately not beyond the bounds of our habitual tolerance when interpreting acoustic signals.

The speed of sound in water can hardly be of much consequence to a musician, though it has other bearings both theoretical and practical: it is considerably faster, at about one second per mile. But the speed of sound in metal, at perhaps around one third of a second per mile with some variation by temperature, apparently affects brass instruments very appreciably; and other substances including wood and ivory may exert some similar influence upon instruments made of them (it is uncertain how much influence or in quite what ways). The substance, most often wood, of which the floor is made, is of detectable though ordinarily negligible significance since some very small proportion of the perceived sound may be reaching us through this unlikely medium. But for broad purposes, the speed of sound may be regarded as a constant within the range of pitches and intensities reaching us in the ordinary way as music.

Because the speed at which sound travels under given circumstances is broadly a constant, the frequency and the length of sound waves are related factors. Thus if the frequency is high, there is little time for the wave to travel between one cycle and the next; hence the wavelength, which is the distance between one wave crest and the next, is small. But if the frequency is low, there is more time; hence the wave can travel further between one cycle and the next, and the wavelength is greater. If two men wish to walk at the same speed, but one man has short legs while the other man has long legs, then in order to keep together, they must not keep in step: the man with shorter legs must take more frequent paces, while the man with longer legs must take less frequent paces. But whereas the frequency of a sound vibration is thus necessarily correlated with its wavelength, its amplitude is not. When the amounts of energy imparted so determine it, notes of the same pitch can impart a different loudness, and notes of the same loudness can be at a different pitch.

The range of vibration frequencies to which the human ear and its linked nervous and cerebral systems can respond with the sensation of sound is not precisely delimited, since it varies substantially between individuals, and still more so with disease, abnormality or advancing age. But in the best of conditions, less than about 20 Hz or more than about 20,000 Hz almost certainly make no aural impression whatsoever, though slower vibrations may thud at our body as a whole, while faster vibrations, if intense, may cause a most uncomfortable or painful reaction which is not sound, but distresses us as if it were just over the perceptible edge of sound. When steam engines were the normal locomotives on railway lines, and steam was escaping at high intensity causing vibration just above the audible frequency, you learnt not to stand too close because of the unpleasant sensation it set up in and around your ears: and of course electronic equipment can be used for experiments of this and other kinds. At the opposite extreme, very large and low-pitched organ pipes can be felt throbbing away without actually being heard. People have been known to fall in step with pulsations too slow and deep to be perceived as sound. And dogs can hear and obey a whistle at too high a pitch for any human to detect at all.

The squeak of a bat at about 15,000 Hz may be quite audible to keen and youthful ears, but not to old people, or to some people in any condition of health and years. Indeed, it is doubtful if any frequencies higher than about 12,000 Hz produce musically significant effects upon the quality of the tone in practice, although they might quite reasonably be expected to do so in theory. The lowest standard note of the piano is tuned to 27 Hz. Organs may often go lower; but it has come to seem very unlikely that we hear notes even as low as the bottom of the piano directly. They may more probably be constituted or reconstituted for our hearing system by subjective processing of component vibrations at much higher pitch. There may be other complicating factors, such as a possible effect of great intensity on pitch, but they do not invalidate the broad working principle that our sensation of pitch comes from vibration frequency.

The more regularly a sound settles into periodic vibration, the more distinctly we perceive it as tone definite in pitch. The more irregularly a sound fluctuates through unperiodic vibration, the more indistinctly we perceive it as noise indefinite in pitch. Yet this is in practice a difference only of degree. No sound can start in steady state, because the impetus which starts it is itself a disturbance; no sound in music achieves a wholly steady state such as can be closely approximated in an electronic laboratory; only some sounds in actual music last long enough to settle nearly as steadily as many laboratory experiments imply; no sound ends without some stage of decline. But once again, these situations which may be so complicated in practice in no way invalidate the basic principle that tone is regular vibration and noise is irregular vibration, however diverse the proportions in which we may expect to find them mingled.

The element of noise which enters into all music is no longer regarded as an undesirable though unavoidable impurity. On the contrary, it is necessary for the defining and recognition of instrumental colourings, and the irregularity which it introduces adds a spice of individuality to what might otherwise be too monotonous a symmetry. Mere background noise is always present in a room or hall, but is in the main ignored, in part because it is normally at small loudness, and in part because our attention is not being given to it. There is a very considerable marginal noise from fingers, keyboards, keywork and the like which is also ignored, though subliminally it may help our recognition. But into the actual tone of instruments, including voices, noise brings other, far from negligible characteristics of which neither the extent nor the positive value were until recently appreciated.

Instruments of percussion in which noise is intentionally prominent or decisive have, it is true, always been much used, and in recent music have taken a far greater share than previously, both for their timbre and for their rhythmic qualities (as well as their pitch in so far as it may be distinctly defined). But it is a new discovery how necessary an element noise comprises in the sound of voices, strings and wind, for the enjoyment and even for the recognition of their tone itself. This is particularly the case during the onset of a note, before it has had time to settle into a more or less regular and periodic mode of vibration. If the start of a note recorded on tape is cut off, and the note is then played back deprived by this means of its onset, the difficulty of recognizing what instrument is playing can be very considerable. Under these conditions, an oboe has been mistaken for a clarinet, a cello for a bassoon, a horn for a flute and other such seemingly improbable confusions. After the onset, the proportion of noise to tone diminishes steeply as a rule (without however disappearing) on such instruments; but the significance of the onset (where most noise occurs) under the actual conditions of music could not be more clearly indicated. It is really quite crucial. Conversely, however, the character of the onset is itself conditioned by the same factors which may then condition the steady state and also the decay. It is only that we must take the package as a whole, not simply its middle portion.

The state of a note at onset may include such mechanical noises as that due to the relaxation of a guitar's body when the plucked string is released, or the 'chiff' of an organ pipe as the air emerges from the flue (together with any noise from the movement of the pallet); but during onset there are also irregular vibrations while the string or the air-column is settling down. The qualities thus imparted during this initial period are transient and can be described as transients. The state of a note after its onset may, if it is long enough, become relatively stable, and the qualities then attained can be described as its steady state. The decline of a note, which can be described as its decay, may begin as soon as what would be its steady state is momentarily reached, if no further energy is being imparted: plucking or striking are ordinary instances. If further energy is being imparted, the steady state may continue, subject to lesser fluctuations, until the source of energy ceases, whereupon the decay similarly takes over: bowing and blowing are ordinary instances. Sounds unmaintained do not cease at once, but persist for a while by momentum and reverberation; and this stage of persistence while decay is taking over is also characteristic and significant. The overall shape of rise and fall, from onset through relative stability and eventual decay, is sometimes described as the envelope of the note; and we have now learnt to treat this factor with a proper respect at all its stages. They all contribute to our recognition of instruments and to our pleasure in the music.

The tonal spectrum comprises the relative amplitudes of the harmonic components of the wave and is more closely related to the shape of that wave (i.e. its behaviour as a sine wave, square wave, sawtooth wave or other description) than to the envelope. But always it is our ears which confirm the differences of quality when listening to music.

SIMPLE TONE AND COMPOUND TONE

It is possible for sound vibrations to be of so simple a character that the sound resulting from them can properly be described as simple tone: pure tone as defined in physics, but this term will be avoided so far as possible here as too liable to be misleading for musicians, and less self-explanatory. It is also possible for simple (pure) tones to be combined in any degree of complexity, the result of this combination being described as compound tone. Maintained compound tones, however complex, of which the components are simple tones, can always be analysed down into those simple tones, each of which may be shown graphically as a sinusoidal curve standing for a sine wave.

Now simplicity and innocence are allied qualities; but in music as in life we should find unmixed simplicity unnatural and unconvincing; and as a matter of fact, it never quite occurs in traditional music, although in electronic music it can be substantially approximated. The traditional tones which come nearest to being simple tones are low, soft notes on the flute, and some comparable organ stops. Even these have certain irregular complications, and in particular they have onset transients which add as much to the interest as they detract from the tranquillity of the tone. Higher or louder flute tones are less simple acoustically and more colourful artistically; but flutes as a whole stand in the cool region of a spectrum whose other areas include piquancy from the oboes, plaintiveness from the clarinets, warmth from the horns and brilliance from the trumpets, as simplicity gives place further to complexity, and in different ways.

The simplest of sounds is the (pure) tone resulting from the periodic vibration of a sounding substance in its entirety. We shall usually perceive the frequency of such entire vibration as determining a pitch which is the note in question. A tuning fork, once its high and jangling onset transients have died down, gives a substantially simple tone, scarcely variable at varying temperatures. Hence its utility as a standard of pitch. But there is or was a very odd little keyboard instrument of which the source of sound consisted entirely of tuning forks: the dulcitone, a compact, reliable and economical substitute for a piano, whose one disadvantage was that it sounded too innocent to be true and in fact soon got to seem almost hypocritically monotonous. It was never important, but it does illustrate the uselessness in art of unrelieved simplicity, and in music of virtually simple tone uncontrasted with something rather less perfect and therefore more interesting to us human beings.

Blowing gently across the mouth of an empty bottle will yield a fairly simple tone. Sounding a tuning fork across a bottle gradually filled with water until its note is the same will yield a decidedly simple tone. The flute itself is less simple, though it is still best on the whole when not too long continued in the orchestra, since its tone has not the complexity to hold our interest on its own account for prolonged stretches at a time. The oboe may require the same caution for an opposite reason: its tone is very complex, and might emotionally fatigue us if heard too unremittingly in an orchestral situation. The violin, on the other hand, spans an amply but not unduly complex range of colouring, and since it is also capable of great variety, runs no inherent risk of growing wearisome.

There are defects for every virtue, and virtues for every defect. Simple tones can be readily generated by electronic devices. In the electronic music for which they are employed, their effectiveness may be very great indeed: but what makes the difference here is once more the context. The electronic situation is very dissimilar from the orchestral situation. No sound, not even simple sound, can be excluded from the resources of music. Simple tone and total sound are two extremes, and both have found their uses in electronic music. It is a brave new world of sound, with values of its own.

I am not suggesting that innocence would be a sufficient word for this use of simple tone. Going the limit to see what happens may well be part of the inspiration, and there is no reason why not. But such experiments may well be subject to the law of diminishing returns. When simple tone and total sound (all frequencies together, described as white noise on the analogy of light) are deliberately opposed, that is the theoretical limit for contrast of timbre, but it may not necessarily sound like that, because no one parameter in music is actually experienced independently of the others. In the traditional situations of orchestral and chamber music, the contrasts of timbre available are all that the heart could desire; and there they are integrated with other parameters through centuries of experiment and experience.

From the flute to the trumpet, from the oboe to the violin, the instruments of our symphonic orchestra are distinguished by contrasts of tone ranging from moderately simple to exceedingly complex. This complexity lies in the combination of frequencies occurring to some extent in any tone excepting simple tone. All tone which is not simple tone is compound tone. It is compounded of frequencies additional to that which results from the vibration of the sounding substance as a whole, and from which the note we perceive as the fundamental ordinarily takes its pitch. These additional frequencies result basically from the simultaneous vibration of the sounding substance in component parts, such as half-parts, third-parts etc.

A crude test may be tried on a length of wire fencing neither too tense nor too slack to be twanged. The full-length vibrations between the posts will be visible as well as audible. The simultaneous part-length vibrations which complicate the tone may or may not be clearly visible, but they will certainly be audible, particularly if the posts are made of wood. The tone in sum will be quite complex, and sound like it. Yet each constituent is in itself a simple tone. And likewise in a choppy sea we may notice small waves superimposed upon large waves, and smaller wavelets superimposed on small waves. They do not in fact have the shape of sound waves; but they give the idea of smaller impulses combining with larger impulses to produce compound movement. It may look disorderly; but every constituent in it is ultimately simple, and the resulting complexity can always in principle be analysed into multiple simplicities.

Of the whole-length vibration and the associated part-length vibrations crudely demonstrated by the fence wire, and subtly exploited by
the strings of a violin or other instrument of the stringed order, the
following basic characteristics may be postulated in common: they
occur simultaneously; they are of the same simple form; they would
each of them, on their own, produce a simple tone in our hearing
faculty; and they all of them, together, make up a total pattern of
vibration which our hearing faculty accepts as a note. Such a note, however, is not a pure or simple tone. It is a compound or complex tone.
For the ear's mechanism has generated the simple tones for itself from
the total vibration, and the brain has then recombined them into the
note with all its timbre or colouring complete. The means by which this
everyday miracle is brought about will be considered more explicitly in
the following chapter.

The simple tones from which a compound tone is generated are
called partial tones or partials. They may under certain circumstances
fail to be fused by the brain into a single note, in which case we may
hear one or more of them individually as separate notes. But when they
are fused, which is the ordinary situation in music, we do not hear them
as notes but as tone-colouring. We hear a note, ordinarily, at the lowest
in pitch of the series. This lowest possible partial tone is called the first
partial, or the prime, or (most commonly) the fundamental. And all
the remaining partials are then called the upper partials, or overtones,
to any height at which they do or might theoretically exist.

There is a very real and practical distinction to justify this terminology. Not only is the fundamental ordinarily perceived as the
pitch of the whole series, while the upper partials are ordinarily
perceived as tone-colouring. That is only one half of the story. The
other half is that when for any reason the fundamental is weak (as it
often is in practice) or even absent (as in certain cases occurs), then the
upper partials, if present in sufficient strength and numbers, will be
perceived as supporting it or even as supplying it closely enough to
serve the need. It is for this reason that we give the fundamental a
certain distinction over and against the other partials in our terminology, though it is, in all other respects, merely the lowest possible
of a set of partials.

Or we could equally put it that the pitch perceived from the fundamental, on its own, corresponds quite closely with the pitch perceived
from the combined set of partials when heard simultaneously. When
the fundamental vibration is weak or absent, then so long as enough of
the upper-partial vibrations are present, the pitch perceived will be

found to be the same as if the fundamental were present in strength. This is a most valuable acoustic characteristic both for speech and for music. It helps to keep pitches clear and distinct, and tone colouring varied and interesting. It also makes the transmission and reproduction of sound possible and tolerable with very imperfect or limited apparatus. This factor is deliberately exploited in telephones in order to avoid giving them natural vibration periods within the range of speech, where they would set up distorting resonances.

TONE AND NOISE

Pitch, we have seen, depends mainly on frequency. Vibrations which form a single segment occupying the whole length of a vibrating substance such as a string or an air-column are the longest, and thus necessarily the slowest (since the speed of sound in a given substance under given conditions is substantially a constant); hence they yield the lowest partial, which is the fundamental. Vibrations occupying two or more sub-divisions of the length are shorter, thus more rapid: their time-cycles (periods) are less; hence they yield the upper partials in ascending order, as they decrease in length and increase in speed.

If the total pattern of vibration is substantially a regular one, repeating itself more or less exactly in the time taken for the fundamental vibration to complete one of its cycles, then we have one common situation. The vibrations of most, though not of all, important musical instruments are in this sense substantially regular. In this situation, the ratios of the number of complete cycles which the vibrations of the individual partials will perform in the same time will form a series of substantially exact whole numbers. The partial vibrations are then said to be harmonic. They produce in the ear correspondingly harmonic partial tones. Such regular partials are often called harmonics for short; and this term may refer either to partial vibrations occurring and measurable objectively, or to partial tones perceived in the ear subjectively.

But there is another, still more common situation, in which the total pattern of vibration is not regular but irregular, so that the physical and mathematical symmetries described above do not obtain. In that event, while we may still encounter partial vibrations, and while these will still result in partial tones, we can no longer correctly describe them as harmonics. On the contrary, such irregular partials are said to be inharmonic.

The ascending order of harmonic partials constitutes a harmonic series which used to be called, in this connection, the Natural Harmonic Series, a somewhat redundant term now discarded as misleading in its implication that there might be such a thing as an unnatural harmonic series. The whole-length of a sounding structure vibrates at the fundamental frequency we hear as the note. The half-length vibrates at twice that fundamental frequency, an octave above. The third-length vibrates at three times the fundamental frequency, a twelfth (i.e. an octave plus a fifth) above. The quarter-length vibrates at four times the fundamental frequency, a double octave above. The same ratios obtain up the arithmetical progression 1 : 2 : 3 : 4. . . . It does not signify which members of the series are actually receiving sufficient energy to be perceptible in practice. It merely signifies that in so far as they are perceptible, and in so far as they are indeed harmonic, these will be their mathematical ratios. Their musical appearances may well be approximate rather than exact, and none-the-less artistic on that account. See Fig. 28 on p. 222.

The term harmonic did not arise historically from any particular connection with harmony in the sense of chords. It arose from an alternative and prior method of calculating not by doubling, or trebling or quadrupling frequencies (and so on), but by the opposite process of sub-dividing string-lengths, in the ratios 1, $\frac{1}{2}$, $\frac{1}{3}$, $\frac{1}{4}$ etc., which is mathematically a harmonic progression. The term overtone is equivalent to upper partial; for an upper partial can correctly be called an overtone of a fundamental partial, but a fundamental cannot be called an overtone of anything. Thus the first overtone is the second partial, or possibly (e.g. on the clarinet, which uses the odd-numbered harmonics while omitting the even-numbered harmonics from its basic scale) the first overtone is the second partial but the third harmonic. This is altogether a source of such confusion that the term overtone is now usually avoided for this purpose.

Harmonic partials have an importance for music which cannot be exaggerated. We do not ordinarily hear the upper partials as notes but as a blend more or less at the pitch attributed to the fundamental, and having a tone colour and loudness depending on their numbers and relative strength. Harmonics and tone colouring go together; to some extent, they may also affect our impression of the pitch.

It has long been possible by mechanical devices, and is now very easy and accurate by electronic devices, to record curves which plot visibly the behaviour of sound vibrations. Some early specimens (but they are still valid) and some specially recorded are shown below in Figures 1–20. The undulations of such curves do not depict the physical outlines of the vibrations, which may not even be transverse at all, but longitudinal. They may not be up-and-down, or side-to-side, but in-and-out or to-and-fro. In all cases, however, they are oscillations or disturbances of a sounding substance, centring upon a position of equilibrium or point of rest.

In order to record such oscillations visibly and two-dimensionally, they are translated by a well-understood convention into lateral curves with up-and-down displacements around a straight line which represents the central position of equilibrium. The horizontal dimension represents one scale of reference: for Figures 1–13, the time elapsing. The vertical dimension represents another scale shown in relation: for Figures 1–13, the form and amplitude of vibration. Once the convention is known, the visible representation of the acoustic happening (in these figures, pressure waves caused in the surrounding air by the tones concerned) is graphic and suggestive, and indeed indispensable for purposes of discussion and comparison. Graphic is the operative word. Such figures are a species of graph.

There are some reservations to be borne in mind when responding in imagination to these vivid illustrations. This particular selection (apart from Figure 5, p. 18) is confined to illustrating tones which have already settled to an approximately steady state. No sound, however regular, actually begins that way. At its first onset irregularities are unavoidable; nor would it be in the least desirable to avoid them. Much of the individual character of an instrument, as already stated, comes from its behaviour during onset: this can, indeed, be varied greatly by the different methods of attack which most instruments allow at the performer's option; nevertheless, it is always recognizable and it also contributes a considerable share of our pleasure. Individuality usually is enjoyable, and it is not only the individual tone colouring but its subtle fluctuations which please us. When a mere steady state is electronically presented it is uninteresting, regardless of how rich it is made in harmonic content; half the problems of electronic music are in trying to simulate the transient waywardness which traditional music has no need to invent because it is unavoidable there in any case.

Irregularities are also unavoidable during the decay of the sound; and these, too, find no illustration in the following specimens. Coming, as it does, not as the initiation but as the termination of the tone, the decay presumably cannot influence that instantaneous recognition which is so crucial to our appreciation; but it certainly enters significantly into the experience, and must be electronically simulated for any sort of comparable effect if traditional instruments are not being used. For purely electronic effect, all possible alternatives, including an overall steady

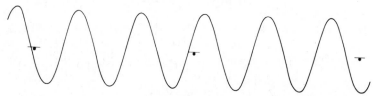

Fig. 1   Sine curve, indicative of the simple tone of a tuning fork

state, are valid; but it still remains our experience that perfection or near-perfection sounds mechanical and in practice dull.

Subject to these considerations, we may pick out several aspects worthy of attention. Figure 1 shows the curve given by a single simple tone. Since no tone in this world has been going on for ever and any tone must eventually stop, we have to conceive of a straight line leading through some preliminary irregularities into the regular curve here plotted, and also of some terminal irregularities leading back to a similar straight line at the end after the source of sound has ceased. All the same, the beautifully smooth and regular curve itself, as we see it, is not misleading. Its simplicity corresponds to a like simplicity in the vibrations of a tuning fork or other source of substantially simple tone. It does suggest what is the basic unit of acoustic material from which sounds are built up in music, so far as these sounds consist (as by and large they generally do) of tone resulting from regular vibration rather than of noise resulting from irregular vibration.

Figures 2–5 show the integrated (in effect, superimposed) curves from tuning forks under different circumstances. Figure 2 has an obvious unity within diversity; and so with rather more discrepancy does Figure 3. The reiterated waxing and waning of the amplitude of vibration shown in Figure 4 illustrates a phenomenon to which we shall later come: it represents the alternate reinforcing and diminishing of one simple tone by another simple tone when their vibrations are at

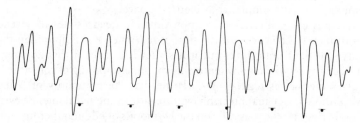

Fig. 2   Integrated curve: just chord on four tuning forks

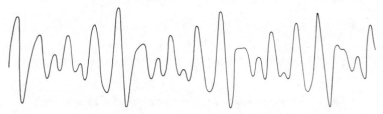

Fig. 3   Tempered chord on four tuning forks

Fig. 4   Beat tone produced between two tuning forks

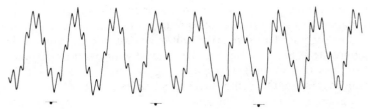

Fig. 5   Preliminary high jangle of tuning fork

slightly different frequencies. Figure 5 shows the quite complicated vibration at high frequencies which produces the unwanted jangle when first a tuning fork is struck: these may therefore be regarded as onset transients, but the figure does not continue long enough to illustrate what happens as the jangle dies down and the fundamental emerges virtually simple, as at Figure 1 above.

Figures 6–13 illustrate the approximately steady states of several instruments. The curve for the flute is not much less simple than the curve for the tuning fork; but it has already a little of that apparent irregularity which actually represents the superimposing of constituent curves themselves regular. The clarinet has the peculiarity of being weak though not inappreciable with regard to the harmonics of even numbering; it relies basically on the harmonics of odd numbering; and its integrated curve, tending to show skew (a sort of mirror-image)

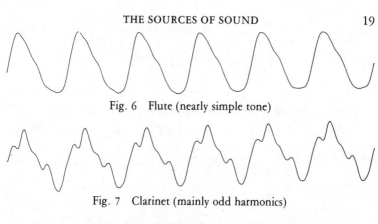

Fig. 6   Flute (nearly simple tone)

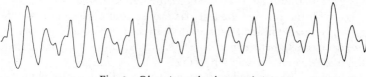

Fig. 7   Clarinet (mainly odd harmonics)

Fig. 8   Oboe (complex harmonics)

Fig. 9   Trumpet (more complex harmonics)

Fig. 10   Violin (balanced harmonics)

symmetry, suggests this peculiarity. The oboe is rich in moderate to high harmonics, suggested by its rather complicated curve; the trumpet somewhat more so; the violin looks as well balanced as it sounds. These notes are all at A 440 Hz, so that the differences visible are basically of tone colouring. The note for the French horn is G 196 Hz and for the tuba is F 174.6 Hz, but the traces have been processed by the computer to have the same repeat for easier comparison. All these variously complex curves are integrations of simpler curves superimposed. The biggest of the curves thus integrated will result from the slowest,

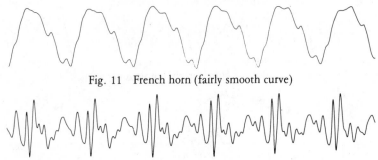

Fig. 11   French horn (fairly smooth curve)

Fig. 12   Tuba (fairly jagged curve)

longest vibrations, i.e. from the fundamental harmonic, where this has objectively the greatest intensity (it may of course do so only for the ear). The smaller indentations result from the faster, shorter vibrations, i.e. from the higher harmonics. The slight variations from one cycle to the next are genuine and repeatable.

These aspects are made clearer by Figures 14–20, which show frequency analyses, prepared by the computer, for Figures 6–12. Here, the horizontal dimension represents frequency on a scale of which the units are 1000 Hz; the vertical dimension represents relative levels (equivalent to amplitude of vibration) on a scale of which the units are 10 dB. The components of the harmonic series stand out as high points on the scale of amplitude; but it is very interesting how many non-harmonic components show up as well. And it must of course be appreciated that the traces illustrated here are not definitive for these instruments, but are merely samples each lasting a little over 1/100 second and showing one note, on one instrument, played at one loudness by one player. The frequency analyses, on the other hand, show one instant of time, about 1/10 second after onset.

Other notes of an instrument will sound differently (in some cases, very differently, like the lower, middle and upper registers of the clarinet); different moments during the same note will sound differently; all notes can be influenced at all stages by the performer (whose personal tone as a whole may be just as recognizable as the generic tone of his instrument). But it is probable that these differences, too, are basically expressed in the harmonic content, and will therefore show up on fine examination in the visual curves. There are indeed other factors known to be involved of which the explanation is at present more or less uncertain. But on the broad approach envisaged for the present book, it is a sufficiently indicative summary that pitch is

Fig. 13 Piano (less regular) (N.B. this pattern does not repeat quite exactly, showing that the vibrations are not quite periodic, hence that the partials are not quite harmonic)

a function of frequency, and that tone colouring is a function of harmonic content. The tonal spectrum may be variable, but nevertheless it is characteristic; and that is the interesting aspect for musicians.

Bowed and wind instruments replenish in performance the energy of their vibrations, thus keeping them essentially to the patterns which their acoustic characteristics basically require. The vibrations remain substantially periodic; the partials are and continue to be reasonably harmonic; and until the energy ceases to be supplied, no great change necessarily ensues. But the piano, as illustrated in Figure 13, does not have its energy replenished with the note, but only renewed when that note or another is once more struck. Thus the supply of energy is not continuous but intermittent; and meanwhile nothing is happening to keep the partials harmonic. They might remain harmonic of their own accord if the strings were infinitely flexible. This cannot of course occur in practice: on the contrary, these strings are exceptionally stiff and tense, and as each note decays after being struck, friction and resistance and beats cause the vibrations to be quite considerably inharmonic. This is shown visually in Figure 13, of which the smaller indentations can be seen to recur a little altered with each periodic repetition. The period is basically maintained, but it is not closely maintained; and the higher up the piano this discrepancy occurs, the greater its relative extent. In this and certain other respects, the piano is in theory a somewhat delinquent instrument. In practice, its very considerable irregularities give life to its tone and are a very considerable advantage. There is a slight uneven and pulsing throb to the tone of a well-made and well-tuned piano: too slight for us to notice directly but not too slight for us to appreciate without knowing quite what it is that we are appreciating. Once again it is the theoretical imperfections which are the making of the practical result.

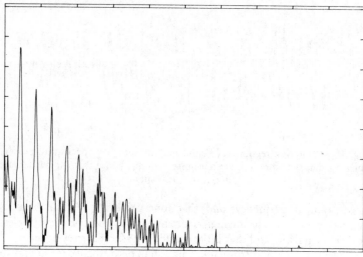

Fig. 14   Flute analysed

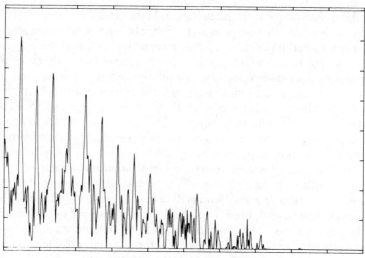

Fig. 15   Clarinet analysed

INTENSITY AND LOUDNESS

Pitch and tone colouring are two main elements in music. Another, viewed objectively, is intensity; and viewed subjectively, is loudness.

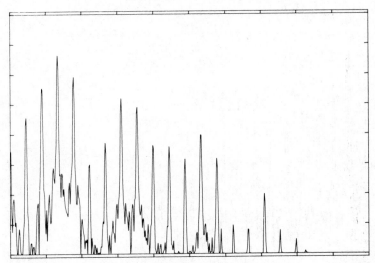

Fig. 16   Oboe analysed

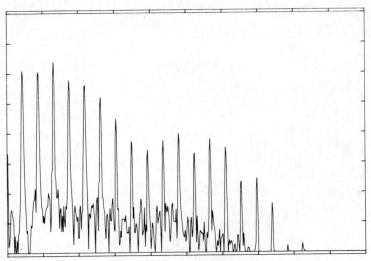

Fig. 17   Trumpet analysed

The intensity of the loudest sound we can endure without acute distress at a frequency of around 1000 Hz (say, c''') is fully a million times greater than the softest sound we can, under favourable circumstances, detect. But the astonishing extent of this range of intensity can be

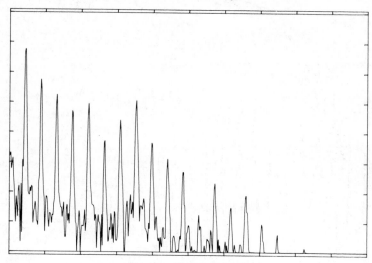

Fig. 18   Violin analysed

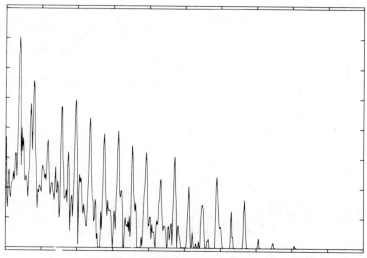

Fig. 19   French horn analysed

brought within our comprehension by measuring its relative rather than its absolute differences. This is done on a scale of 130 decibels, where one bel represents a tenfold change of intensity, and one decibel equals one tenth of a bel.

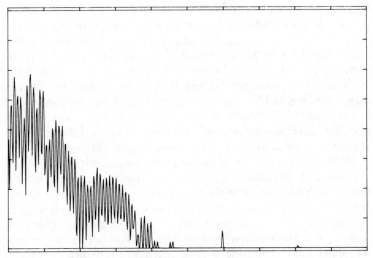

Fig. 20 Tuba analysed

There are numerous factors influencing the intensity of sound, one of them being the frequency or frequencies involved, and another being their respective amplitudes. Broadly speaking, the lower the frequency, the greater the amplitude of the sound pressure required for a comparable intensity, whence the need for a good supply of bass instruments in the orchestra. There is also an element of mutual interference. Sounds that are close in pitch may readily mask each other; but only a low pitch can mask another low pitch, and only a high pitch can mask another high pitch − except that if a group of high frequencies generate a low subjective pitch, then high frequency sounds may mask that low subjective pitch. Very low and very high sounds require much greater intensity in order to be heard at all than sounds of intermediate frequency: our most sensitive hearing is about from 250 Hz (say around middle c') to 6000 Hz (only as harmonics). Sounds may intermittently strengthen and negate each other as their vibrations alternately coincide and conflict, producing the curious oscillation of intensity known as beats: for which see the next chapter.

The level of loudness we may perceive is affected by any such complications. Loudness is approximately indicated by a further scale of 130 phons. Decibels show sound-pressure levels, i.e. intensity; phons show loudness levels, related to intensity but not the same, since other factors enter in, especially those related to frequency. A very low note

having an intensity of 80 decibels may be perceived at a loudness level
of about 40 phons, which is more or less as we hear an orchestral *pianissimo*. A note which is not quite so low, but is at the pitch of the bottom
C string on the cello, having the same intensity of 80 decibels, may be
perceived at a loudness level of about 75 phons, which is more or less as
we hear a quite moderate orchestral *forte*. But a note two octaves
higher, which is middle *c'* having the same intensity of 80 decibels, may
be perceived at a loudness level of about 80 phons, which is more or less
as we hear an orchestral *fortissimo*. The notes mentioned above are each
assumed to have originated from a single simple vibration.

At this frequency, therefore, the two scales approximately correspond; and they continue to do so for about another two octaves
higher, which brings us to the C above the treble stave (*c'''*). At two
octaves higher again (important only for upper partials) 80 decibels
may be perceived at a loudness level of about 85 phons; higher than
that in pitch, the loudness level perceived will decline steeply away as
the upper limit of hearing is approached where higher frequencies
become inaudible. The upper level of loudness which the ear can perceive without distress and eventual risk of damage is somewhere in the
region of 120 phons. (These statements likewise apply with respect to
simple vibrations sounded one at a time.) When sounds of different
frequencies, pressure amplitudes and loudness levels are heard in
combination, as they are in any ordinary experiences of music, their
reactions upon one another become very complicated.

The impressions of pitch made on a normal listener by different
frequencies of vibration are fairly predictable, though not without
complicating factors. The impressions of tone colouring made by
different combinations of harmonics are at least sufficiently predictable
for us to recognize familiar instruments and timbres. The impressions
of loudness made by different amplitudes under varying conditions of
frequency and harmonic content are so individual that measurement is
hardly applicable. It is, of course, interesting to learn that ten violins
playing at the unison can be expected to impress us not as ten times but
only as twice as loud; or again that when they are playing not unisons
but separate notes they will impress us as considerably louder. But this
is not really a measurement of quantity; it is a suggestion of quality. It
tells us something about how we may expect to respond, other things
being equal, which since we are human, they seldom are.

THE ELEMENTAL QUALITY OF THE HARMONIC SERIES

Pitch, tone colouring and volume: these are the primary constituents of music, disposable in every variety of melodic, harmonic or rhythmic pattern. Their behaviour as sound vibration is measurable in principle, and has been measured in practice with an exactness to which this chapter provides only the broadest and most elementary introduction. There are measurable aspects to melody, harmony and rhythm also; but none of music's parameters depends on measurement alone, however calculating the composer may wish to be.

Household mains in the UK supply electricity as an alternating current at a frequency of 50 Hz. This gives a periodicity which may be picked up by any apparatus possessing a tendency to free vibration at corresponding frequencies. For example, a small room-heater, generating heat from wire-bound bars, may have a metal reflector which serves in effect as a coupled resonator, and may be heard humming away with a fundamental around *G* and upper partials through the harmonic series. The second harmonic an octave up should be especially clear, and also the third another fifth up; the sevenths both major and minor will be jangling away; others may stand out momentarily and be lost again, now heard as notes, now as tone colouring.

A small transformer for an electric shaver may do the same; or much more impressively, a large transformer for a district supply or an electric railway. No wonder the periodic vibrations of which these are samples were at one time known as the Natural Harmonic Series: they are indeed a phenomenon of nature. So, under suitable circumstances, our physical universe resounds; from such a property of matter can music be produced. Electronic equipment can, of course, not only generate harmonic vibrations readily, but in any strengths and proportions. One or more can be brought up at will; and if clusters or chords are thus stressed, we notice that however dissonant or out of tune on any normal scales or temperaments, they have a rightness in their sound as if from some underlying compatibility of their own. That is a consequence of their being periodic.

Very broadly speaking, the more energy in the lower harmonics, the solider the timbre; the more energy in the higher harmonics, the edgier the timbre. Always there is the connection between the acoustic spectrum and the emotional response. We may turn to a further stage of this connection in the following chapter, where the transmission of sounds from source to hearer will be given consideration.

3 SOUND INTO HEARING

How do sounds occurring outside travel to our ears? They mainly travel through the air, as pressure waves. It is these waves, these small but complex variations of atmospheric pressure, which impinge upon our hearing apparatus, there to initiate the process which results in our perceiving the sounds. Outer disturbances become inner sensations, and we hear.

The disturbances in the air which bring sound to our ears are the continuation of those vibrations in sounding substances which are the source of it. The substances are various, and include air itself when this is contained in an instrument and forms part of it. The correspondence is close between the vibrations which are the source of sound and the vibrations which transmit the sound, and between these and the vibrations with which our ears respond. But many complications can occur during the journey to modify the message.

Vibrations transmitting sound through air are, as we have seen, longitudinal. They exert and relax pressure in their direction of travel. Unlike the graphs by which we can plot them two-dimensionally, they go not up-and-down and side-to-side, but to-and-fro in all directions outwards. Particles of air, being elastic, are pushed on so that they become compressed, and rebound so that they become rarefied, in the normal course of oscillation. They do not themselves pass on substantially; they pass on the succession of energy-impulses. It is not the air which travels from this cause; it is the pressure waves in the air. Compressions and rarefactions alternate until an obstacle is reached, which may then receive and transmit them in another form, as our ears do.

Visual analogies are apt to be misleading; but there is something in common with a billiard ball impelled by the one behind it, and impelling the one in front of it, without itself departing from its previous position. Waves in water, again, can be seen to rise and fall as they spread and travel; but the water itself does not move forward from this cause, as can be seen from any floating objects bobbing up and down. Only when the height of a wave pours it over a rock, or the impact fragments it or carries it up the beach, does substantial forward motion of the water result; and these rising and falling waves in the water, of course, are transverse waves, instances not of longitudinal but of lateral vibration. Tides, currents and to some extent surface winds may be moving the water on, but the waves in themselves move through it, not with it. Another instance of relatively slow longitudinal vibration may sometimes be seen when a loosely coupled freight train is jerked forward, so that the wagons jolt in both directions from the alternate compressions and expansions of the buffer springs, before settling down into steady forward motion: sudden braking of the engine may produce a similar oscillation before the wagons settle steadily together again.

When longitudinal oscillations of sufficient magnitude in the surrounding air reach our ears at frequencies within the relatively rapid range of sound, we hear sounds. The path of travel between source and ear will, in the first instance, be the straightest possible, along the shortest distance, requiring the least time in which to arrive; and the speed of travel, which is the speed of sound in air subject to variations of temperature, will be about twelve miles a minute, say 1133 feet or 345 metres a second. However, the shortest possible path may be lengthened by obstacles needing to be circumvented; and, moreover, this lengthening may be different for harmonics of different wavelengths and frequencies, the shorter and faster getting round more easily than the longer and slower. This can modify the harmonic spectrum on its journey to the hearer, and can make a considerable difference to the sounds reaching him. And that is only a beginning to the complications of the journey. For the sound does not only travel by the shortest and quickest of the routes available. It also travels by way of echoes, and echoes of echoes, each at its own longer distance and later time of arrival, with unlimited opportunities for mutual interference and influence as the sound waves cross and recross at every angle. Out of doors, these echoings may be slight and perhaps inappreciable; but indoors, they are bound to be significant, the more so as the room is the more resonant; and the total acoustic situation may become very complicated indeed.

One such complicating factor is reflection; another is absorption. These two factors stand in a complementary relationship; for when the sound in its travel meets with an obstacle, some part of that sound is reflected on a new stage of its journey, while some part is absorbed and ceases to share in the travelling vibrations. The proportions which are absorbed or reflected vary greatly in accordance with the substance and dimensions of the obstacle. Hard, smooth surfaces reflect more than they absorb, and soft, rough surfaces absorb more than they reflect. Large and even surfaces reflect with little or no appreciable change in the pattern of vibration; small and broken surfaces reflect with significant changes. A compact and solid obstacle may send out in all directions a modified version of the vibration pattern falling upon it. A sizeable obstacle but relatively of limited area may introduce distortions, but the reflection will not be in all directions; it will tend to be at an angle equal to the angle of incidence. A large, unbroken surface behaves for sound very much as a mirror behaves for light: the reflection is undistorted, and the angle of reflection equals the angle of incidence with substantial accuracy. Rough or broken surfaces, on the other hand, not only absorb more sound but also cause more diffraction in such sound as they do reflect; while diffraction may also be caused when sound vibrations pass round the corners of larger objects. There can be, so to speak, acoustic dazzling and there can be acoustic shadows.

Any sizeable obstacle will cause some diffraction of the sound. This also occurs somewhat comparably for light. But light vibrations are themselves so small that they are affected almost equally by any obstacle of appreciable size. Thus even the dust floating through the air may cause diffraction, but in this case the obstacles are small enough to scatter the shorter vibrations of the blue light, while allowing the longer vibrations of the red light to pass unimpeded. We see the effect of this very attractively in sunsets; but sound vibrations are altogether much longer, and a fairly large obstacle like a pillar may be of a size to scatter the shorter vibrations of high-pitched sound while allowing the longer vibrations of low-pitched sound to pass unimpeded. The effect of this is to take out all or much of the brightness, as is made obvious by sitting behind that pillar in a cathedral or a concert hall.

Not only diffraction but also absorption acts differently in accordance with the frequency (and therefore with the pitch). It is the lower sounds which tend to lose least energy from absorption, and the higher sounds which tend to lose most energy. Other things being equal, sound decreases in intensity (and therefore basically in loudness) in proportion to the distance travelled, since the same energy is spread over an ever larger area, not to mention losses from friction or other causes. In principle, the intensity of the sound is inversely proportional to the square of the distance travelled. In practice, the energy never will have been evenly distributed in all directions, and all manner of inter-reactions will have been occurring as the journey proceeds.

Although the principles by which sound travels are not affected by circumstances, the practice is; and one practical distinction of importance is that already mentioned between an open and an enclosed environment. Out of doors, there may be much absorption from the ground and the vegetation, and few if any objects to give much reflection, so that the intensity may decrease with distance very much more steeply than the theoretical decline.

A further factor results from the greater outdoor possibilities for refraction. The speed of sound is appreciably faster through warm air than it is through cold air. Thus in the open air, if there is a cold layer near the ground, and a warm layer higher up, then the more lofty sound vibrations will travel faster than the less lofty sound vibrations. The result is refraction: the more speedy vibrations are bent down towards the less speedy vibrations. It is a little like a column of men marching, who can be got to wheel round by having the rank on the outside of the curve march faster than the inside rank. The result for the sound is to concentrate it more on one level, so that less energy is diffused up and away: the concentrated sound persists more loudly over farther distances and does not so soon dwindle to inaudibility. (A speaking tube applies this principle of concentrating the direction of the vibrations, and so in a small measure does an ordinary, i.e. unamplified megaphone.) The converse also applies, of course, if the ground level temperature is higher than the upper.

Another cause of refraction is wind stronger at a height than near the ground. If the wind is blowing with the sound, the diffraction is downwards, and the sound thus concentrated travels exceptionally far and loud. If the wind is blowing against the sound, the diffraction is upwards, and the sound may be so rapidly diffused that it carries hardly any distance at all.

Indoors, the circumstances are radically affected by the enclosing of the space. There are normally four walls, a ceiling and a floor. Not only do these afford very variable but substantial proportions of absorption and reflection: they also provide a contained volume of air; and this contained air has its own peak resonances and its own natural periods of vibration, which are activated by the very same disturbances as the air is in course of transmitting sound. The air in the room therefore becomes a partner, and a very active partner, of the source of sound, and its natural resonances enter very significantly into the combined pressure waves arriving at the ear. The source and the room form a coupled acoustic system, just as effectively as the reed and the tube of an oboe or the strings and the body of the violin. We shall find in due course that the ear, the aural nerves and the brain themselves take shares in shaping the acoustic patterns: it is a coupled acoustic system in sum, and the point at which the acoustical material passes over into mental and emotional response is by no means so sharply defined as was previously supposed. It is not only that the acoustics impinge on the psyche; the psyche also conditions the neural processing of the acoustics.

In the room or hall, the chief factors are the reflections which follow more or less closely after the direct travel of the sound, and the natural resonance peaks or formants which characterize the room itself. Since the speed of sound at twelve miles a minute is relatively slow, those vibrations which reach the ear after reflection, by a path longer than the direct path, arrive perceptibly later; and those vibrations which have been reflected more than once arrive that much later still.

The mere fact of an orchestra being set out over a substantial area causes the farthest instruments to be heard later than nearest, but our hearing has sufficient tolerance to tidy that up mentally. The succession of reflected vibrations, however, can go to remarkable extremes: there may be a hundred or more distinct reflections of the same source-sound reverberating for several seconds before total inaudibility supervenes in a sufficiently resonant environment. We do not disregard the extraordinary build-up of overlapping vibrations which results from this; on the contrary, we turn it to our advantage, using it to increase very greatly the information we extract from the acoustic events occurring all around us. When it is considered that the whole of this information reaches the ear solely in the form of pressure variations, and that these pressure variations are combined and superimposed into no more than one single pattern at a time, yet are scanned and analysed and passed intelligibly forward to the brain and the mind and the responding psyche, the delicacy of the whole complex process becomes remarkably impressive.

Consider, then, a room ringing with direct and still more with indirect and reflected oscillations, partly from the source of sound, partly from the room's own acoustic contributions as activated by the source of sound. Consider an interplay of these oscillations to produce yet others in a succession only to be interrupted by eventual loss of energy. Consider further that there will be points at which vibrations themselves periodic may fall into phase with mutual reinforcement, or out of phase with mutual interference, and that the resulting fluctuations in their effective amplitude may likewise be periodic and audible in their own right as repercussive beats or even as independent notes. Consider yet again that the onset of each and every constituent differs from its settled state, while the decay also repeats in reverse something of the character of the onset. Nothing decays at once: the overlapping of sounds, one across another, varies with the resonance of the room, but is never inappreciable and is commonly very extensive indeed.

It may perhaps be useful to make a very rough and ready comparison with troubled waters, of which the waves big and small are piling up and sloshing around, now with their peaks and troughs colluding and now competing, until they break on the same shore with multiple additional reflections. Unlike the shore, the ear-drum is designed to accept and transmit vibration; but it can only accept and transmit what reaches it as combined pressure waves. Changes of pressure in relation to the time elapsing: these are the only variables of which the eardrum can detect the communication. All further processing by which sound is experienced relates to that.

Every source of sound includes its own spectrum of partials: harmonic in so far as the vibrations are periodic and of the broad nature of tone; inharmonic in so far as the vibrations are unperiodic and of the broad nature of noise. In many circumstances, two partials other than the fundamental of a series will be so prominent that they may be called formants, because of their specially formative influence on the main quality of the sound. The room will also have its own formants of given frequency, and potential oscillations at many other frequencies. Wherever the source and the room coincide in these respects, particular activity results; but since the sources of sound may be multiple, and constantly on the change, the total situation may be fluctuating with bewildering rapidity. Yet the ear is not bewildered, as a rule; on the contrary, its ability to accept complex information is equal to all ordinary situations and some which are indeed extraordinary.

The overall reverberation within a room depends basically on its balance of absorption and reflection. Reverberation may be measured by averaging the time in which sounds decay, and the reverberation time may be defined as the time in which the sound pressures thus averaged decay to a one-thousandth part of their original amplitude when energy ceases to be supplied. In an enclosed space, the total energy of the sound at first builds up faster than it is being absorbed, so that its loudness is on the increase. When the build-up is balanced by the absorption, loudness may remain constant; when the source ceases, the energy may be gradually and dwindlingly absorbed, until silence supervenes. But in a resonant room, absorption will overtake build-up more tardily: greater loudness may build up; decline may likewise be tardier. And in an unresonant room, absorption will overtake build-up more speedily: less loudness may build up; decline may likewise be speedier.

There is a certain conflict of advantages in this factor of reverberation. Since high sounds tend to lose more energy by absorption than low sounds, a resonant room is more favourable than an unresonant room to the high harmonics on which brilliance of sound depends. If absorption is too great and the room is too unresonant, the build-up will be too tardy and inadequate, so that performers and audience alike will feel burdened by a sense of unavailing effort; every small blemish will be left uncovered; sufficient brilliance will seem unattainable. On the other hand, everything can be got extremely clear and definite. If resonance is too great, however, and reverberation is excessive, nothing can be got clear at all, since the overlapping of successive sounds will go on for longer than the ear can sort out.

A moderate overlapping is not confusing, and is indeed necessary for any sense of liveliness or naturalness, being a highly desirable part of the complex information which gives the ear its needed clues. An extreme overlapping is very confusing indeed. And when the time of arrival between the most direct, quickest travel and the most reflected, most delayed travel exceeds the smallest time in which we can detect sounds separately (it may be from about 30 to about 50 milliseconds), then we experience not a compound sound but an echo. Suppose such an echo is focused by reflection from a curved surface (as in the Albert Hall before obstacles were put up under the domed roof to alleviate the problem), then its loudness and its distinctness can be catastrophically exaggerated. The ear cannot assimilate the irrelevant information, nor can the mind accept it. Occasionally on a trans-continental telephone call you can hear your own voice speaking, and also an electronic repetition of it just long enough afterwards not to fuse with your speaking voice: it then becomes difficult, and can become impossible, to go on speaking at all. The mind cannot contend with that much contradictory information.

The reverberation of a hall is not necessarily a fixture, but can be changed by judicious alterations. For example, if two opposite walls are flat and rigid, an unpleasant exchange of echoes, known as flutter echoes, may be set up between them; but it can be sufficiently remedied by breaking the smoothness of these surfaces with irregular protruberances. Echoes from the ceiling are usually valuable and should not be suppressed unnecessarily; the floor will normally be prevented from exchanging flutter echoes with it by the seats, especially if these are made absorbent with upholstery; and this will also avoid too disconcerting a difference between rehearsing in an empty hall and performing after the audience has come in. Clothes, and indeed any cloth (particularly if it is soft and thick) will absorb heavily, the higher partials being the most affected. Painted plaster and polished wood are good and impartial reflectors of sound; thin wooden panels are however unsuitable, since they tend to swallow up low partials, which in any case are apt to suffer some considerable depletion in large halls. It is always wise to provide ample basses for large-scale performance.

On the basis of many comparative experiments, the best reverberation times for music seem to average from about one second in small halls and chamber music, through one and a half seconds in moderate halls and ensemble music where clarity is more needed than momentum, to two seconds in large halls where fusion and power come first. But for speech, partials are largely associated with the steady state of the vowels, to which the consonants largely supply onset transients – but all moving at considerable speed; and here, from half a second to less than a second of resonance is most appropriate, while anything approaching two seconds may make it almost impossible to be understood. An all-purpose hall will have to be something of a compromise, assisted tactfully, perhaps, by movable screens and curtains to vary the effective resonance.

Because sound travels with almost the same speed at any level of sound ordinarily used in music (very loud noises travel faster), and because sound travels with almost the same speed at all pitches used in music, we do not hear the partials of a note or the notes of a chord out of turn. We do hear reflected sounds out of turn because of the different distances over which they travel at substantially the same speed, and we shall have next to consider the ways in which our ears, our nerves and our brains make sense of that. Other things being equal, louder sounds take longer to sink to inaudibility, while our hearing remains more sensitive to higher sounds at low levels of intensity. Some small proportion of the sound vibration can actually reach us through the floor, with detriment to the high harmonics, but apparently in no significant degree of strength.

THE RECEPTIVE LISTENER

We have now to think of the listener surrounded by this sea of sound. If he is at a concert, he will probably be sitting in one place for the duration of the music. Under certain circumstances, such as at the Proms, he need not do so; and we may realize with something of a shock that as he alters his position, so he alters his experience of the music. For the sound is not the same in different places, any more than it is the same at different moments. The sum total of direct and reflected sounds, with all the combinations and contradictions and diffractions and diffusions which they undergo, varies with the relationship between the situation of the sources and the situation of the listener. Walls and ceiling, angles and corners, obstacles and objects large and small, reflective and absorptive: all such factors affect the sound on its travels, and none of them can be quite the same for any two listeners in the room. Yet no one doubts that their basic experience of the music is the same.

Moreover, suppose at a rehearsal a listener is moving round the room on purpose to get an overall impression of how the music is sounding. He may try it at the front and the back, at one side or another, upstairs and downstairs, testing for balance, blending and ensemble. It is a sensible conductor who may occasionally leave his orchestra playing for a few moments while he listens to them from the back of the hall. Under these circumstances, the listener is aware of getting new slants on the performance, but he is also aware of the performance being the same. He is not misled in the least, but somehow takes an educated average of the sounds reaching him; and while the conductor may well wish to alter the balance a little when he picks up his stick again, he has made the necessary allowances in his mind already.

The ordinary listener who stays in his seat is also taking an educated average. As he enjoys the smooth flow of orchestral sound, the surge of the strings, the warmth of the brass, the cool flutes, the pungent double-reeds and the strangely hollow and haunting clarinets, he does not have to work it out that the total harmonic spectrum is fluctuating wildly from instant to instant; or that every note on every instrument has its own onset transients and, if it is long enough, its own steady state and certainly its own decay, by which time it is overlapped by a hundred or a thousand reflections reverberating from what has gone before. He does not have to work it out because his aural system has worked it out already.

Certain virtues and certain limitations of our aural system combine for our advantage here. One of the virtues is its extraordinary capacity for detecting very small distinctions of frequency, and therefore of pitch, as well as not quite such small distinctions of harmonic content, and therefore of tone colouring, and of amplitude, and therefore of loudness. One of the limitations is our inability to distinguish separately

any acoustic events occurring within an interval of about 50 milliseconds: say from 1/20 to 1/18 of a second. The effect of this for sound is
a little like the effect for light of the persistence of vision. Within so
short a time, impressions carry over sufficiently to blend, so that we see
the successive frames of a motion picture as continuous movement, and
hear the successive impacts of a harmonic spectrum as a continuous
stream of sound. If we could detect each impact individually, the confusion might be greater than our hearing could sort out.

It is this merging of our hearing across a mini-interval of time which
may in part account for the blending of harmonics into tone colouring,
as opposed to their separating into individual notes. For the relationship of harmonic partials is a time relationship: so many oscillations in
such-and-such a time; so many Hz or cycles per second. Oscillations
more than about 50 milliseconds apart from one another may not blend
into tone colouring but may set up other notes, though there is quite a
wide margin within which we can hear them either way according as we
direct our mental attention. Oscillations slower than about 20 Hz (i.e.
of greater duration than 1/20 of a second) are not detectable as sound at
all.

How we direct our mental attention has a very great effect upon how
we perceive the impact of sounds. We have unconscious expectations
and preferences to which native disposition and early conditioning
alike contribute, as well as training and experience. We have a
tendency to hear (acoustically) what we expect or wish to hear. It quite
often happens in ordinary discussion that we hear (semantically) what
we expect or want to hear rather than what is actually said; indeed, our
human capacity for self-deception and mutual misunderstanding is
always with us. Sometimes, let it be added, our illusions are valuable or
necessary to our well-being, just as the persistence of vision is necessary
to the motion picture and the persistence of hearing is necessary to the
musical experience.

One advantage of the delay of about 50 milliseconds before the next
impact is detected as a separate event is the margin of time which this
delay allows to our hearing for scanning the vibrations and averaging
them into one blended impression. What arrives at our ears first during
that margin of time impresses us as being the source of the sound; what
follows may add volume or colouring or other attributes without
appearing to be a further source of sound. This effect is sometimes
called the precedence effect, because what comes first within the
margin takes precedence over what comes later, which only reinforces
and does not displace the first impression. Some other such subjective

effects are the fatigue which may briefly set in after a rather loud note of rather long duration (so that, for example, our impressions of loudness are momentarily altered, and a loud after a soft may seem louder than it is); and the remarkable tolerance with which we may adjust mentally to what we really very well know are quite gross errors, e.g. of intonation. (Equal temperament, for example, only becomes acceptable through this tolerance.)

Our scanning of all the available information with a view to averaging it out as one combined and comprehensible impression is greatly assisted by our having two ears, separated by perhaps seven inches and a moderately dense and bony obstacle, namely the head. The head diffracts or scatters sound like any other obstacle of comparable size and density. The two ears receive signals by no means identical, especially for the higher frequencies above some 1000 Hz. Not only are the ears slightly apart; we can and do move our heads, and turn our ears this way and that, and lean a little one way and another, thereby considerably increasing the amount of information made available for averaging up; the frequencies which can be thus researched go down to about 500 Hz. The performers are also liable to move about to quite a substantial extent. Every such small variation in the paths of travel is eagerly accepted by our hearing for further processing and scanning and eventual reporting to our brain centres as the sound perceived. So far from being confused by such a multiplicity of information, the ear makes all possible use of it, and reports the complications as a compound perception of extraordinary richness and fidelity – superimposed, in musical people, upon a more or less poetical and creative factor of imagination. For in music, as elsewhere, what we are bringing to an experience may count for just as much as what we are getting out of it.

THE MECHANICS OF HEARING

The mechanics of our aural perception really begin at the eardrums; for the outer ear in humans has only vestigial utility in gathering the sounds. The eardrum is a membrane of the requisite elasticity to pick up the pressure waves in the air which constitute sound vibrations, and to vibrate almost exactly in response. The vibration of the eardrum passes through the middle ear by a link comprised of three small bones or ossicles which form a system of levers, reducing the motion but increasing the pressure transmitted to the flexible oval window, where the inner ear begins. Here comes a coiled cavity called the cochlea; it contains fluid, and is divided lengthwise by the basilar membrane, to which the fluid imparts vibrations still in close correspondence with the source of sound. Since the fluid is incompressible, there is also a flexible round window leading back into the middle ear, so as to relieve the pressure after it has passed across the basilar membrane.

The explanation of the basilar membrane, elaborated by Helmholtz and for some time afterwards accepted, has not in the main stood up to later researches. The basilar membrane has a very large number of hair-cells arranged in rows, possibly totalling something in the astonishing region of 30,000. Helmholtz thought that what he described as the fibres of the basilar membrane resemble the strings of a piano, tuned to different tensions in such a way as to pick up the vibrations imparted to them by sympathetic vibration. If the dampers of a piano are raised by putting down the 'loud' pedal, its strings can readily be heard resounding in sympathy with any tones within range, such as a radio sounding in the room; and so it was thought that the fibres might resound in sympathy with the oncoming vibrations. This theory assumed a scope and fineness of distinction within a tiny organ which further investigation has not confirmed. The distinctions of which the ear is capable are just as fine as was supposed, or finer; but they are made at later stages in the auditory process.

The pressure waves received by the eardrum and transmitted by the ossicles and the oval window pass hydraulically along the basilar membrane, causing bulges in it positioned and conditioned by the frequencies occurring. The higher frequencies press harder near the oval window, where the basilar membrane is stiffest; the lower frequencies press harder away from the oval window, where the basilar membrane is slackest. The passing amplitude of each successive wave is greatest within a small area governed by the frequency, but not so small that it could by itself determine the fine distinctions which we know from experience to obtain. There are bands of response, not lines of response. The fine distinctions must, therefore, be coded at some further stage by the nervous system.

Many rows of sensory cells receive mechanical impulses from the places at which the basilar membrane is bulging most, and relay corresponding electrical signals to the brain. What may be loosely compared to a system of switches is operative here, but how it is operative is not certainly known. The nearer to the brain, at any rate, the more complex the coding. Within the brain, further processing is introduced which cannot be described merely as coding, since it takes account both of prior experience and of present intention. The entire subject of neural and cerebral activity continues to be studied with an elegance and precision which are extraordinarily impressive up to, although not across, the very threshold between the mechanical and the psychological realities of human experience.

There are some mechanical characteristics of our hearing which further complicate the already very complex information as it reaches our ears. For example, beats are set up in the oncoming vibrations when these are of close but not identical frequency. For such vibrations get periodically into phase together, thus intensifying their combined amplitude; and out of phase with one another, thus diminishing their combined amplitude. Wholly in phase, they may double their loudness: wholly out of phase, they may reduce it to silence; and the periodicity at which they produce these alternations may itself be heard as an oscillating frequency, and therefore as a sounding pitch. Such induced frequencies of the first order may themselves relate to other neighbouring frequencies, inducing other but weaker beat tones of the second order; and so on to any extent in theory, although quite negligibly thereafter in practice.

Not only can beats occur objectively, however, but in certain respects (as perhaps in all second-order effects) subjectively as well. It is one fairly well established characteristic of our mechanism of hearing that it may be (as outside sources of sound may be) not quite symmetrical in its activity. Its response to vibration is therefore not quite linear: it introduces some vibration conditioned by its own non-linear behaviour, in addition to its conditioning by the oncoming vibration. It is not, however, at all certain whether such mechanical lack of symmetry is located in the ear (as was originally supposed), in the sensation cells and nervous system (a stage further along the line) or even in the brain itself (with its not by any means subservient influence upon the perception of sound).

Beats in the form of oscillations of amplitude due to mutual interference can certainly be established as objective tones when their oscillations recur at frequencies within the audible range. Harmonics due to non-linear interference with our hearing faculty are still an area open to conflicting explanations, but that something is happening subjectively, since it does not show up on objective measurements, is generally accepted. One term which defines itself is subjective tones; but a more explicit term is combination tones, on the assumption that two objective tones may combine to produce a third tone which is subjective.

One combination tone which is not always credited and is certainly of no great importance is ascribed to a frequency equal to the sum of the two objective frequencies, whence it was called by Helmholtz a summation tone. Far more important and less controversial tones are those called difference tones, because their frequency is equal to the difference between the two objective frequencies. They are therefore lower than either of their generating tones in pitch. When these generating tones are of sufficient loudness, the combination tone may itself be loud enough to have very substantial consequences for music.

The great violinist Tartini claimed, in the mid-eighteenth century, to have discovered difference tones; and indeed they are very easy to produce audibly by playing double-stops accurately upon the violin. Helmholtz in the mid-nineteenth century built up a considerable area of acoustic theory on the strength of them. Their musical importance rests mainly on one remarkably helpful feature: it is that any two objectively consecutive harmonics of a given series may generate subjectively a difference tone at the fundamental frequency of that series.

It is extremely important for music that we normally perceive a note at the pitch of its first or fundamental harmonic. Yet when objectively measured, that fundamental may be found to have very little intensity, or to be virtually or entirely missing. The bottom g of the violin, for example, has been measured at a mere 0.1 per cent of the intensity of its harmonic series as a whole. But that, of course, is not in the least how we perceive the note. It is very probably the accumulation of difference tones, subjectively generated, which brings to our perception of the fundamental enough loudness to cause us (aided by our expectations) to accept that fundamental so readily as the note in question.

Suppose there were to fall upon the ear no more than four or five consecutive upper harmonics of a series, of reasonably equal intensity, but with not a trace objectively of the fundamental: we shall hear the pitch of that missing fundamental subjectively. Suppose some 10 to 30 consecutive harmonics to be generated electronically quite high up in the series, with none of the lower harmonics objectively present; still the fundamental rings through with uncanny solidity and conviction. The listener is supplying what the source of sound does not, and supplying it all the better because it is just what the acoustic situation familiarly implies.

A telephone diaphragm must avoid vibration peaks within the fundamental range of human speech, since these would cause acute distortion. It transmits, objectively, enough upper harmonics for the ear to reconstitute from them, subjectively, the suppressed fundamentals, probably as difference tones. The expense and size of very large organ pipes is sometimes avoided by juxtaposing two smaller ranks a fifth apart, of which the difference tones are heard as the low notes required. In fact, it seems unlikely that fundamentals can be heard directly from the vast 32-foot (or even 64-foot) pipes at all, nor perhaps from the low notes of the piano. It is more probable that we are reconstituting them anyhow from upper harmonics which we know can be directly heard. We are not just imagining them: they have acoustic origins. But we may well be taking them from our inner processing rather than from the outer conformation.

The structures of sounding substances in the shape of instruments are themselves liable to non-linear oscillation, causing harmonic or inharmonic partials which would not be present if their oscillation were exclusively linear. In actual circumstances, that can never quite occur. Friction and stiffness and inertia and resistance are inherent in our physical universe: it is only the extent of them that may so widely vary. It seems quite certain, however, that the resulting irregularities are not only tolerated but welcomed for their part in giving to actual instruments their individuality. Life itself is individual and imperfect. Music of any wide range of feeling must be able to take into account the hard and the bitter sides as well as the smooth and the sweet sides of life; and in the following chapter, we may consider in principle some of the underlying connections through which this might occur.

4 HEARING INTO MUSIC

CONFLICT AND RESOLUTION

The connections between physical and physiological occurrences, on the one hand, and emotional and psychological experiences, on the other hand, operate primarily in the unconscious. We never enquire about them when hearing or performing music, and scarcely when composing. The composer's craft is, indeed, both conscious and unconscious, but he does not seem to know or need to know any more than the rest of us about these underlying connections, being well content if as an artist he knows how to make them work. As a problem in philosophy the relationship of sound to sense has been given some very persistent attention, some of it uncommonly perspicacious, some of it rather more academic and unrewarding, but from the nature of the case none of it at all conclusive overall. As a problem in psychology, and perhaps still more in those refinements of physiology which verge upon and are often called psychology, the subject has been approached through many series of controlled experiments, some of them of the most remarkable ingenuity and insight, some once again oddly remote from the human objects of the enterprise, and as a whole no more conclusive than the philosophical speculations with which they are of necessity bound up. There is always the limitation that the psyche in so far as it is unconscious cannot be directly observed, still less measured. In so far as the experience of music is conscious (and of course it very largely is), we can still observe only its subjective character as reported by individuals. In certain of their more elemental aspects, such as for example impressions of pitch, of loudness, of timbre or of speed, these reports can be averaged, measured and compared mathematically. But however scrupulous the statistics thus obtained, and however valuable on the borders of the musical experience, they are not measurements of what comes out of these elements, namely the musical experience itself. It is not the emotions which are being measured. Nor is it the psyche which is being measured. The psyche deals in images, not quantities. The meaning of these images may be variously explained, but it certainly cannot be measured.

Thus when we set up an objective scale for measuring amplitude, and when we find that a comparable scale for our subjective impressions of loudness has to be logarithmic in order to keep in approximate correspondence, we have a most useful yardstick, but not for the emotional imponderables of the situation. It is the emotional realities of music which so elude us in our attempts to give them an intellectual status and definition. They are definite, but they are resistant not only to measurement but to verbalization. Music is non-verbal, which has led to the question whether it may not have certain source-springs which are pre-verbal. Our emotional sources do go very far back, and though we change as we grow older we do not discard so much as assimilate the earliest modes of our being. That glory of warmth and containment which we know so well in music but can only describe with such difficulty may derive something of its feeling-tone from our state before ever we came to the use of words. Then indeed for good and bad we must have felt at one with the universe. Outer reality seemed part of us, neither separate nor substantial, but a continuum bounded by the mother who sustained us and comprised of the emotions which possessed us. In so far as later on we grow to accept that there is a reality out there and that *we* are parts of *it*, there may be great reassurance in finding samples of it so controlled and interiorized as music has to offer. For while we are in the music, once more the world is feeling, and feeling is the world. There are more treasures in that borderland of the unconscious than we could or need to bring to rational account. Just occasionally a hint gleams through, unprovable yet suggestive. There are, for example, dreams on record of music appearing as rebirth, that perennial symbol for a new start in life, or as a flow of milk, in some comparable fantasy of inner nourishment and renewal. We are really in the region here of myth and ritual, and of those archetypal images which run through the products of human imagination as Alph the sacred river ran through caverns measureless to man. Coleridge knew: he was himself a prime dealer in archetypal imagery.

Since musical images essentially lack verbal or even pictorial correspondences, it seems untenable to call them representations of anything. But it is not untenable to call them analogues, along the lines of that lively musical philosopher, Susanne Langer and her followers. Art and feeling are not identical, nor are they interchangeable, but somehow the shapes of them may run in parallel. The music unfolds analogously or 'isomorphically' with our feelings and our intuitions, needing no words because it is itself a wordless form of awareness. There is nothing vague about this awareness, consisting as I think basically it may of insights into the inwardness (as opposed to the out-wardness) of our ordinary lives, which however individual in the working-out are nevertheless conditioned by archetypal themes such as love and hate and courage and despair. We all know something of those themes at heart and can respond at least in principle to their analogues in music.

It was Beethoven who once spoke of his music going from the heart to the heart, implying, of course, that it was feeling he most wanted to communicate. Intuition certainly comes in as well. We could speak about music going from the unconscious to the unconscious, but also to and from consciousness, nearer to which on the whole lie those abund-ant technical resources, the links, the repetitions, the balances, the contrasts and the transformations of thematic material. Even so, a composer may often surprise himself later on by noticing relationships of which he had no deliberate intention at the time. And to find a problem solved overnight in the unconscious which would not yield (though it may well have been prepared) the day or the month or the year before is not uncommon. Artists are not the only people to benefit from this sort of uncovenanted assistance (it can also be hindrance) from one's lower layers; but they do so very markedly, and not least in music.

As can happen in all the best conjuring, you may have a very fair idea of how the magic is being worked yet still experience it as magic. The resources of music are in fact largely accessible to trained analysis, especially when that analysis is guided by an empathy which comple-ments the training. The magic will gain, not suffer, from being better understood. But even when we are only giving a subliminal attention to the cunning contrivances which both consciously and unconsciously have gone to the making of the music, it is wonderful how they im-pinge on the underside of our awareness, and where necessary on the overside. We take in what we need to take in, and the more so as we are the more musically adapted. We may be taking conscious pleasure in some of the finer felicities, while assimilating others at varying levels; but it is the felicity itself which takes hold of us. We are in happy state; and of this happiness we most certainly are conscious.

There are, then, these two faces of musical experience: it glows with meaning; and we are hard put to it ultimately to say what that meaning might be. But short of that ultimate solution, much important work is being done, for a sympathetic and perceptive summary of which the reader may be recommended to the article 'Psychology of music' written in part by Natasha Spender and in part by Rosamund Shuter-Dyson for *The New Grove Dictionary of Music and Musicians* (1980, Vol. 15, pp. 388–427, London) under the general approach known as experimental psychology. True, our chief research finding in the field appears to be how variable our research findings are, and how flexible the links must be between the objective conditions and the subjective responses of an ordinary musical experience. Yet is that surprising? The human psyche is autonomous, incalculable and very potent in its own right; and music certainly plumbs its deeper levels, bringing up rewards which far exceed our conscious expectations.

For, of course, what we should like to know even more than the many details illuminated by experimental psychology is how our response in detail adds up to our experience in sum. Our experience in sum is a totality of feeling and intuition. We cannot even begin to measure that side of life. Perhaps we can really only live it, and notice that other people appear to be living it in comparable fashions and degrees. It is the fact of our sharing so much in common with other people that makes music potentially a channel of communication. We share images both individual and inherited, as the many common features in dreams and in mythology alike suggest. We draw on associations from our own childhood and from the childhood of the race, as well as on others which may lie much closer to the surface. Our human arts are all in some degree conditioned by this interior stream of associations, but none more so than music, in which references to the world outside are few and unimportant and verbal messages have no place at all.

The interchange of mind and matter is also more mutual than had been supposed. The ear signals to the brain; but so, in return, does the brain signal to the ear, modifying its receptivity. The channels in between are multiple and complex, likewise modifying the signals in either direction. Not only will an acoustic stimulus induce a mental state; a mental state will condition an acoustic stimulus. The end result may owe as much to interpretation as it does to stimulation. We hear to some extent as we expect and even as we wish to hear: not only our capacities but our preferences affect our hearing. The implications of these facts for philosophy and for psychology alike are full of interest. They are interesting for music, too. They will be differently viewed under the divergent hypothesis of behaviourism (unrewarding here), of Gestalt theory (certainly relevant), of information theory and cybernetic theory (both of them suggestive) and of depth-psychology (highly appropriate). It is chiefly necessary for what follows to accept the psyche as an actual and not merely as a theoretical fact of life. We *have* ears, nerves, a brain. We *are* people, which is not just another way of saying the same thing.

Art in its more searching operations functions primarily by contrasts. These must be sharp enough to generate tension, not so sharp as to baffle understanding. Now of course our understanding is itself a variable, depending as it does on many factors both innate and acquired. There are degrees of natural bent and talent, of social background and tradition, of training and experience, of exposure and committedness. But always it is the contrasts which set up the tension. A one-sided statement is not a sufficient statement until its opposite is also stated or at the least implied. A work of art which is only sentimental, for example, or only brutal, is unbalanced, and lacks that tension which comes from resembling life in being a conflict of opposites. Good and evil, sweet and bitter, light and dark, male and female: with all such opposites, the one pole can only be imagined in relation to the other pole. We ourselves are alive, yet mortal; human, yet animal; in unavoidable conflict, yet in search of reconciliation. It may be that the ultimate scenario is just such a search through conflict for reconciliation. Contrast is the stuff of art because contrast is the stuff of life.

Music can show the clash and reconciliation of opposites in many idioms; but these idioms have it in common that they use symbolic images, namely sounds. We should never underestimate the power of images. An image of which the associations, and more particularly the unconscious associations, are strong enough, as in great music they evidently are, can focus our feelings and stir our intuitions, conditioning our moods and carrying them through inner dramas of the spirit. The emotion with which such associations may be charged, however, is certainly not decreased, and indeed it may on the contrary be in some manner defined, by their being very much of the body, too. For there are organic factors which while not, in all probability, making a biological force of music, nevertheless bring music into an area where biological forces operate, as a few very elementary considerations may next suggest.

One such consideration is that a rise in pitch may require more tension physically on vocal cords or lips or strings or reeds: hence more energy. Similarly with a rise in loudness, requiring perhaps more manual exertion or more pressure from the lungs. There is, indeed, a certain acoustic and artistic relationship between a rise or a fall in pitch and volume: they tend to go together. In this way, we may have the sensation of rising to a climax and falling to a resolution. Now raising oneself uphill is indeed more effortful than lowering oneself downhill, except in so far as effort is needed to prevent oneself from going down too fast. Gravity is a force we all experience; and the effort of raising the pitch or the volume has enough in common with our experience of gravity to give substance to the metaphor by which we call pitches of greater frequency high and pitches of lesser frequency low: just as, of course, we call greater numbers high and lesser numbers low. High and low volume reflect the same basic metaphor as high and low pitch.

A rise in speed will also demand more energy in terms of physical movement, and may suggest it in terms of musical meaning. In greater physical effort, too, our hearts beat faster and harder, as may also happen in mental agitation; tempos and rhythms in music take on a comparable significance. Our breathing is liable to similar inflexions. Our legs swing steadily at the walk, with a resemblance to pendular motion closely reproduced in 'ordinary time' (*tempo ordinario*) or 'common time': that is to say, in duple measure at moderate speed; or faster, but still in duple measure, at the run; for not until we feel disposed to skip rather than to run will our legs break into a triple measure, but when they do, our spirits are likely to be as translated as our movements, real or imaginary. Or perhaps a slow triple may feel more like lingering than skipping, but at any rate with a certain elegiac lilt and asymmetry. And all these bodily associations, together with our far subtler rhythms of electrical charge and discharge, are deeply ingrained, normally unconscious, and the stronger in their hidden influence on that account. Music does not merely feel like a sort of dance: it is a sort of dance, but as much in the psyche as in the limbs, and indeed for essential purposes not in the limbs at all. The 'as if' experience takes over from the 'as is' experience so characteristically that the mental effect comes out much the same; while in performing music there are indeed actual bodily movements akin to dance.

The point here is that our symbolical experiences are every bit as potent in their own way as our literal experiences. Music really can take us through it all, for while our bodies may be stationary our minds are travelling. Our journeys of the imagination pass through far realms of fantasy. But fantasies however incorporeal are experiences too, and none the less so when they remain below the threshold of consciousness. We do not need and we are better without conscious imaginings about the music; but our state is different from usual, and it is the flow of feelings and intuitions with which we are responding, largely beneath the surface of awareness, that make it so. Mendelssohn once put it that music is not too indefinite to be expressed in words, but too definite. The meanings of music may indeed be definite, resting as they do on associations so positively defined. But they would not be so valuable to us as they are if they could as well be expressed in any other way.

BEATING AS A LINK WITH THE EMOTIONS

Our associations of musical patterns with organic occurrences are only one front of the multi-dimensional interface of mind and matter which we experience in music. The physical characteristics of sound vibration themselves invite associations. There is a physical plenitude and intensity about those tone colourings which arise when the higher harmonics are plentiful and vibrant: we pick it up emotionally as bright and fascinating. There is a physical sparseness and solidity about those which arise when the lower harmonics are preponderant and massive: we pick it up emotionally as dark and powerful. Harmonics of which the ratios are complicated give rise to stronger mutual interferences and combinations, and therefore it may be supposed to more prominent beating, than harmonics of which the ratios are simple: we pick it up as rich, or if carried farther, we pick it up as harsh. For as we have seen, beating may occur when two harmonics of different pitch sound together. In more complicated situations, beating becomes more complicated also. The ways in which such beating affects our musical responses are not so clear as they appeared to be before recent experiments revealed certain previously unnoticed discrepancies: but there can be no doubt that beats are relevant, and that we have therefore to bring them at least tentatively back into the discussion here.

We may recall broadly how beating may happen. Faster vibrations giving higher pitch may overtake slower vibrations giving lower pitch. Then their peaks and troughs may alternately coincide (putting them in phase, with maximum reinforcement) and cross (putting them out of phase, with maximum interference); the transitions between the two extremes are intermediate (at every stage of being partly in and partly out of phase, with every proportion of reinforcement and interference). It is broadly the case that the lower and the closer together two tones are sounding in relation to each other, the more slowly the oscillations of amplitude perceived as beats will be produced; the higher and the more separated, the faster. This may be tested by playing loudly together two rather low notes on a piano, when they will be heard to beat quite slowly and clearly. Higher up, the rate increases; and between wider intervals, it can be so distinct, and so distinctive for the intervals being sounded, that piano tuners are in the habit of counting the beats as a check on the exact pitch relationships they are tuning. Yet higher, the rate of beating gets to be too fast to be distinguished, let alone counted; but it does not follow that the subliminal effect is negligible. On the contrary, it may well influence our sensations and condition our responses as one factor in the combined musical situation.

Beating at the rate of about six or seven times a second is perceived as distinct pulsations of amplitude, and in general with a pleasing effect. This is approximately the rate of a good vibrato, which is a frequency modulation, ordinarily combined in some degree with an amplitude modulation, used more or less deliberately to alleviate the deadening effect on the ear of an absolutely constant acoustic signal if too prolonged. Organ builders may deliberately introduce beating at about this rate between two ranks of pipes by tuning them just off the unison. Piano tuners also tend to mistune the three unison sets of strings in the instrument's middle register to give enough beating for a sort of life and sparkle additional to the inharmonicity already inherent in those tense, stiff steel wires: all of which works to our advantage, since it is in our nature to prefer this shimmering ring to a deadpan regularity. Machinery can be undeviating: we are not; and we have here a typical collusion between an acoustic imperfection and a human need.

But as beats get faster, so they may come to seem restless, until they are fast enough to merge indistinguishably yet still disagreeably. Faster again, they become inappreciable. For tones moderately high in pitch, the most disagreeable rate of beating seems to come at about the rate of thirty beats a second. And here a most interesting speculation arises, though not all impediments to it have been cleared, and it must therefore represent a part of the explanation rather than the whole. The speculation is that consonance and dissonance represent degrees, from zero upwards, of subliminally disagreeable beating. On this assumption, dissonance actually feels a little uncomfortable or rough; and consonance actually feels more comfortable and smooth. It is, of course, obvious that a mild discord feels harsher in a smooth context, and smoother in a harsh context. A discord harsh enough to need resolving in Palestrina may be mild enough to resolve a harsher discord in Stravinsky. The results of familiarity are important here; for if the harshness is in any way a product of the complexity of the vibrations present, then it is reasonable to suppose that our auditory system gets used to resolving greater complexities with growing familiarity. Thus it is that at different periods, different choices are available to us. What does not come within our choice, although it is quite wonderfully at our disposal, is the physical behaviour of the acoustic material around which our use of consonance and dissonance revolves.

A single, simple (pure) tone by definition has no upper harmonics; and it is one of the unresolved impediments to the theory of beats as the physical cause of dissonance that even two soft and undistorted simple (pure) tones may apparently yield an effect of dissonance not only when mistuned at the unison and beating there, but also at wider intervals where their upper harmonics could no doubt be supposed to beat – if only they had any upper harmonics to beat! I shall refer the reader to Charles Taylor's *Sounds of Music* (1976, pp. 151ff., London) for an indication of the lines along which this problem can perhaps be met. What in all probability can be taken to happen, though it cannot be all that is happening, may be summarized as follows.

Suppose two approximately simple (pure) tones to be sounding within a pitch-range in or around the treble stave. The dissonance attributed to beating becomes harshest around the interval of a semitone, and vanishes around a minor third. Just short of the octave, dissonance somewhat less harshly reappears. At the exact octave, beating and dissonance are virtually as absent as they are at the exact unison; whence in part it is, perhaps, that an octave feels more like a higher replica of the unison than like a wholly different note. Just beyond the octave, beating and dissonance return. Further up, beating and dissonance become inappreciable. But in all this, there are great possibilities of confusion between beats objectively observable and combination tones subjectively experienced. It is only legitimate to assume that beating does happen and that its connection with dissonance is at least one contributory factor in the explanation.

Next suppose not two approximately simple (pure) tones, but two compound tones of more or less considerable complexity, such as actual music uses. The beats will no longer be confined to fundamentals (and any subjective by-products) but may occur between any audible harmonics. Thus at the interval of a minor second between c and c sharp, for example, the fundamentals and all the upper harmonics beat to produce a maximum of intelligible dissonance as normally encountered in equal temperament. At the major second between c and d, the same harmonics beat, but not quite so harshly. At the minor third between c and e flat, there may be a combination tone at d' flat: there is certainly some beating between c'', as the fourth harmonic of c, and b' flat, as the third harmonic of e flat; still more is there beating between e'' natural, as the fifth harmonic of c, and e'' flat, as the fourth harmonic of e flat (the bottom open C of the cello, for example, will sound this major third as a very clear harmonic).

While the minor third has been fully accepted as a consonance for some hundreds of years, this was not always unreservedly the case. There is a certain ambiguity, a trace of unavoidable uneasiness, because while the harmony is declaring minor, the harmonics are ringing through hauntingly with major, and the conflict, however subliminal, is not altogether to be ignored. It remained customary during the Renaissance to avoid the minor third at least on final closes, by turning it into a major third on the last chord (sometimes called *Tierce de Picardie*, Picardy Third); and many people would still feel that the minor mode tends to a less confident or brilliant feeling than the major mode.

No such ambiguity affects the major third, as between c and e. But there is beating, for example between c'', as the fourth harmonic of c, and b', as the third harmonic of e; and again between g', as the sixth harmonic of c, and g'' sharp, as the fifth harmonic of e. Since the lower the pitch, the more prominent this beating, care must be taken when using thirds in a low register, where they will sound much more thick and lumpy than in a high register, as every good teacher or craftsman of harmony and orchestration is well aware.

At the perfect fourth between c and f, there is some beating between g', as the third harmonic of c, and f', as the second harmonic of f; and between g'', as the sixth harmonic of c, and a'', as the fifth harmonic of f. The effect is consonant, though there has always been that faint suspicion that nevertheless a fourth may need resolving on to a third just as if it really were a discord. A matter of degree, evidently; but that is only to be expected in this elusive region where so much depends upon familiarity and custom. At the tritone (augmented fourth, c to f sharp, or diminished fifth, f sharp to c') there is a quantity of beating, but the chief impression is not so much dissonance as uncertainty about which way the tonality is leading; for the scale is divided just at the middle and we sense C major and F sharp major indeterminately (or simultaneously in much music of the twentieth century – Bartók, for example – where the tritone acts a little like the dominant in classical and romantic harmony).

At the perfect fifth between c and g, there may perhaps be a very consonant combination tone at e'; there is some appreciable beating between c'', as the fourth harmonic of c, and d'', as the third harmonic of g, and between this and e'', as the fifth harmonic of c; the overall

1   Apollo with Renaissance lyra da braccio

2   Renaissance rebec and lutes

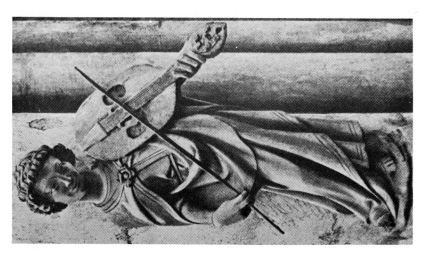

3–5 Late-medieval lyra, portative and gittern

6 St Cecilia playing a Renaissance portative

7 King David playing a late-medieval harp

8   Late-Renaissance masque with broken consort (Sir Henry Unton at dinner)

9 Orlando di Lasso and the late-Renaissance chapel of the Duke of Bavaria

10 An early-baroque consort of six viols played by the choir-school at Troyes for Louis XIII

11   A baroque recorder, with typical cross-fingering

12 A baroque lutanist, playing a theorbo with long diapasons

13 A late-baroque chamber orchestra

14 Henriette, daughter of Louis XV, playing a late-baroque, seven-string gamba, with a two-manual harpsichord in the background

effect is almost wholly consonant. At the octave between c and c', there is no beating among the first six harmonics, while any beating between b'', as the seventh harmonic of c, and c''', as the fourth harmonic of c', is too high and rapid to produce dissonance. Intervals which are themselves partials of one harmonic series have a way of sounding consonant in sonority even when not in grammar, so that the unison itself is experienced not as an interval but as an identity: there is no beating between the harmonic series of each, because they are the same. Since this is very nearly true of the octave also, we can see yet again why each octave feels like a repetition in another register, and why we name our notes in repeating order at each octave interval.

Beating between very high harmonics, even if strong, may be too rapid to have much if any influence. Between the lowest few harmonics (and any prominent combination tones), on the other hand, beating is likely to have a powerful effect; and it is somewhere in this effect that there almost certainly lies one physical and objective cause of distinction between grades of consonance and dissonance. Our subjective distinctions can then elaborate, as usual, on the objective potentialities. We may do well not to press this explanation too literally, but it almost certainly applies in principle.

THE BALANCE OF SIMPLE AND COMPLEX ELEMENTS

It remains to draw attention to one more physical property of intervals which may help to condition their mental and emotional associations as the ear interprets them. This is the mathematical simplicity, reflecting an acoustic simplicity, in the ratios between the vibration frequencies of the primary or diatonic intervals within the octave. It is the smoothest consonances which tend to show the simplest ratios. Once again, we are not required to take the calculated ratios in too literal a significance. The exact figures will vary in practice with, for example, the temperament or tuning chosen, not to mention any unintended discrepancies of intonation. But there is no mistaking the broad principle that simpler ratios go with less beating and therefore somehow or other with less dissonance. Our very perception of consonance and dissonance is perhaps a mode of experiencing degrees of simplicity and complexity. We have seen reason to think that in any artistic response, what holds our attention is something neither too simple to be interesting at all, nor too complicated to be interpreted at all, given the habits and the capacities we ourselves may be bringing to the situation at any particular time or place. A proper balance between the

baffling and the intriguing is surely the most acceptable artistic challenge. The blend of discord and concord in music is a variable blend;
but it will always bear some relationship to the prevailing conditions of
acoustic simplicity and complexity.

The simplest of ratios ranks grammatically as the most perfect concord: the unison at 1:1. The octave comes next at 2:1; then the fifth at
3:2, and the fourth at 4:3. These all rate grammatically (in the old
dispensation) as perfect concords (even though in certain contexts the
fourth may need to be resolved). Then come the grammatically imperfect concords: the major third at 5:4; the minor sixth at 8:5; the minor
third at 6:5; the major sixth at 5:3. And the grammatical discords:
minor second (as diatonic semitone) very harsh at 16:15; major
seventh, fairly harsh at 15:8; major second (as major tone), fairly harsh
at 9:8, or (as minor tone) at 10:9; minor seventh, not very harsh at
16:9. The above are intervals diatonic to their scale. Chromatic
intervals are basically less simple, and less distinctly defined, so that
their tuning is apt to be neither so close nor so critical. The minor
second (as chromatic semitone) comes out, for example, pretty dissonant and ill-defined at 135:128.

The augmented and diminished intervals are neither very dissonant
nor very definite: their chief effect is to be tonally ambiguous, turning
this way or that, elaborating plain progressions with subtle alterations,
modifying classical directness towards romantic mystery. The augmented second is calculated at 75:64, but may be tuned quite satisfactorily at 7:6; the diminished third stands officially at 256:225; the
tritone as augmented fourth stands at 45:32, but may be tuned well
enough at 7:5; the tritone as diminished fifth stands at 64:45; the augmented fifth stands well enough at 25:16, and the augmented sixth
may be well tuned at or very near to 7:4; the diminished seventh, a
slippery customer facing just about in any direction desired, catches the
official eye at 2048:1215.

Intervals larger than the octave are regarded grammatically as transposed replicas (e.g. the tenth, at the octave plus a third, as if it were a
third). For some purposes, this is realistic; for others, not. The beating
of the compound interval will resemble the beating of the simple
interval, but not altogether: as we saw, thirds low down beat more
roughly than thirds high up, and tenths in that register will sound both
sweeter and more resonant; while thirds high up give a sparkle and
brilliance which tenths do not. Yet for voice-leading and progressions
and harmony generally, any third or tenth shares a common behaviour
far outweighing the acoustic unlikeness. Tone colouring and harmony

may sometimes come into conflict there, and it takes a good craftsman to know just how best to balance it out.

Two notes together make an interval: more than two notes together make a chord. If such complexity can be found between two notes, their upper harmonics and their combination tones, what must it be like between more than two? There should never be any difficulty in understanding how music can find enough raw material for its manifold operations. The acoustic material is there in abundance; the only difficulty is in understanding how we, with our limited hearing system, can take it all in and sort it all out, arriving at our ears as it does solely as minute variations in the pressure of the outside air. But we do take it in and sort it out, and the hidden bridge which music crosses between mind and matter is certainly a fact of life. So is the bridge between our more conscious and our less conscious levels. This bridging of boundaries between outer and inner, and between conscious and unconscious, can work abundantly to our advantage, and is one of the chief bonuses which the arts can bring to us in our ordinary living.

5 WORKING METHODS

SIMPLE AND COUPLED ACOUSTIC SYSTEMS

Instruments are the working tools of music. They are the practical devices by which the acoustic properties of nature are managed for the artistic purposes of music; and they are for the most part examples of intuitive discoveries developed by craftsmanship, rather than of methodical discoveries developed by science. Nevertheless, scientists have a great deal that is to the point to say about them, and it is easier to get a systematic view if they are scientifically distinguished.

Perhaps the most elementary distinction among instruments is between those which are themselves an effective sounding substance, propagating vibrations directly through the air to our ears, on the one hand; and those which have a primary source of sound propagating vibrations indirectly by means of a secondary resonator, on the other hand. The first of these classes has the scientific description: idiophones, or self-sounders. The sounding substance is its own source of vibration, receiving acoustic energy and transmitting it in the same action. Gongs, wooden blocks and the powerful little reeds of the harmonium are examples of this self-sufficient principle.

The second class, however, is much the commoner and more important. The vibrations are excited in one source, not by itself sufficient, but needing the resonant support and collaboration of an associated structure such as the body of a violin or the air column of a flute, the two elements together forming a coupled acoustic system. The violin body has its own peaks of resonance, and so does the air which it contains; these do not decide the note heard as a fundamental, which the string determines, but they do greatly affect the tone colouring of that note; indeed, the felicitous placing of the peaks of resonance makes all the difference between a good violin and a bad one. It is certainly reasonable, therefore, to refer to the chief of those bands of natural resonance as formants. The pipe of the flute itself has probably little influence, but the air shaped by it and contained in it basically determines the pitch, and very largely conditions the tone colouring, of the note heard.

Whether they are simple idiophones or coupled systems, all instruments enlist the environment (i.e. normally the room) and also our ears themselves as acoustic partners. Hearing itself is a coupled acoustic system, as well as having neural, cerebral and psychological connections to complete the operation. The air which is our atmosphere always or almost always enters at some stage into the partnership. The air itself can under certain circumstances be a source of sound. When parted by a flash of lightning, the air can rebound with the clap of sound which, with its many echoes, we hear as thunder. When penetrated by a solid such as an aircraft travelling at supersonic speed, i.e. faster than the rate at which it can yield by permitting the passage of vibration at the normal speed of sound, the air reacts with a sonic bang very like a clap of thunder. But when all is said, the chief acoustic role of air is to accept and transmit vibration from an independent source of sound.

A rhythm struck out on a solid wooden log is sounded on an idiophone: the vibrations set up in the wood are transmitted from its surface to the surrounding air, which takes them to any listening ears. But a rhythm struck out on a hollow wooden log is sounded on a coupled acoustic system of which the resonating partner is the air inside: the vibrations set up in the wood excite further vibrations in the contained air, conditioned in part by the natural resonance-frequencies of the wood, in part by those of the air-cavity (and governed by its shape and size), and altogether by the combination of these two contributory factors. The pressure waves represented by this combination are transmitted to the air outside, more particularly through any opening but also in a measure by the wooden surfaces as before. The sound may be louder, from the greater amplitude imparted; it may be more definite in pitch, from the greater proportion of periodic vibration; and it may be more colourful from the greater complexity of the partials vibrating.

A contained body of air is, in fact, a highly susceptible recipient of periodic vibration. According to the dimensions given it by the containing object, there will be resonance peaks which are excited easily and strongly by any vibrations at or in the close neighbourhood of their natural frequencies: either as fundamentals; or as upper harmonics to those fundamentals. And conversely, the presence in strength of such peaks of natural resonance makes it easy to excite at strength the corresponding vibrations in any attached source of sound serving as the primary stimulus. It is for these reasons that one of the partners in the coupled acoustic system of an instrument is so likely to be a cavity of air (as in the violin) or a column of air (as in the flute).

Thus to take the example of the violin, the string gives the primary stimulus. It is the source of the vibrations; yet neither the amplitude of its vibrations, nor the total surface offered to the air, will be sufficient to make any effectual impact. But the wooden body of the violin, and the air cavity contained within it, can both be excited by the vibrations of the string into strongly sympathetic vibrations of their own, which the air inside imparts to the air outside through the sound-holes, and the wooden body through its ample surfaces. This is a splendid speci-men of a coupled acoustic system, and much more characteristic of sophisticated instrumental construction than, shall we say, that simple idiophone, the gong. Yet the gong has its subtleties of construction and performance too, and like any other instrument of satisfactory design, holds its place and its value somewhere within the wide range of pitches, tone colourings and volumes which together provide the raw materials of music.

This elementary distinction between idiophones on the one hand, and coupled sound-producers on the other hand, is less familiar to ordinary musicians than the distinctions next following.

FOUR ORDERS OF MUSICAL INSTRUMENTS

On the basis of a long and honourable tradition, most ordinary musicians would recognize three great orders of instruments: the strings, the wind, and the percussion. To these we have added in the present century another great order: the electrophones. That classifica-tion works out very well for straightforward purposes. It is not quite precise or logical, and in particular, the percussive order groups together a number of instruments, both idiophones and otherwise, which may not literally be struck, but perhaps coaxed into vibration by stroking them or rubbing them or rattling them. The strings and the wind are grouped by sounding category, the percussion by performing category, which is not logical classification at all; but it serves. If we picture a traditional orchestra, those are indeed the three basic group-ings which come to mind.

The electrophones are a fairly self-explanatory category: they range from electronic amplifications or modifications of conventional instru-ments (electric piano, electric guitar, etc.) to the synthesis or generation of sounds by electromagnetic, electrostatic or electronic circuits fed into loud speakers (electronic organs, electronic synthesizers, etc.); but they all have it in common that they depend upon oscillations of electric current rendered faithfully into acoustic oscillations and thereby made audible.

It must not for one moment be imagined that we are considering here four different kinds of sound. On the contrary, as we have seen from the beginning of this book, sound vibrations are sound vibrations however various the means used to produce them. Difference of frequency for pitch, of amplitude for loudness, and of harmonic (or inharmonic) spectrum for timbre: these are the basic variables which music manipulates.

In this sense, it makes no difference whether a string, or an air column, or a plate or a bar or a membrane, or an electric circuit, has set the vibration into motion: it is still neither more nor less than fluctuations in pressure waves when it arrives at the ear. We recognize the source of the sound at least as much through its incidentals, and especially through its onset transients – through what happens when a note is getting into action – and its manner of decay – what happens when it is dwindling away. And all of this, too, is conveyed as pressure waves. Not even electronic music has produced new kinds of sound. It has chiefly produced new ways of combining and controlling sounds: filling in a few gaps in the harmonic spectra conventionally available, but not adding so much as might be thought to the wide range already covered.

In conventional instruments of whatever order, certain working principles are shared in common. The chief of these relate to the natural peaks of resonance. It now seems quite certain that these affect the tone colouring in conjunction with the player's skill, and that of such natural peaks, two are likely to be so influential as to deserve the name of formants, while there may be a third and perhaps others which are much less influential; and none in theory would wholly lack influence, even though in practice negligible. It is the exact disposition of its formative resonances which distinguishes an excellent violin from one less excellent or not excellent at all. And yet the player, by his personal management of the string which is the primary source of sound, can get such an individual tone from almost any violin that it will hardly be mistaken – very possibly, as much as anything, by his manipulation of the onset transients.

There is a mutual influence between the behaviour induced by the player into the primary source of sound, on the one hand, and the response induced by that source into the resonating partner, on the other hand. There is always a connection; but it is not a fixed connection. Each note sets up the factors differently. For suppose a note sounded: such of its harmonics as accord best with the formants of the instrument will tend to be selectively reinforced. Suppose another note sounded: the same formants will reinforce harmonics at the same frequencies as before, but they will not be the same harmonics of that different series. Meanwhile the player will be favouring some harmonics by his technique, disfavouring others; thus the primary source of sound will already be feeding different strengths of harmonics into the secondary resonator, which in its turn will be favouring some of the primary vibrations and disfavouring others: there will be feed-in and there will be feedback. The room or other environment adds other formants, not to mention those brought to bear in our own auditory systems. Truly, coupled acoustic system is the proper term for it.

SYSTEMS OF TEMPERAMENT

A factor which arises for all instruments giving a choice of pitches, including the voice, but which only presents substantial difficulties for instruments of fixed tuning (chiefly keyboards and the harp) is temperament: the necessity to temper our intonation in order to keep any such fixed notes in relationship with the acoustic realities of the harmonic series.

Because our music (unlike Eastern music) is and for many centuries has been attached to harmony, we are more circumscribed in our choice of intervals than is the case when melody alone is in question. Harmony requires as just a ratio between its component fundamental frequencies as the circumstances allow, since it is otherwise apt to sound more out of tune than we should find agreeable. By 'just' is meant here an interval evincing the least possible roughness due to beating, in so far as consonance and not dissonance is the intention. It is, in fact, desirable for discords to beat, since that is basically what makes them dissonant; and music without dissonances would lack the very strength which makes returning consonance a welcome relaxation. But that in turn implies that our concords should indeed be consonant.

The most consonant intervals and the most stable in any ordinary tonality are the octave, the fifth and the major third. The octave is (after the unison) the least given to beating, but for that very reason, it is also the most narrowly hedged around by dissonance: the contrast between its virtual beatlessness when justly tuned and its conspicuous beating when imperfectly tuned is greatest. The remaining intervals are progressively more given to beating, however well tuned. By the time we get to the augmented fourth, we find it beating so little the worse for being out of tune that it is really quite difficult in practice to give it a definite tuning at all.

The octave has a ratio between its frequencies of $2:1$. The fifth has $3:2$. The major third has $5:4$. Now 2, 3 and 5 are all of them prime numbers to one another. This means that if we calculate intervals up from a given note by octaves, by fifths, and by major thirds, not one of these three calculations can bring us out to exactly the same note. For suppose we start from $C_{\prime\prime}$ and calculate upwards. Since $\frac{2}{1} = 2$ and $\frac{3}{2} = 1.5$, to reach the octave we multiply by 2, and to reach the fifth we multiply by 1.5. Then 2^7 which is 128 gives us the seventh octave, c^v; and $(1.5)^{12}$ which is 129.75 gives us the twelfth fifth, b^{iv} sharp. We have come out very nearly the same, but not quite the same. The difference is that tiresome little gap, almost a quarter of a semitone, known as the ditonic or Pythagorean comma. The mathematical calculation, of course, is merely a language for expressing it in figures. It is not the mathematics that so stubbornly opposes us; it is the hard facts of periodic vibration, and we cannot alter them. This is the material out of which we have to make our music.

Or we can look at it the other way up. The $D_{\prime\prime}$ double-flat reached by going twelve fifths down from c^v, is almost the same note as the $C_{\prime\prime}$ reached by going down seven octaves, but it is not quite the same, being flatter by a ditonic comma. And likewise with any other notes, so that, for example, B flat as reached by a succession of fifths is not quite the same note either as A sharp or as C double-flat. Likewise, you can reach quite a different b^{iv} sharp again, by going up three major thirds from c^{iv}: flatter by a gap very slightly smaller than the ditonic comma, and known as the syntonic comma or merely as the comma. And the chief musical consequence thus mathematically expressed is indeed musically important. If we tune our fifths consistently true, we mistune our major thirds; and if we tune our major thirds consistently true, we mistune our fifths. In practice, we can and we do adapt flexibly as we go along; but with the fixed tunings of keyboard instruments we cannot do this, and we have to settle for a temperament which cannot be perfect, yet cannot be altered in course of any given performance.

How near to just temperament can we come? Consider the diatonic scale on c' with just intervals to the octave at c'', the fifth at g', the fourth at f' and the major third at e''; with d' as a just fifth to g; with b' as a just major third to g'; and with a' as a just major third to f. This makes the diatonic major seconds from c' to d', from g' to b' and from a' to b' (called major tones) larger by a comma than the major seconds (called minor tones) from d' to e' and from g' to a'. The diatonic minor seconds (having different letters, without accidentals) from e' to f' and from b' to c'' are called diatonic semitones; they are larger than chromatic minor seconds (having the same letters, with accidentals) such as c' to c' sharp, called chromatic semitones. This in theory is as pure as you can tune; but if you think it might be a little daunting in practice, you would not be wrong.

For now if you rise the major sixth justly from c', you will arrive at a'. Or if you rise the fifth justly from d', you will likewise arrive at a': but not, unfortunately, at the same a', since a major tone c' to d' plus a fifth d' to a' is a comma wider than a major sixth c' to a'. In practice, the d' will probably be flattened slightly if reached from the a', or the a' sharpened slightly if reached from the d'; this cannot be done at all on instruments of fixed temperament. Again, even as a major sixth c' to a' less a major tone c' to d' gives a comma short of a fifth d' to a', so also a fourth c' to f' less a major tone c' to d' gives a comma short of a minor third d' to f': a shortfall of almost a quarter of a semitone, which renders supertonic harmony quite unacceptably ill-tempered. And yet again, most good musicians have a melodic preference for going up a little sharp and coming down a little flat. As a just interval, the leading note is in theory a major semitone from the tonic, yet in practice it entices us up, and we tend strongly to make it narrow (i.e. we sharpen instead of flattening the leading note). So too we are enticed down by a rising semitone which falls immediately back again (e.g. c', d' flat, c' – in just intonation a major semitone). In short, whether from necessity or from preference, justness is not our only consideration for good intonation; it all sounds and is so much better if we play it, literally, by ear – in a word, flexibly.

But of course on instruments of fixed intonation, we cannot play it by ear. An extreme attempt was made by Bosanquet with a harmonium of fifty-three subdivisions to each octave (and even so, it gave faintly tempered major thirds): though described as smooth and sweet, it quickly cloyed. And fancy playing on it! Our normal keyboard with twelve notes to the octave is at least feasible and familiar, and in fact it is susceptible to a choice of temperaments. One of the best of these within certain limits of modulation is called mean-tone, because you tune your major thirds just and abolish the inequality between major and minor tones by splitting the difference at the mean (or half-way) point of those major thirds. Fifths are made a little narrow, i.e. flat as you go up (e.g. by four fifths from *c* to arrive exactly at the *e″* a major third above *c″* rather than overshooting); and by twelve of them, to arrive at a *b^{iv}* sharp about two syntonic commas short of *c^{v}* (not at a ditonic comma beyond). That reconciles the major thirds (beautifully just) with the fifths (only a little tempered).

On a keyboard having twelve notes to the octave, modulation can be provided in this way through a sequence of eleven fifths; but there the cycle breaks, for lack of new notes to continue it. Say your chosen twelve notes are: E flat, B flat, F, C, G, D, A, E, B, F sharp, C sharp, G sharp. For an A flat you would then have to use the G sharp, nearly three-fifths of a semitone off the just major third with C, and nearly one-third of a semitone off the just fifth with E flat. It was this unacceptable yet unavoidable discrepancy which got the name of 'wolf'. Providing A flat instead of G sharp, or D sharp instead of E flat, merely changes the position of the discrepancy; tuning these notes to a compromise is not really much help; adding extra notes by dividing, say, two of the keys only puts the problem back a little. Thus in its good keys (usually B flat, F, C, G, D, and A major; G, D and A minor) mean-tone tempera-ment works very well indeed, but outside its good keys, there is this inherent barrier to modulation. It is not, however, as insuperable in practice (give and take a little here and there) as it seems in theory; and among many variations upon mean-tone temperament which were devised and advocated, there is one which may have been Bach's for the Forty-eight Preludes and Fugues, and which approaches (though it is not) equal temperament by slightly widening (sharpening) its major thirds (but not all to the same extent).

Temperaments which cannot modulate through the complete cycle of the fifths (at least without being somehow a shade manipulated) are termed non-cyclic. Some of those which are cyclic may not be practic-able (e.g. because of using 19, 31 or 53 notes to the octave). Equal temperament, however, which is now normally in use, is a cyclic tem-perament using twelve notes to the octave and possessing great practical advantages. By dividing every semitone equally (whence the name) as one twelfth part of an octave, tones are made twice the size of semi-tones; major thirds, four times; fifths, seven times; etc. Enharmonic neighbours like G sharp and A flat are amalgamated, so that you can use the same note for either. Thirds, fifths and octaves are reconciled, so that you can go up twelve fifths to a B sharp which is the same as C, or up four fifths to an E which is the same as the major third above C. The infinite spiral of non-cyclic temperaments has closed to an un-broken cycle of fifths, through which modulation in both directions is unrestricted. Everything is possible: nothing is absolutely right. But then, where in art or in life is anything absolutely right?

Mean-tone and other early temperaments are being successfully used again in music designed and suitable for them. On an organ, the difference is particularly desirable because the tone remains in sufficiently steady state, with sufficiently harmonic partials, for the effects of temperament to be conspicuous; and in baroque organ music, it is especially enjoyable to hear the ring and sweetness of some well-adjusted mean-tone tuning or related temperament. On a harpsichord, with its less sustained but reasonably harmonic partials, the improvement is still substantial, and our current experiments with various temperaments have proved their worth; but the ear much more readily tolerates the slight added inharmonicity due to equal temperament, and for general purposes this is perfectly acceptable. On the clavichord, the temperament is not quite fixed (because the pitch responds a little to the touch); on lutes, guitars and viols, discussion was considerable (particularly during the late Renaissance) but academic in so far as the frets do not actually preclude fine tuning by the fingers.

On the piano, equal temperament is made necessary by the wide range of modulation in most of its music; moreover, there is relatively so little of a steady state, and so much endemic inharmonicity, in the tone production of an average piano anyhow, that it would be unrealistic to object: its inharmonicity is so much greater than anything more which equal temperament is adding to the acoustic confusion. And still our aural system accepts it as effectively in tune. In fact we might put it that what our aural system perceives really is in tune (always provided, of course, that the piano basically is); for this is exactly the kind of subjective modification which occurs during our nervous, cerebral and mental processing of the objective sounds. We simply do not under ordinary circumstances perceive a well-tuned piano as out of tune on account of its equal temperament. In short, equal temperament is always an acoustic but it is not necessarily an artistic compromise.

6 STRING METHODS

The vibration of strings (or wires) under tension is the source of sound for the first of the great classes of musical instrument to be considered here: the strings. In this case, the direction of oscillation in the source of sound is lateral, and the vibrations (except for a few unintentional squeaks or scratches) are transverse vibrations. For a crude visual comparison, wave one end of a piece of fairly thin rope from side to side and watch the undulations pass along although the rope as a whole does not. Attach the end, say to a wooden door, and some of the energy will rebound while some may be picked up audibly by the door: a coupled acoustic system in which the exciting vibrations of the rope, cord or string may still be slow enough to see, yet fast enough to hear at a low pitch which rises as more tension is applied.

The fundamental pitch at which a stretched string is heard depends upon its length, its tension and its mass: its amplitude varies with the energy imparted and transmitted; its tone colouring with the harmonics aroused. The entire sounding length of a string sufficiently stretched between supports will (unless otherwise prevented) vibrate as a whole with a substantially periodic frequency giving the first or fundamental harmonic. It will also vibrate in its quotient parts: in half-lengths, giving its second harmonic an octave up; in third-lengths, giving its third harmonic a twelfth (octave and a fifth) up; and so on through its upper partials until the energy going into the ascending series dwindles to negligible amounts.

The energy going into the different partials of the harmonic series, on which tone colouring depends, is affected by a variety of factors in addition to their height or position in that series. There is, for example, the method by which the vibrations are being excited: plucking, hammering or bowing, as will be seen below. Moreover, brighter colouring due to higher harmonics is encouraged by plucking with the fingernails or a hard, narrow plectrum; by hammering with a hard, small hammer; by bowing swiftly with the edge of the hair; and by choosing a point of contact near one end of the string. Solider colouring is encouraged by plucking with the fingertips or a soft, wide plectrum; by hammering with a soft, large hammer; by bowing slowly with more width of the hair; and by choosing a point of contact farther from the end (even, with plucking, at or near the middle).

And all this is no more than the start of the matter, since the contribution made to amplitude and to tone colouring by the other partners in the coupled acoustic system (the wooden box, the air it contains, or the soundboard and the frame and other factors) has still to be considered. Factors of technique and construction and stringing conspire to produce a resultant sound far other than they might be thought to be contributing individually: their mutual feedback is of the utmost importance; and the acoustics of the room itself further enter into the conspiracy. Nor is this resultant distribution of energy among the constituent partials by any means a constant through the duration of the note. On the contrary, it varies at all stages. And finally, it differs substantially on every different note which the instrument produces. That we nevertheless retain an overall impression of uniformity, or at the very least of consistency, is further tribute to our mental powers of assimilating discrepant signals into a meaningful whole: a pattern, a *Gestalt*.

Nevertheless, we can broadly take it that whatever vibration frequencies are being energized, and with whatever distribution of energy at whatever moment of their duration, they are partials more or less harmonic to the series. And we can broadly take it that the net resultant is a compound tone, heard (unless otherwise prevented) at the pitch of the fundamental partial (the first harmonic) but in a tone colouring governed by the distribution of energy among the upper partials (any higher harmonics present in appreciable strength). For this is a principle of such periodic vibration, whether on stringed or other instruments. With appropriate reservations, the principle may again be stated: tone colouring is upper harmonics, and upper harmonics are tone colouring. The whole is a complex tone reducible to a series of simple partial tones. The partials are the constituents, each of which is a simple tone of sinusoidal form. All of these partials are reinforcing jointly their own fundamental, and colouring it with their own fluctuating yet individual ring. So we hear a note complete with tone colouring.

The ends of the vibrating string are rendered stationary by whatever supports or fixes them. The usual name for such a stationary point, at which no vibration can occur, is node. Thus the full-length or fundamental vibration has a stationary point, a node, at either end. Half-way between nodes, the string is most free, able to make its most ample excursion from the state of equilibrium: the usual term for such a point of maximum vibration is antinode. Thus the full-length or fundamental vibration has a point of maximum excursion, an antinode, at the middle of the string.

This is confirmed when the violinist places a finger lightly upon the middle of the string. For this makes a node of it, just where the fundamental partial needs its antinode. This immediately inhibits it; for without its central antinode, it cannot go. So it falls silent; and in place of the first partial, the fundamental, we hear the second partial, an octave higher. The tone colouring also changes; it has what is sometimes miscalled 'flageolet tone'; at all events it sounds veiled and disembodied, quite beautiful in its special way, but not for ordinary use. The second harmonic has taken over the function of the first, but with a difference which the ear can well detect.

The second harmonic vibrates over the total as two halves, so that it requires a node in the middle (which is what the finger lightly pressing, as described above, reinforces); but an antinode at the middle of each half-length, i.e. at a quarter of the total length from either end. When the violinist places a finger lightly upon the string at a quarter of the length from its upper end (the pegbox end – though the other end would give just the same effect), then the same inhibition as before now falls upon the second harmonic: it must needs become silent too; and the third harmonic is compelled to take over, at the twelfth (octave and a fifth) above the fundamental. All such effects are described by violinists and others as using 'natural harmonics'. They can be carried a stage further by stopping any chosen length of the string with a finger hard pressed down in the ordinary way, then touching some nearby antinode lightly with the fourth finger: a sub-division of a sub-division, we might say; and the eerie sounds thus to be extracted are very properly described as 'artificial harmonics'.

Each harmonic in the ascending series has nodes and antinodes along the string in greater numbers and at smaller intervals, always subject to the necessity of having one of its nodes at either end of the string, where the fastening or support enforces it. The end by the pegbox serves no acoustic purpose but to reflect as much of the vibration reaching it as it does not absorb. But the end resting on the bridge has a double acoustic significance: in part, vibration is likewise reflected; in part, it is taken over by the bridge and transmitted to the body. The vibrations of the bridge are partly sideways, that is to say to and fro in relation to the length of the string. For high frequencies, there is also a lever action of which the fulcrum is at the foot held stationary by the sound post, while the motion passes through the foot allowed to rock by the relative flexibility of the bass-bar. When the bridge is loaded by having a mute clamped upon it from the top, the damping affects the higher more than the lower frequencies, so that the upper harmonics are reduced in proportion, and the tone colouring sounds veiled: an effect of some poetic value in suitable passages, but otherwise very much inferior to the undamped vibration.

The vibrations of the bridge are transmitted by its feet to the top plate of the body (also known as the table or the belly). String instruments having no bridge, but a crosspiece glued to the table as a holder for the strings (lutes and guitars exemplify this method) transfer vibrations directly. The ribs or side pieces join the top plate to the back, thus forming a box of which all the members take some part in the ensuing vibration, though the most influential member, and the most important for the maker to get exactly right, is the table. In violins (and in viols at least of baroque and later dates) a bass-bar glued lengthwise to the underside of the table near to one foot of the bridge strengthens the box against the downwards pressure of the strings; and it also imposes nodes, points of no vibration, which influence the tone. Nearly beneath the treble end of the bridge, but a little lower, a sound post is wedged in (under fairly tight friction) from the table to the back, giving further support: this also is now thought to have been absent from some or all Renaissance viols, but the evidence is not quite conclusive. One effect of the usual sound post is to impose a rigid node, the exact placing of which is of crucial influence. The shape and position of the sound holes also conditions the patterns of vibration in the table, as well as allowing communication between the contained air inside and the surrounding air outside. Violins and viols have a table more or less arched against the pressure of the strings; lutes and guitars have a flat table, with quite a variety of bars but no sound post; and one or more ornamental roses (found also in a few viols) may often be cut, but not as a rule sound holes. In any case, the vibrations of the contained air impinge much more through their influence on the plate vibrations, which mainly radiate the sound, than through communicating holes.

The vibrations in the wood of such a resonating body are extraordinarily complex, and depend for their quality on very fine adjustments of sizes, proportions and thicknesses. It is what the body makes of the strings which counts for quality, although not for pitch. The air contained should have one main band of resonance, which for a violin should be at about the frequency of the note a semitone below its D string. The wooden box should have many, of which the lowest should be at about the frequency of the note a semitone below its A string. It is not only these notes themselves which will be thus reinforced, however, but any of their partials in sufficiently harmonic relationship. The whole fiddle will be ringing with sympathetic vibrations, heard not ordinarily as notes, but as contributions to that glorious quality and variability of tone colourings which go to the making of a good stringed instrument.

Stringed instruments may have several strings of the same length but of different gauges, masses or tensions, on which the fingers stop off widely differing lengths to give the pitches desired. Too slack a tension sounds feeble, too thick is hard to get vibrating and restricts high harmonics; thus low strings later than the mid-seventeenth century are commonly gimped (wound with fine wire on a moderate core) to allow sufficient tension without excessive mass or stiffness. Stringed instruments played through a keyboard (harpsichord, clavichord except in so far as it is fretted, piano) give the desired pitches from strings of which the length is fixed and cannot be altered in performance. Since even on the longest harpsichord or piano it is not practical to vary the length of the strings to an extent proportionate to the full range of notes, an adjustment is arrived at partly by more or less heavy gimping, and partly by a balanced choice of gauges, tensions, and materials. On such an instrument, some vibration occurs in the body and its frame (especially when this is made of wood, as in harpsichords, clavichords and early pianos); but the main resonance, instead of coming from a box, comes from a soundboard whose function it is to reinforce and transmit vibrations at all required frequencies with as even a response as possible. Its material is some closely and evenly grained wood of which pines and spruces are representative; its thicknesses are finely judged and tapered; its mounting is as free and flexible as structural requirements permit. It can never be quite impartial, since it is bound to possess some natural resonances of its own. But it will be as impartial as its makers can contrive it within the space and price ceilings allowed.

EXCITING THE VIBRATIONS IN STRINGS

There are three basic ways of exciting sound vibrations in strings: plucking; striking; and bowing.

The most general characteristic of plucking is that it tends to excite a good and active range of high harmonics, whose rate of decay is relatively rapid. This makes for attractive and interesting tone colouring, capable of considerable choice and variation at the performer's disposal, but no very great duration of the sound. Plucking imparts energy by a single impulse, and there is no means of maintaining the vibrations, as there is with bowing. The next impulse follows as a separate event when the string is plucked again.

Both the timbre and the amplitude are conditioned by the manner of plucking. The harmonics potentially available from a string of suitable length, mass and tension are very numerous; these harmonics are actually sounded only as the plucking is adapted to their varying requirements. Each has its particular nodes and antinodes distributed along the string: for example, the first or fundamental harmonic has its only antinode at the middle point, the second harmonic has two antinodes a quarter from either end, etc. Any plucking at an antinode takes advantage of the maximum excursion of the string for this mode of vibration, and will produce maximum amplitude in the corresponding harmonic. Any plucking at a node encounters the zero excursion of the string for that mode of vibration, and will not activate the corresponding harmonic at all. Any plucking at intermediate positions between nodes and antinodes will take just so much or little advantage as the excursion of the string allows at that point for that mode of vibration. And as usual the result will be the combination of whatever amplitudes each mode of vibration is being given individually: in short, a compound tone.

A string plucked in the middle favours its fundamental harmonic and will yield a sober sound of no great amplitude or brilliance: indeed, it may seem a little veiled or muffled, without enough impact or interest unless that is just what the music happens to be requiring then. A string plucked very near one end favours only high harmonics from rapid, short vibration, since no others have space enough for an antinode within so small a distance from the node imposed by the end of the string. A string plucked between about one-seventh and one-ninth of its length from the end will favour an excellent selection of harmonics, putting plenty of amplitude into the fundamental and enough others of moderate rather than extreme height to give solidity and interest in suitable proportions for average musical situations; and experience has confirmed this as a good basic position for plucked instruments in general. But many other positions will work well, giving a splendid variety of tone colouring and loudness suitable for different musical situations from the most poetical to the most robust. To hear an accomplished guitarist running his plucking fingers along from nearly the end to the very middle of the string, with every nuance of timbre and dynamics, is to understand this distinction in its most practical application. Bowed instruments can only use this resource to a more limited extent.

Timbre and amplitude are further conditioned by the size, the density and the shape of the plucking implement; and also by the speed and firmness with which it is manipulated. When the implement is relatively hard and narrow, the string is displaced at a sharp angle, and quickly released. Only the shortest vibrations, yielding the highest harmonics, are of a size to be incommoded by such an implement; most harmonics will be excited, especially if the plucking is swift and vigorous. But if it is swift and vigorous to an extreme, the lowest harmonics may not be so fully involved, which is why harpsichord touch must not be violent or pianistic if the sound is to be produced in full warmth and sonority.

When a string is plucked with the soft end of a finger or the side of a thumb, the angle at which it is displaced is not very sharp; the length of string covered is relatively wide, so that vibrations of quite moderate length and frequency may be incommoded; the tone colouring will therefore tend to be somewhat rounded, neither very veiled nor very brilliant, but suitable to a broad average of musical situations. When a string is thrummed across with fingers or thumb or both, the angle is still less sharp and the tone may be still mellower, though the rapid reiterations will set up a good deal of rather clanging sonority. When a string is plucked with a narrow-edged plectrum of hard material, or with the fingernails, the angle of displacement is decidedly sharp, the higher harmonics are considerably favoured, and the tone colouring may range from brilliant to jangling, especially if the point of contact is kept fairly near to the end: not only are harmonics of short length and high frequency encouraged, but they may also be rendered rather less accurately harmonic (i.e. appreciably more inharmonic) than they would otherwise achieve (and no partials are absolutely harmonic in actuality). Hence the possibility of a jangly sound.

The most general characteristic of striking or hammering a string is that it encourages a longer persistence and slower decay in the higher harmonics, though if the string is relatively stiff and tense, as with the modern (not so much with the early) piano, most of the energy may be going anyhow into the lower harmonics (perhaps something like the lowest six in a medium register of the modern piano). As with plucking, there is a single impulse for each note sounded, and no further maintaining of the energy of vibration until the next note is struck. In the piano, the persistence is much greater than in the harpsichord, but so also is the inherent inharmonicity. They are indeed very different instruments in mechanical and also in musical respects.

The factors conditioning the timbre and amplitude of a struck or hammered string, nevertheless, are basically similar to those conditioning a plucked string. There is the same relationship between the position at which the string is struck and the nodes and antinodes governing the various harmonics potentially available. And as before, the result will be whatever the combination of harmonics actually excited, at whatever amplitudes, in fact produces. There is also the same sort of relationship to the size, the density, the shape and the energy of the striking implement. A hammer or a beater may be large or small, resistant or resilient, sluggish or swift of impact. When it is wide and soft and gently applied, it tends to cover more of the string for a longer period of time, thereby incommoding harmonics of greater length and slower frequency: the tone colouring is thus fuller but less brilliant than it is with narrow, hard hammers vigorously applied and rebounding sooner, which only incommode harmonics of a shorter length and more rapid frequency.

Moreover, the gentler the impact, the less the compression of any elastic material (such as leather or felt) with which a hammer may be covered, and the slower the relaxation; the more vigorous the impact, the greater the compression and the quicker the relaxation. Since the compressed material is harder than the uncompressed, this, too, affects the space and the time within which harmonics of each length and frequency are incommoded. It takes less space to cover a shorter vibration, and less time to interfere with a higher frequency: that is why high rather than low harmonics suffer from any departure from a theoretically fine-pointed and instantaneous plucking or striking. But it is also fortunate that these variables exist. They increase enormously the opportunities for diverse musicianly expression.

The general characteristics of bowing a string differ from plucking or striking above all in maintaining the supply of energy for vibration, thus allowing a much more steady state to develop, and a possibility of controlling it through its duration which would not otherwise exist. The same basic principles remain, since the position of the bow along the string, and the width of bow hair brought into operation, are in like relationship to the nodes and antinodes encountered, and with a like influence upon the harmonics encouraged and discouraged. There are, however, other factors to be considered in addition.

The action of the bow depends upon the alternate establishing and overcoming of friction. A bow is a stick of moderately springy wood, worked to a fine straightness laterally and to just the needed resilience longitudinally, and having in its modern design a slight inward camber of logarithmic curvature: pre-baroque bows are of all shapes and sizes; baroque bows have a varying but usually slight outward camber favourable to the characteristic articulation of baroque music. Between the ends anything up to some hundred hairs from the tail of a horse (or substitute material) are stretched at a tension which can be relieved or modified by a screw and knob. The hair has roughnesses, made rougher by being rubbed with fine resin; these pull the string sideways until its tension overcomes the friction, and it rebounds, only to be caught again; and it is this rapid oscillation of pulling and recoiling which excites periodic vibrations in the string.

This method is favourable to a wide range of accurately harmonic partials, kept so by the energy which is being steadily imparted. There are, moreover, several variables under the continuous control of the performer. For example, the width of hair brought on to the string can be changed by tilting the bow at different angles, and also by pressing harder or less hard. The greater the width of hair, the more it eliminates or incommodes high harmonics; the greater the pressure, the greater the total amplitude and loudness. The faster the bow is drawn, the louder the sound, but the greater the risk of not biting firmly, thereby throwing more energy into higher than into lower harmonics. The nearer to the bridge, the louder the sound, and the brighter its tone colouring (and beyond a point, the harder); but too near requires undue pressure, disfavours low and moderate harmonics, and eventually leads to disembodied sounds or even squeaks. The further from the bridge, the softer the sound, and the more veiled its tone colouring; but too far finds the string so yielding that it cannot accept a sufficient pressure, and the sound fades out from lack of energy. The normal limits are from about a seventh to about a fifteenth of the string length away from the bridge; the average is about a ninth.

The use of 'natural harmonics' and to some extent of 'artificial harmonics' has already been mentioned as an element in violin technique; it is mainly for bowed strings, excepting that the harp makes good use of it. A normal note at the full length of the string is called an open note, or an open string; stopped notes have shorter lengths produced by different fingerings. Mention has also been made of a mute clipped or sprung on to the bridge: this increases its weight and therefore its inertia, penalizing high harmonics and causing a veiled and distant tone colouring of very restricted utility. Further special effects are plucking (*pizzicato*); bowing very near to the bridge (*sul ponticello*) so that the fundamental almost vanishes in a tone colouring of metallic glitter; bowing very near to the fingerboard (*sul tasto*) so that the total energy is impoverished and the tone colouring thinned and harshened; bowing not with the hair at all but with the wood of the bowstick (*col legno*), or bouncing the stick on the strings, which is bad for the varnish and not much good for anything else. For no one can really complain that bowed instruments lack for anything in variety; there is no need to pick at them or tap them or slap them on the back. The natural resources of the bowed strings are surely ample for any demand that need be put upon them musically.

7 PLUCKED STRINGS

OPEN AND STOPPED STRINGS

Plucked instruments may have many strings of different lengths for each note required (e.g. harp, harpsichord); or fewer strings of the same length stopped by the fingers at different points to give any other notes required (e.g. guitar, standard lute); or occasionally a combination of these two basic methods (theorbo and other archlutes).

THE HARPS

The twang of a hunting bow, amplified by contact with a resonant body such as a hollow gourd, may underlie the family of harps and (less directly) other plucked instruments. Many Oriental harps have a bow-shaped arch with strings reaching down to a bowl-shaped or box-shaped resonator, and no front pillar to strengthen their rigidity: some ancient Egyptian models have proved their excellence in modern reconstructions. Occidental harps have that more or less triangular frame, consisting of a resonant box or bowl with a soundboard as lid, an upper member curved to accommodate the graduated string-lengths required, and a vertical member for strength, so familiar in all manner of robust or delicate variations. It is, indeed, a superlative construction for plucked sounds each originating from its own string of appropriately adjusted length, mass and tension.

Small harps are commonly depicted or described in medieval sources; their tone, to judge from modern reconstructions, is clear and bell-like; their presumed use is for melody and rhythm rather than for chords and harmony; a plectrum is shown more frequently than the fingers for plucking. There may have been an unwritten bardic tradition of harp playing on the Celtic fringes, using vertical chords for two hands (what may be late written remnants survive). There were certainly harpists at many medieval and some Renaissance courts, such as that of the Tudor dynasty in England with their Welsh connections. There was by the fifteenth century a large *simple harp* with gut strings, and a compass upwards of two diatonic octaves, increasing to three or even four under early baroque influence. There was also an *Irish harp* with metal strings, giving remarkable resonance, and numbering up to forty or more (so that some, among so many, seem likely to have been chromatic).

As the Renaissance merged into the baroque, a variety called the *double harp* became prominent, in Italy especially. There are two, or sometimes three, parallel ranks of strings, divided in various manners between diatonic and chromatic notes. 'Double', at this period, probably means exceptional in compass, which might be around four and a half octaves. This is the *arpa doppia*, the double harp for which Monteverdi wrote out the brilliant solo interludes and accompaniments to the aria 'Possente spirto' (Powerful spirit, i.e. Charon the ferryman of the underworld) in his *Orfeo* of Mantua, 1607, showing us thereby something of the expressiveness and virtuosity which would ordinarily have been expected to have been improvised by the performer. The effect here does not depend on chords, but on rapid scale passages and figurations of which the undamped resonance builds up a glitter of dissonance all the more striking in this mainly melodic context. The part sounds reasonably well on a modern symphonic harp, but really requires the much more cutting sonority of its own contemporary instrument. The difference is particularly marked if the harp has, as early harps including the double harps (but probably not the Irish harps) often did, a set of bray pins: small angle pieces so fitted as just to touch and jangle against the bottom ends of the strings, with an extraordinary increment of dissonant upper harmonics, and a buzzing effect which appears to make the sound travel farther and last longer. In some instances, at least, the bray pins could be rotated to turn the buzzing on and off. The yet more resourceful *triple harp* largely took over from the seventeenth to the eighteenth centuries, especially with the Welsh.

Another seventeenth- and eighteenth-century variety of harp, the *hooked harp*, was given a diatonic tuning, which can be modified chromatically by a set of pivoted hooks. These can be turned individually to press on their strings, to produce the rise of a semitone. A stage on from this, there developed the single-action pedal harp, on which the feet are used for operating similar devices in course of the performance, so that some chromatic modulation is available. And this is the principle which was applied, with yet greater ingenuity and versatility, by Erard early in the nineteenth century, to produce the double-action pedal harp of our modern usage, which has pivoted disks, bearing pins, in place of hooks. Here the pedals can be set in advance, and re-set in performance, to give a choice of raising any notes in all octaves either by one or by two semitones; and if the composer is aware of the wide possibilities and practical limits of this technique, modulation can be used as freely as he wishes and as the performer has the skill to carry out. Both close chords and open arpeggios are highly effective; runs and glissandos add to the brilliance; and while the tone is more veiled than in earlier harps, it is also more powerful and more suited to the symphonic orchestra. Wagner's multiple harp parts in the *Ring* are excellent examples of idiomatic composing, in a romantic idiom, for this splendid instrument, which can send gentle ripples or surging waves through the full orchestra with remarkable effect. Discretion is needed, since the harp can lend itself to a sort of obvious sentimentality quite out of fashion now; but its ability to impart a special thrill or to cap a mounting climax is extremely valuable in the proper context.

The proper context is indeed the operative guideline for all good instrumental practice. The illusion that instruments, or anything else, can only improve in course of development is no longer found convincing: there can be gains and losses; and the real issue is not what is better in the absolute, but what is better in relation to the music. The sonority best suited to the music is normally that nearest to what the composer planned; and that is the broad reason for using contemporaneous rather than anachronistic forms of instruments whose historical evolution has been considerable.

THE HARPSICHORD

Of all plucked instruments whose notes are varied basically by having strings of different lengths, the *harpsichord* has the greatest scope and versatility, and is the least dispensable for its own (chiefly baroque) music. There are various sizes and designs, having various supplementary resources, but all have harp-like strings, coupled to a resonant soundboard, and excited by plucking through a keyboard mechanism.

Incisiveness and transparency are the chief characteristics of such an instrument. It is of no use asking a harpsichord to sound elusive and mysterious, as the piano can; its poetry is quite otherwise achieved. On the other hand, though its duration of sound is considerably shorter, it does not have to be evanescent, and with a good instrument and a proper touch it need not in the least sound dry, but on the contrary is capable of a splendid flow of warmth and brilliance. This brilliance will not be massive or opaque, but crystal-clear both in solos and in accompaniment;

and the incisiveness and transparency thus imparted are the very qualities which make the harpsichord so necessary for baroque music.

The mechanism of a harpsichord consists of keys each of which raises one or more jacks, according to the set or sets of strings on which a note is to be played. The jack brings into contact with its string a small, hinged plectrum of quill, leather or some plastic substitute for quill (which can work very well indeed): the harder and the sharper the plectrum, the more favourable to high harmonics and the brighter the tone. The position, relative to the bridge, at which the plucking occurs has its usual influence, and will not be quite the same for different sets of strings. The initial impact is hammer-like, causing a minute but appreciable rebound, the vibrations from which are heard as a slight buzz extremely characteristic of the instrument. Arnold Dolmetsch once evolved a harpsichord action by-passing this initial buzz in favour of a preternatural purity which was not characteristic at all: it was afterwards abandoned.

The plectrum now pulls firmly on the string and slips away from it, leaving vibrations typical for a plucked string though slightly enriched by remnants of the impact sound. When the pressure of the finger on the key is released, the jack falls back. The plectrum on its return past the string again touches it, but lightly because the hinge is free in this direction; there is, however, a slightly longer recurrence of the initial jangling. A moment later a narrow damper (usually made of felt) drops on to the string, from which the jack has raised it by its upward travel. The width is small, the material is fairly hard, the weight is light and the damping is by no means sudden, so that a perceptible sound briefly persists of which the harmonic content includes a portion added by the impact of the damper itself. So complex overall is the onset, the continuation and the decay of the harmonic spectrum for a good harpsichord that it has an individuality which adds greatly to its artistic value.

The strings of a harpsichord are much thinner and much less tense than those of a modern piano. This tends to throw much more of their energy into a wide range of partials, and also to produce them with a much lesser degree of inharmonicity. On the other hand, there are in effect more such partials to build up inharmonicity; and also these thin strings, being less massive, store less energy, which is therefore radiated more rapidly by the soundboard to the surrounding air, causing a more rapid decay of the sound as a whole. This is tantamount to saying that the basic tone of a harpsichord is more colourful but less sustained, as experience confirms.

When the mechanism of a harpsichord is properly designed and adjusted, it is sensitive to variations in the player's touch. A feeble touch reduces the sound on impact and does not get the string into its firmest motion. A violent touch sends the plectrum past the string too rapidly for a focused effect, decreases the amplitude of the lower partials and increases the inharmonicity of the higher partials to the extent of sounding not only (again) rather weak, but also rather tinny. It is necessary for good harpsichord touch to grasp the keys with a certain prehensile determination, quite different to good piano touch. But this can be done with less or greater power, and the difference of loudness, though small, is sufficient to keep the player in human contact with his instrument, without his having any depressing sense of the machinery getting in the way. The machinery may include, in the more elaborate instruments, variations of timbre and of loudness comparable to those of a small organ; but these resources are valuable only as supplements to the excellence of the player's touch and of his phrasing and articulation. Like the organ, the harpsichord is an instrument whose most characteristic effects depend upon a certain stability of dynamic levels and a certain dignity of tone colourings, subject always to the finer nuances of attack and separation.

There are three main factors of elementary technique on the harpsichord. The first is the firm and masterful grasp on the keys which gives the tone its solid foundation. The second is spreading the chords with a powerful roll which builds up their force as no absolutely simultaneous plucking can do. The third is holding down all notes in the same harmony except where good phrasing or articulation requires a break. The least possible spreading of the chords may be hardly detectable to the ear; but it must be there as a matter of unfailing habit, or the vibrations will clash unpleasantly. Wider spreading may often be desirable, up to any appropriate degree of arpeggiation, which in some cases can recur up and down (especially on final chords, or for filling out the accompaniment in recitative). But whether the spread is little or much, swift or slow, it normally starts with the bass note on the beat. And because no normal harpsichord has or can have a damper-raising pedal, holding the harmony down is essential so that sonority can accumulate and tone colouring develop through sympathetic resonance. Thus, for example, if the C major prelude which begins J. S. Bach's '48' is played with the fingers coming up after each note, as would appear to be what the notation indicates, the result on the harpsichord becomes intolerably dry, and was never actually intended. Not only must the fingers stay down; they must be put back and stay down again as the arpeggiation passes over them. But, of course, the separations needed where the harmony does change or the phrasing does need interrupting are all the more conspicuous and important. As so often in baroque music, one main consideration is to sustain the line, and another is to break it decisively wherever the pattern implies a separation.

Nowhere is this more obviously the case than on the harpsichord. So slight is the dynamic difference made between one note and another, by the touch alone, that small silences of articulation and larger silences of phrasing are just as primary for the expression as they are (and for similar reasons) on the organ. In particular, an effect of accentuation can only be got directly to a very limited extent; but it can be created indirectly by taking a small silence of articulation out of the note before. This gives to the accented note an illusion of prominence greater than it actually possesses, and serves to supplement such dynamic emphasis as the nature of the touch permits. Similar considerations apply on any instrument, but less exclusively in that dynamic nuances will usually be taking a much larger share in the note-to-note and phrase-to-phrase moulding of the line.

The simplest harpsichords use a single set of strings, operated from a single keyboard. Any variation of loudness or of tone colouring, beyond the little which the touch affords, has to be suggested, as for example by thinning down or filling out the chords played in accompaniment, or merely by a more or less relaxed style of performance. It is extraordinary how adequate these methods are for the satisfaction of our musical requirements, except where the piece itself requires something more showy for its proper effect. In most harpsichord music, the simple instrument sounds so well that any further variety by more complicated resources will probably not be missed: if they are available, they may have much to add; if not, a fine performance need not leave us wishing that they were.

When a second set of strings is added (complete with its own jacks but generally worked from the same keyboard and coupled in or out as required by a knob, knee-lever or foot-pedal) the pitch may be at the unison, in which case it may be tuned just enough out to give a pleasant beat; or it may be at the octave above. On the analogy of organ pipes, the standard register will be called 8-foot; the register an octave above will be called 4-foot; there is very occasionally a 2-foot register another octave up; and sometimes (but hardly ever on baroque instruments) a 16-foot register at the octave below 8-foot, which is not so desirable as has sometimes been believed in modern times; for while it brings depth to the combined sound, and a striking solo timbre when heard alone, it also puts so much extra tension on the soundboard that it probably takes away more resonance than it has to offer. It was, with a very few and untypical German exceptions, avoided in the past, and should preferably be avoided now.

A harpsichord with one manual keyboard and two 8 ft registers is a very versatile and admirable instrument for most solo work and almost any accompaniment. When further registers are added, the next stage is ordinarily 8 ft, 8 ft, 4 ft. A second keyboard is now very advantageous, since the hands can then pass almost instantly, say, from a softer registration on the top keyboard to a louder registration on the bottom keyboard, and the other way about, so that the dynamics can be changed without waiting for a break between sections of the music. That is all the variety which most harpsichord music requires, and even this should not be done too often unless something rather gimmicky in the music does really suggest it. All three sets of strings work from their own row of jacks, but may be moved either from one only of the keyboards, or if the mechanism permits it, from both. There is commonly some device, called a coupler, for joining the keyboards so that playing on one (the bottom) also works the other, with any jacks which may be arranged to rise with it.

A set of strings may be brought into or out of action by sliding its row of jacks near enough to pluck, or far away enough not to pluck. When the jack-slide is controlled by knobs or hand-levers, a hand must be raised to do this at some appropriate break in the natural flow of the music; and this limitation may really be thought a blessing in disguise, since it is almost invariably better from a musical point of view so to restrain oneself. However, some early harpsichords had knee-levers, and one or two extreme rarities had pedals for the feet: that these never came into general practice is itself a comment on their basic undesirability. They became a commonplace when the harpsichord was newly being revived in the twentieth century, but the best makers and performers have for the most part preferred recently to dispense with them. They are a convenience which, it is true, does not have to be abused; but they form no part of the basic harpsichord. Nor does another resource which they render possible: sliding the jacks into play or out of play gradually, thus giving a more or less perceptible crescendo or decrescendo. There can also be a half-hitch to the pedal, setting the jacks to pluck at half their usual volume: it does not work very satisfactorily as a rule, being hard to keep in adjustment; and it is not necessary at all.

Pronounced louds and softs on the harpsichord are properly produced by a change of register or stop made decisively at those points where some new event in the music itself gives cause for it. If the music itself suggests crescendos and decrescendos, it is unlikely to be very characteristic music for the harpsichord. True, a few late eighteenth-century harpsichords were made with movable shutters across the strings (the so-called Venetian Swell) in imitation of the Swell box on some organs; it has very little effect, and that little deleterious, since the high partials are most reduced and with them the brilliance. It was nothing but an ill-conceived attempt to keep pace with the dynamic freedom of that quite different and increasingly successful instrument, the piano. And the piano is different because it emerged through different musical requirements, which certainly include every shift and transition of dynamic level.

Other more or less valid devices are, however, found on some harpsichords. There may be a different set of jacks so placed as to pluck the same set of strings at a different position, nearer to the bridge (the lute stop properly so called); high partials are favoured, and the tone colouring is hard and bright and piquant, very useful in a plangent situation. At the other extreme, there may be a slide to bring small felt or leather pads into light contact with a set of strings (the buff stop, sometimes called the harp stop with some slight aural justification, or less properly called the lute stop, with very little): most of the resonance goes and all the brilliance, so that the sound is muffled and quite against the native splendour of the harpsichord. It is an effect far less pleasing in a concert hall than the performer may fondly imagine, and is especially unsatisfactory in accompaniment because it does not give the soloist enough sonorous support (in an ensemble it is merely apt to be inaudible). But another device has every musical justification, though it is not necessary nor very usual: fitting leather plectrums and quills on contrasting registers. The warmth of the leather and the sharpness of the quills are alike within the basic nature of the harpsichord. A few German harpsichords were made in the eighteenth century with a pedal-board additional to their manual keyboards: useful for practising organ music, but never taken up for much other use.

It will be appreciated that various periods and nationalities came up with very different kinds of harpsichord, suited to very different idioms of music, and that so far as possible the right kind for the music should be used. Thus there are, from the sixteenth century, sharp-sounding Italian harpsichords of most attractive assertiveness, slightly clarinet-like from the prominence of their fifth harmonics. There are Flemish

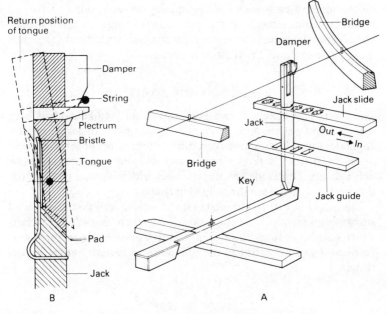

Fig. 21 Harpsichord action

harpsichords and English harpsichords of the late sixteenth and the seventeenth centuries, rich in tone and clear in articulation. There are German harpsichords of deeper mellowness and more sober attack. Above all, there are the glorious French harpsichords of the eighteenth century, profoundly influenced by the Flemish heritage (in fact, actually making over and extending many older Flemish instruments), and combining a great warmth (especially in the bass) with a clarity and a transparency which complement it very well. A French concert harpsichord with two manuals, having two 8 ft and a 4 ft, worked by handstops which include a very direct form of sliding coupler to unite or separate the keyboards: such an instrument is rightly the starting-point for many modern makers in some of their very best original work today. For Couperin or Rameau, for Bach or Handel, for Domenico Scarlatti, and even in fair measure for Frescobaldi or John Bull or Froberger or Purcell, this French-style instument is always admirable. No harpsichord can be an all-purpose instrument in the strictest sense, since from Frescobaldi to Bach is a vast range only to be met closely by varying the instrument; but the nearest approach may well be an instrument in this classic tradition. Robust on the one side, and poetic on the other, a harpsichord of this quality will spin out a melody or elucidate a counterpoint or maintain a figuration with equal fitness, and accompany a soloist or support an orchestra with equal grace. It is indeed one of music's noblest instruments.

PSALTERY AND ZITHER

The *psaltery*, a common medieval instrument, is like a small harp strung laterally across a soundboard on a triangular, trapezoid or rectangular frame. Plucked with a plectrum – sometimes one in each hand – or the fingers, it gives a bright and resonant tone needing to be deftly damped by hand as required. Struck with beaters, it becomes the dulcimer, for which see the following chapter.

The *zither* is a current representative, sometimes having five metal strings over a metal-fretted fingerboard, on which the melody contrasts with a number of supporting open strings of uncovered or covered gut. Numerous variants persist in the folk music of Eastern Europe in particular.

LUTE, GUITAR

Of all plucked instruments whose strings are basically of the same length stopped by fingering for other notes as required, the *lute* came to have the most delicate construction and expressive technique. It arrived through the Moors, probably in the thirteenth century, relatively small in size and used, like the medieval harp, for melodic lines; a plectrum rather than the fingers picks out the notes. But in the Renaissance, large lutes and virtuoso idioms emerged, not only for melodic ornamentation but for a very effective kind of sketched-in polyphony, where the imagination readily supplies any notes which are not struck owing to the limits of the technique. By the late fifteenth century, the plectrum was replaced by the fingers and thumb, and both chords and counterpoint flourished. The construction became lighter, with finely coopered ribs replacing the carved-out bowls, and usually eight movable gut frets tied round the slender neck.

The lute thereafter became the most regarded of all courtly instruments. At the turn of the fifteenth and sixteenth centuries, we read in Bembo and Castiglione of courtiers of either sex accompanying their own singing exquisitely on the lute or the viol. Dances and other solos were elaborated with largely improvised ornamentation; vocal transcriptions and free fantasies were in similar idioms. The Italians and (on the lute-like vihuela) the Spaniards were greatly to the fore; the Germans were early in the field; the French and the English came to the front later in the century. There was a characteristic French style of great brilliance, which passed much of its figuration on to the French harpsichord composers. Both for the polyphonic accompaniments to his lute songs, and for his still more highly elaborated solos, John Dowland stands out upon the very boundaries of the Renaissance and the baroque periods.

The lute in its Renaissance and early baroque eminence was to music then much what the piano became in the nineteenth century. But the contrast is also instructive: for where the piano is powerful and well suited to the great outer world, and particularly the romantic world, of public music, the lute is sensitive and apt for the inner circles of chamber music at its most intimate. The lute remained active through the seventeenth century, but more for accompaniment than for solos, and particularly in those more or less expanded forms, with added bass courses carried to an upward extension of the pegbox, which in moderate size might be called *theorbo* and, in almost any large size, *archlute*. There was a revival of the lute during the eighteenth century in Germany, to which J. S. Bach made a small but valuable contribution. The lute then went into virtual oblivion until the present century, when it has been successfully revived on a wide scale.

The acoustic properties of the lute are very interesting, tending as they do to the greatest freedom and not at all to the greatest amplitude of vibration, so that the tone is highly coloured with upper partials, but by no means loud. The shape of the classical lute may be compared to one half of a pear which has been sliced through in the plane of its stalk. The table (made of pine) is flat; the back (made of various materials including ivory) meets it in the form of a bowl without being separated from it by ribs. This bowl is built up of narrow strips glued edge to edge. The wood in all parts of the body is exceedingly thin (especially the bowl – but the table is little thicker); and there is no sound post to stabilize the connection between front and back. There are, however, barrings glued beneath the table in various designs, the exact nature of which has an important influence upon the patterns of vibration natural to this part of the instrument. There may be an ornamental rose, or roses, piercing the centre of the table. As usual, the wood itself has a main resonance, the air contained has others, and the sound pressures consequently impinging on the air outside are of the customary complexity.

To pick up a lute for the first time is to be astonished that it can be so light for its size. In fact, some of its first revivers in the twentieth century made their instruments too thick and too heavy, with fatal consequences for the tone (some of our more recent makers are very good indeed). You have only to speak while holding a proper lute to feel it picking up sympathetic vibrations. It is, in short, an instrument eminently conducive to the high partials which give it colouring, but much less so to the lower partials which might give it volume. It is suitable in public only to small halls and attentive audiences; but in private rooms and chambers, for which it was originally intended, it is a prince of instruments.

It is also a very difficult instrument to play well. The technique has to be extremely accurate merely to get a good tone, and any carelessness will lead to dry and prickly sounds in place of the warmth and resonance of a well-played instrument. It is also difficult, but necessary, to keep all the fingers down so long as the harmony requires and the hand can manage, thus letting the notes ring on. The strings are numerous and unusually thin, so that a common instruction for finding the right pitch of the top string was to tighten it until just short of its breaking. Thin strings go out of tune more readily than thick strings with changes of temperature and humidity, so that a lute player may need to make swift adjustments to his pegs, though with skill he can usually overcome this difficulty.

Except for the single topmost string of fine gut (or nowadays nylon), the strings of the classical lute are tuned in pairs (courses) at the unison or sometimes (for the lowest three courses) at the octave. It is necessary to pluck both pairs evenly with the fingertip or the edge of the thumb to produce a solid tone; and up to four courses may have to be plucked at once. If the fingernails are used in place of the soft ends of the fingers, a much sharper and more penetrating tone results; this was not, however, the standard technique, though it was in use. The little finger may rest on the table to support the hand and most paintings show it so; or it may remain in the air as in modern guitar technique. Occasionally, a finger and thumb are stroked in opposite directions simultaneously across the strings, producing a compound arpeggiation very effective on certain full chords.

On a sixteenth-century lute, there might be from five to six courses, lying over the broad fingerboard, and stopped with the left hand as desired. But from the latter years of that century, there may be further low courses (diapasons), often lying outside the fingerboard, and plucked open without stopping, so that they add bass notes of extraordinary resonance and depth; they also add to the sonority by vibrating in sympathy even when they are not being played. The theorbo carries this principle to the extent of mounting a vertical extension to the bass side of a vertical pegbox, thus allowing extra bass strings of greater length. When a lute of more or less ordinary size, as to the body, has a second pegbox reaching anywhere up to twice as far from the lower end-piece as the first pegbox, the name *chitarrone* might be used; or this, or any other lute of exceptional proportions, might be called archlute. There are also lutes in smaller sizes than usual, lacking diapasons. Out of a considerable diversity of tunings, G, c, f, a, d', g' ('Old Tune') is the most typical for the sixteenth century. $G, c, f, a, c',$ e' ('Sharp Tune') and G, c, f, a' flat, c', e' flat ('Flat Tune') are typical for the seventeenth, together with added basses on the various forms of archlutes, equally various in tuning.

The neck of the lute now always carried frets of gut tied round it at intervals corresponding to successive semitones above the open strings. They are very easy to replace, and they can also be tuned at need by pushing them up and down. The knot must be tight enough not to let them slip inadvertently. There were contemporary arguments about how to temper them (Pythagorean, mean-tone, etc.); but in practice their tuning is not fixed so definitely as it is on keyboard instruments, and the player retains at least some measure of control by managing his fingering. Indeed, the frets alone will not locate his fingers, though serving as a guide. The best tone results when the fingers lie very closely behind (but not on top of) their frets, which is not easy to achieve in chords. The fret then cuts off the string to sound much like an open string, and the tone will ring. Fingers less accurately placed will probably sound the notes, but they may not be quite in tune and will certainly lack that ringing edge which neater playing brings.

As usual (though not invariable) with plucked instruments of this general kind, there is no bridge on the lute to raise the strings in the manner needed where a bow is to be used. At their lower end, the strings are attached directly to an end-piece glued on the table at a point determined by its effect upon the patterns of vibration. Nor do the sides have to be in-curved to allow a bow to tilt; hence the noble simplicity of outline, as favourable to this type of tone production as it is grateful to the eye.

A more plebeian relative is the *mandora*, of which the *mandolin* is the smallest size, having mainly wire strings normally plucked with a plectrum, so that the tone is less poetical and the technique less subtle: it may well be nearer to the medieval than to the Renaissance lute. The Spanish *vihuela* is an instrument hard to classify, since it has a body resembling a guitar but a technique resembling a lute when plucked with the fingers (*vihuela de mano*), or a mandolin when plucked with a plectrum (*vihuela de péndola*). Equally, however, it could be bowed, when it became a form of viol (*vihuela de arco*); and both in this role and in the role of a lute, its national context and its musical value were alike significant.

In all Europe, the *guitar* itself was and remains prominent. The table is flat, and may be pierced by an ornamental rose. The back may be either flat like a viol (most commonly) or arched like a violin (as is the vihuela). There are sides or ribs; there is barring, but not a sound post; there are slightly incurved waists, not required for bowing but influencing the patterns of vibration. It should perhaps be added that plucked and bowed forms of the same or similar instruments were a normal feature of the Middle Ages, and that the vihuela is an important case of this. The fingerboard of the guitar was fretted with gut like a lute, or (later) with fixed metal frets which have the disadvantage that they cannot be pushed around a little to adjust the tuning – for example, if a string goes false. The Renaissance guitar is double-strung, with five courses, and is perhaps a little easier to play than the lute with which it has so much in common. It can play lute music to good effect, and has also a substantial repertory of its own. Early in the eighteenth century, the double-strung guitar gave ground before the single-strung guitar, having six single strings, in which form it retained, unlike the lute, a continued popularity. The tone of this is excellent, but no longer resembles a lute. The modern instrument exists in Spain as a family of four sizes, which may be called *guitarillo* (having five strings), *requinte*, *tenore* and – the familiar bass guitar – *guitarra*.

There is a regular technique of plucking with the fingers, equivalent in sensitivity and virtuosity to that of the lute: Segovia gave to this form of guitar playing an incomparable reputation in the present century. The variety of tone colouring and the dynamic finesse achieved by good players in this classical idiom are of the highest value. Another technique is by thrumming across the strings. The guitar has also an empire of its own in the great world of jazz. There it is commonly given a very high degree of electrical amplification. The electric guitar properly so called is in crucial respects a different instrument, and will be considered later.

The *cittern* or *cithren* has sides more nearly circular than the lute, and a flat back similar to the standard guitar. The so-called *English guitar* is a form of cittern; the *gittern*, on the other hand, was a late-medieval relative of the guitar. The cittern is found in many sizes, double-strung with four to twelve pairs of strings, which should be of wire; and it is played either with the fingers like a lute or with a plectrum like a mandolin. It was an extraordinarily popular and somewhat lowbrow instrument of the Elizabethan period. The pandora or bandora is in effect an outsize cittern, sometimes replacing a theorbo in accompaniment, and quite an attractive instrument in its own right. It is not to be confused with the mandora, which is more closely related to the true family of lutes.

The *orpharion* is a form of cittern in which the end-piece holding the strings is glued on the slant, giving a greater sounding length to the lower than to the higher strings; the fixed metal frets are slanted accordingly. It is tuned like a lute, for which it sometimes served as a less expensive substitute. The *poliphant* is a remoter cousin of the cittern. The *banjo* has no hollow wooden body, but a shallow metal hoop carrying a stretched membrane for resonator. One form (the mandolin banjo) has four pairs of metal strings played with a plectrum to yield a hard but brilliant tone; the usual form has five to nine single gut strings, played more persuasively with the fingers.

8 HAMMERED STRINGS

THE CLAVICHORD

The working principle of the *clavichord* is by striking the string with a sort of hammer which remains in contact: it is called a tangent. The principle may date at least from the fourteenth century; the instrument, however, acquired no prominence before the sixteenth century, and not very much until the seventeenth. Perhaps its best period was the eighteenth century when it was a favourite both with J. S. Bach and with his most famous son, C. P. E. Bach. Beethoven could still report that 'among all keyed instruments the clavichord was that on which one could best control tone and expressive interpretation' – but this is only relevant, as he well knew, in very intimate surroundings, since the loudest tone to which a clavichord can be raised is extremely soft, and the softest, though still expressive, is not audible against any appreciable outside noises. But the range in between is very considerable, and loud chords on a clavichord, as you might hear them, for example, in J. S. Bach's Chromatic Fantasia near the end, can sound like thunder to an ear acclimatized by the greater softness that has gone before. The clavichord went out of use in the nineteenth century, but has found admirable champions once again in the twentieth.

The tangent is a brass wedge set upright at the far end of a pivoted wooden lever of complete simplicity, the near end of which is the visible key. When this is pressed with a firm but sensitive motion, the tangent is thrown smartly against its string or strings (i.e. one, or for greater resonance, a pair). There is a momentary but audible juddering as the tangent infinitessimally bounces; and the vibrations resulting enter into the subsequent sound as onset transients rather like the consonant which may precede a vowel sound in speech. Since everything to do with the lever, including your finger, is mechanically free, and since the string is elastic, a slow oscillation of the tangent and its string up and down occurs; but the finger is relatively heavy, and the oscillation is controlled by it, either with or without the awareness of the player – he can use it, and normally does, as a deliberate vibrato, but even if he does not, it affects the sound.

Before being struck by a tangent, the strings are slack. When a string is struck, that string (or that pair of strings) is raised and thereby brought to a tension mainly predetermined by its mass, by its length, and by the tuning which has been previously given to the instrument. The string is now divided into two portions, of which the shorter is damped (though not quite completely) with strips of felt, while the longer vibrates actively and transmits this vibration by way of the bridge to the soundboard. The material of the strings is ordinarily uncovered or covered brass; they are quite thin and flexible. The fine tuning is determined by the player's fingers. He must not press too hard, or the note will go objectionably sharp; yet, given the skill, he can certainly control the dynamics with the greatest subtlety, even bringing out one voice in a contrapuntal texture to emphasize an entry, or stressing one note of an expressive harmony. The touch is not at all that of a pianist, and requires considerable experience not just to go through the action with a bump. But it used to be said that if once you have acquired a good touch on the clavichord, you will easily master the touch of any other keyboard instrument.

By closing the finger upon the key more decisively, you can increase the velocity of the tangent, and therefore the loudness of the note, without appreciably sharpening the pitch. By closing the finger more caressingly, you can decrease the velocity of the tangent, and therefore the loudness, without losing the warmth and focus of the sound. For the sensuous beauty of a good clavichord should be very great. The double-strung clavichord is basically an improvement on the single-strung, since two adjacent strings can help each other to build up sonority by sympathetic vibration, and the larger total of strings may also help: the amplitude may be a little increased in this way, and the colourfulness also.

For economy of size and price, clavichords can be designed for several tangents to strike each string or course at different lengths, thus providing the same total of notes from fewer strings (*gebunden*, i.e. bound or fretted clavichord). If two or more notes thus disposed upon the same string are played simultaneously, only the higher can sound, although closely consecutive notes and even trills can be played in succession. Only notes not very likely to be needed together were thus bound on any one string; but even so, the restriction became less acceptable, and by the eighteenth century the unfretted (*ungebunden*)

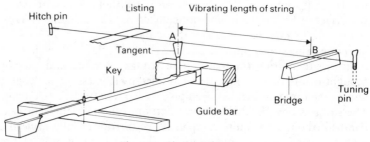

Fig. 22   Clavichord action

clavichord had become general. This is the instrument associated with J. S. Bach, some of whose more poetic keyboard pieces sound at their best on it. C. P. E. Bach appears to have favoured a particularly large and resonant variety of clavichord, such as was being made by Silbermann, whose early pianos were also notable. C. P. E. Bach actually praises the clavichord for accompaniment, a role in which most clavichords are far too soft. These big German clavichords have been revived for concert work, being just about loud enough for the purpose under favourable conditions. Electronic amplification can be used if it is so designed that the direct sound takes precedence at the ear, and recordings can be successful if played back at appropriately low volume. But basically the clavichord is for one's own home and, by preference, one's own playing. It is a pleasure too intimate to be widely shared.

THE PIANO

The *piano* (pianoforte, or in some earlier descriptions fortepiano) takes its name from its most striking novelty when first developed: its power of shading the loudness in course of playing, by touch, as opposed to altering it abruptly, by change of registers. To call such an instrument the 'soft-loud' or the 'loud-soft' was to draw attention to this feature, and very properly, since that is what brought a new resource in answer to a new need, and in turn helped that new need to find expression in contemporary music.

There is no clearer case of this mutual connection between means and ends in the history of instruments; for the working principle of the piano was not new. It had been anticipated in a MS by Henri Arnault in the mid-fifteenth century; and in practice, it seems possible, from the late Renaissance, and certainly from the fully developed and effective pianos made by Cristofori in the first quarter of the eighteenth century.

The action of these was later followed by Silbermann; but when J. S. Bach tried one of Silbermann's pianos, he was reported by Jacob Adlung (*Musica mechanica*, Berlin, 1768, ii, 116) not to have been much impressed. This was perhaps because the keyboard music of J. S. Bach requires the contrapuntal clarity and crisp articulation at which the harpsichord excels, much rather than the chordal fusion and dynamic finesse to which the piano inclines. C. P. E. Bach, on the other hand, actually praised 'a good clavichord' for possessing, 'except that its tone is weaker', the expressive beauties of the piano. That precisely was the point. The piano was not novel just in being highly responsive to touch, or in being relatively loud, but in being both at once. Each instrument to its virtues; but the virtues of the piano were those which went with the trend of music through the classical period, and still more so through the romantic.

The working principle of the piano is by projecting a hammer to strike the string and to rebound so as to leave the vibrations almost unhampered freedom. Since the hammer leaves the key behind in its flight towards the string, no further control is possible; but the force with which the key is depressed conditions the speed and therefore the impact of the hammer. Everything else in piano touch (and there is a great deal else) depends upon the finesse with which one note is joined to another, the effect of which upon the quality and build-up of the sound is indeed crucial.

In order to withstand the considerable impact of the flying hammer, and to let it build up amplitude without so thickening the strings that their partials become unduly inharmonic, they are set in courses of two or three to each hammer over all or some of the compass. The lower strings are likely to be covered so as to increase their mass and flexibility in proportion to their length, which for practical reasons may be considerably shorter than is acoustically ideal. Early pianos have strings and tensions almost comparable to harpsichords, and harmonic analysis confirms their resemblance in tone colouring although not in nuance and articulation. The lower harmonics are not particularly strong, but the upper harmonics are many and well-excited: the timbre is more rich but less massive on that account, and the sound dies down sooner. Later pianos have been given increasingly thick and tightly tensioned strings, with frames of a growing rigidity to correspond. The changes of musical quality thus introduced eventually resulted in a much altered instrument.

Hammering, particularly when the strings are thick and tense, tends to cause more inharmonic upper partials than plucking. But this inharmonicity, uncontrolled as it is by any further sustaining of the vibrations before the next note is struck, brings, together with other factors, that shimmering unevenness which in practice is so strong a recommendation. When the key is depressed, the energy is transmitted through quite a complicated action to the hammer, which flies up to strike its strings with a velocity commensurate with the impetus. Another part of the action at the same time raises the damper. As in the harpsichord, all strings are damped when their keys are not depressed, unless the dampers have been already raised by a separate mechanism which the harpsichord does not (and if it is a normal instrument cannot) possess: the damper-raising (sometimes called the loud) pedal.

This distinction is of great musical consequence. For if all the dampers are raised at once, the whole instrument comes alive with sympathetic vibrations which can only occur in much more limited degree with the dampers all down except for the notes at that moment being played. And this is the most important of the resources within the player's control for allowing the piano to build up colourfulness of tone, in a great surge of mounting sonority if he so desires. True, it is done at the expense of clarity; but then, clarity is often not the aim in piano music, but rather a glowing fusion in the sound at which the harpsichord is neither adept nor intended to be.

The basic tone of the modern piano effectively includes as many as twenty or thirty audible partials up to about its middle C; above that the higher partials reach too high for effective audibility. There is a certain neutrality about basic piano tone, in its relatively modern varieties. That is why a piano can be so useful in composing. If you are thinking strings the piano will sound like strings; if you are thinking horns, the piano will sound like horns. And, of course, this neutral aspect is useful in many pianistic passages too. But generally what happens is that the pianist relieves the basic neutrality by all manner of colourings with the skilful use of his pedalling, which exploits sympathetic vibration in almost unlimited degree. This recourse is extremely typical of the true nature of the piano, so well employed by the music proper to that very individual instrument.

When the hammer has struck, it has to fly back out of contact with the string, which it would otherwise damp inadvertently and catastrophically. It is for this reason that a piano action has to be more complicated than a harpsichord action, and far more complicated than a clavichord action. The tangent of a clavichord is pushed up to the string and held there; the plectrum of a harpsichord is pushed past the string and gets out of the way; the hammer of a piano has to rebound, but in

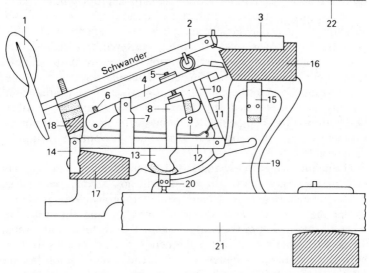

Fig. 23   Piano action

1. Hammer head
2. Grand shank and roller
3. Grand flange and repetition screw
4. Repetition lever
5. Repetition lever regulating screw
6. Repetition spring regulating screw
7. Repetition lever flange
8. Bent block
9. Repetition spring and cord
10. Grand jack
11. Grand jack regulating pin and button
12. Grand lever
13. Grand lever block
14. Grand lever flange
15. Set-off button and pin
16. Grand butt rail
17. Grand lever rail
18. Grand rest rail and baize
19. Grand standard
20. Bass capstan screws
21. Key
22. String

such a manner that it is available for almost immediate repetition. All successful piano actions arrange for this; but by a modification known as double escapement and patented by Erard in 1821, the hammer can be given a new impetus much before the key has returned to its position of rest, and repetition of the same note can then be especially rapid.

When the key itself is released, the damper connected with it will return to silence its strings, unless held up meanwhile by the damper-raising pedal. The damping is heavier and more quickly effective than on the harpsichord, but still not so sudden that some appreciable effect on the decaying sound is altogether lacking. And just as some incidental thuds can be detected from clavichord or harpsichord action, so a rather more conspicuous factor of unintended sound occurs with the piano, although the generally greater amplitude and resonance tend to disguise the fact. Part of this is thudding, conveyed appreciably to the resonant soundboard; part derives from the spread of complicated sympathetic vibrations set up even in the damped strings (on both sides of the bridge), and in those highest strings which, for good reasons of sonority, are not provided with dampers at all. Altogether, the vibration patterns of a good piano are among the most complex of any instruments, while those of a bad piano may be complex in quite a disagreeable sense.

The hammers may be covered with different materials. Leather, as in early pianos, tends to a bright sound. Felt, now normal, can be soft, tending to mellow sounds, or hard, tending to brilliant sounds; for the harder the hammer the firmer its compression and the swifter its rebound, so that less of the string is damped by it, for a shorter time. The shorter vibrations of higher frequency are therefore less liable to have their antinodes suppressed and their harmonic contributions inhibited, especially since the point of contact will also have been chosen to favour them. Soft felts, on the contrary, have a deeper pile, less firmly compressible, and clinging longer to the string. There are pianos like the Bösendorfer of very hard but splendid tone, others like the Blüthner of very mellow tone, others again of fairly mellow tone like the Steinway or fairly brilliant tone like the Bechstein – valuable differences, to which various factors besides the hammer felts contribute. But the felts are certainly important.

A piano tuner can prick the felts with a needle to reduce their hardness, with substantial effect upon the quality of tone; but while tastes will always differ, and while accompaniment will perhaps need less brightness than solos, it is on the whole desirable to keep piano tone rather on the hard than on the soft side. Paderewski used to say that he could draw mellow sounds from hard hammers when he so desired, but not bright sounds from soft hammers. In any case, there is one fortunate incidental feature: the momentary hardening of the felt by compression as the result of its impact is greater, and so is the speed of the rebound, when the impulse is violent and the note is loud. This favours the upper as against the lower partials, so that loud tone gains in brightness and soft tone gains in mellowness, which is exactly what the musical situation will normally require. Felts which are unduly soft forego much of this advantage, and for that reason are not favoured by good makers even of the mellower varieties of piano.

It is a proven truth about hammer action that the pianist can influence only one mechanical factor: the velocity with which the hammer makes its impact. He has no control whatsoever over what happens to the hammer in any other respect, and analysis shows no difference in this respect between the results of his skilled finger pressure and of a weight released on the key to produce the same impetus. But this does not, of course, mean that his touch is unimportant. It simply means that touch on the piano consists of an infinite subtlety in the joining of one note to the next: from staccato through legato to actual overlapping; from even dynamics to every conceivable gradation; everything, in short, that goes to the shaping of a line. The control needed is very great, and so is the musical judgement. Much that happens is on too fine a scale to be separately detected, yet it adds up to all the difference between a poor or indifferent pianist and a good one or a great one. It is not only that the articulation can range from an intoxicating crispness to an almost vocal smoothness, and that such contrasts can be put at the service of deliberate expression; it is also that the transition between notes can affect their acoustic quality. Good touch on the piano, though different from the clavichord or the harpsichord or again the organ, is a very real and essential ingredient indeed.

On modern pianos, the touch, though various, is overall considerably heavier and stiffer than on early pianos. The strings of the early piano soon tended to be made stouter to withstand the blows of the hammer action. No actual string is of infinite thinness and flexibility. The weight and stiffness of a string are matters of degree; but the thicker and the stiffer it is, the less harmonic and energetic are its upper partials, and the greater the amplitude of vibration which it can sustain. That was the direction taken by the piano for most of its history. For the sake of loudness, strings were continually being made more thick and stiff, at higher tension, able to sustain stronger and stronger blows from heavier hammers, but with softer coverings to moderate the tone. Iron frames in place of wooden ones made possible an internal tension which may now amount in the aggregate to over thirty tons. The energy required to activate this potent instrument necessitated a corresponding stiffening of the touch (though in that respect, at least, some reaction has by now occurred). The rewards of this development include a massive volume which is not, indeed, the supreme quality in music, but which can nevertheless be wonderfully exhilarating in its proper place. The penalties include a decline in colourfulness of tone; but this is more than replaced when the dampers are raised to permit sympathetic vibrations which include a multitude of more or less harmonic partials. In keeping with this, unobtrusive arpeggiation and atmospheric figuration take large shares in the pianistic image as it emerged throughout the nineteenth century, particularly from the generation of Liszt and Anton Rubinstein onwards.

The piano in any standard form lacks the choice of registers which allows a concert harpsichord so wide a range of colourings and so strong a sound when everything is brought on. It does not need them, since its own different resources suit its own different purposes better, and its own inherent volume is greater. However, certain variations were tried, of which our standard two pedals are the chief present survivors. The so-called soft pedal may now work in one of the following ways. It may interpose a strip of felt between the hammers and the strings, which operates against higher still more than against lower harmonics, and reduces colourfulness and brilliance still more than loudness. Or it may bring the hammers nearer to the strings, thus reducing their travel and hence their impact, with rather more satisfactory but somewhat similar effect. Or much the best of all, it may shift the hammers sideways so as to strike only two out of the three strings in each course. This not only reduces the total amplitude, but actually enriches the colouring; for the dampers are raised from all three strings of each course as usual, leaving the one which is not being struck to vibrate in sympathy without any damping influence from contact with the hammer. Beethoven and his contemporaries could count on a further variant by which only one out of the three strings was left in line with its hammer: hence his written instruction in some passages to play *una corda* (one string), a haunting effect not literally available on the modern piano.

The damper-raising or 'loud' or 'sustaining' pedal has already been mentioned. It allows sympathetic vibration not merely in adjacent unisons but everywhere, so that the colour and the loudness surge up together, until some musical consideration requires a sudden stop to it – sudden, though never absolutely instantaneous or complete. The sustaining pedal can be operated at very great speed, and contributes not only to the colouring but to the phrasing and the articulation, and indeed to the whole fine shaping of the flow of sonority which both for melody and for harmony moulds the line and makes the pattern. A modern piano without its dampers and its damper-raising pedal would be unthinkable. The early piano makes equally good use of damping and damper-raising; but in a different context.

The pianos of the later eighteenth century included a variety of small, economical instruments, some good, some not so good, which we commonly assort together under the general name of square pianos. Actually they are oblong, with restricted soundboards, rather simple actions, and not always very efficient damping. Their stringing is light, they have leather-covered hammers, their tone is quite colourful and agreeable, and they achieved such popularity that old specimens can fairly often be found in working or repairable condition.

Far better mechanically and acoustically, however, are the concert pianos of this early period. They closely resemble contemporary concert harpsichords in shape, in size, in material and in construction, though they soon tended to become more massive as the years went by, and as what musicians required of them altered. Two distinct branches emerged: the Viennese (its action initiated or perfected by Stein) and the English (stemming ultimately from Silbermann). Their differences are fairly radical; for whereas the English aimed at power and brilliance, and developed a design and an action conducive to these aims, the Viennese aimed at lightness and clarity, and developed a different design and a still more different action. Near the end of the century, the Viennese concert pianos, by us commonly distinguished as forte-pianos (or sometimes as Mozart pianos, since he undoubtedly performed on such) were thoroughly efficient instruments of clear and elegant tone, having an action of such sensitive delicacy that a modern pianist has to practise for some time, rather as he does on the clavichord, not just to go through it with an awful thud and hardly any tone. But when this action is allowed to tell you what it wants, its lightness is a delight and the tone resulting is warm and glowing, and at the same time transparent. This, or something very like it, is the only instrument for letting Mozart's scoring on the piano sound as he conceived it: clear and eloquent in the bass where a modern piano sounds inevitably too thick; bright and innocent in the treble where a modern piano lacks this particular innocence of colouring. That is indeed no disparagement to the modern piano; it is simply a matter of using the original sonorities for getting the original results. But this is a principle which we are now finding it just as necessary to attempt in classical music as we have long found it in baroque; and no doubt the authentically romantic sonorities will soon have to have their turn of intelligent revival.

By the time of Beethoven's middle period, and still more by the time of his last period, the difference between the Viennese and the English pianos, and the controversy over their respective merits, had become very marked. As was natural from the evolution of his own piano idioms, Beethoven became sympathetic to the English aims at least in some degree, but he did not definitely take sides; and indeed his deafness would have made his assessment difficult. The English piano sent to him by Broadwood, and others of the kind made by Clementi and later in France by Pleyel and by Erard, suit his later music very well; nevertheless, the very finest pianos around 1830, and the very best for music such as late Beethoven and Schubert, may well be those by Graf (and next to Graf by Streicher) of which the tone is less loud but very adequate and very beautiful, while the actions are a marvel of quick and sensitive response. It is also typical of the two traditions that the damping on the English pianos is light and sluggish, adding somewhat to the agreeable confusion of the resonance; whereas the damping on the Viennese piano used leather and is very swift and decisive indeed (at first there were actually no damper-raising pedals to arrest the return of the damper so soon as each note is left; from round 1780, knee-levers for this purpose were becoming usual, but not invariable).

The piano music of Beethoven includes much scoring, such as thick chords or closely spaced arpeggios in the bass, which presents ultimately insoluble problems on the modern piano: it can never, that is to say, sound sonorously quite right, however artistically it may be conceived. The modern piano, such as really had its origins in the generation of Liszt and Anton Rubinstein, is a magnificent instrument, but it is not an all-purpose instrument. No instrument can be that; and just as the harpsichord is now taken for granted as an elementary necessity in baroque music, where the piano cannot (as once was thought) replace it, so Mozart pianos for Mozart's music and Beethoven pianos for Beethoven's music are emerging as the one radical solution. Under many circumstances, it is not possible to be radical, and good pianists using modern instruments will continue to make a stylish adaptation; but we miss something of great beauty in this way, and there is every likelihood that the early pianos, and reproductions of them, will come, as the harpsichords have done, into their own wherever the finest considerations of sonority and suitability are expected to prevail.

For its own music of the romantic period, and for modern music designed to exploit it either on its atmospheric or on its percussive side, the modern piano is a splendid instrument indeed. It is also capable of marginal side effects. The pianist can, for example, reach inside while standing on the damper-raising pedal, and pluck it like a harp; or he can prepare it with screws, rubber wedges and other small impediments for special effects (the prepared piano). But it is, of course, as a normal keyboard instrument that the piano counts.

DULCIMER, CIMBALOM

The *dulcimer*, a popular instrument in medieval and Renaissance depictions, is no other than a psaltery struck with beaters rather than plucked with plectrum or fingers. In this technique, its leading modern representative is the *cimbalom*. This may range from a simple but very effective folk instrument with undamped strings, on the one hand, to a large and sophisticated variety with full chromatic compass and a built-in damper-raising pedal on the other hand. This may be played with the utmost virtuosity, especially in Hungarian orchestras having some folk tradition behind them. The tone colouring can be strangely rich and thrilling, particularly when built up with much tremulando reiter-ation. The family resemblance to the piano is clear enough – we might almost think of it, somewhat fancifully, as an ancestral resemblance; but, of course, this modern dulcimer is a very different instrument, just as the psaltery ancient or modern is a very different instrument from the harpsichord. And the difference between plucking and hammering in effect outweighs any structural connections between the two related prototypes. For construction, psaltery and dulcimer are one instru-ment: for technique, two; which just goes to underline how unattain-able a wholly logical classification of musical instruments must inevitably remain. After all, it is the musical usages which matter most.

9 BOWED STRINGS

THE MEDIEVAL LEGACY

The working principle of bowed instruments depends upon a continuously maintained excitement of the string, which causes its vibrations to remain substantially harmonic. This in itself is an important distinction. Furthermore, not only the onset but also the steady state of the note, and to some extent its decay as well, are under the direct control of the player. This is true for tone colouring, up to a point, and even more true for articulation and dynamic nuance. Bowed instruments are not unique in having these advantages, which are shared in varying degrees by most wind instruments; but nowhere else in music are they associated with quite such versatility.

The tone and the technique of a good bowed instrument are not only very adaptable, but in a certain desirable sense they are very ordinary. A flute or a clarinet, an oboe or a trumpet has so special an individuality that it declares itself for what it is in any situation; a violin can do this, but it can also provide a more neutral texture when that is what the situation requires. There is something particularly satisfying about the sounds of the violin family, of which the ear will never tire. The harmonic spectrum must somehow appeal to us as especially well distributed: it is rich and ample, but also it is balanced and moderate. It is never so extreme as to commit the music only to one kind of feeling. There is that within us which loves an impassioned eloquence, yet needs an ultimate assurance of restraint and proportion. For such reasons as these, perhaps, the violin family is the acknowledged foundation of the orchestra. Other instruments are just as fine, and just as indispensable for variety's sake. But they are not so basic. Of course a wind band by itself, or a brass band, can be a noble music: so can a string orchestra, but with a wider range of expression. The string quartet, again, is a world of its own, to whose range of expression no limits can be set.

Bowing appears to be much less ancient than plucking or hammering as a method of exciting vibrations in stringed instruments. However, it was certainly familiar during the Middle Ages in Near Eastern centres of civilization with which the West had many contacts, and it may have reached Europe somewhat earlier than, for example, the lute, and from similar Arabian sources. Our knowledge here remains quite incomplete; but we may picture a great variety of fairly small string instruments, with very fluctuating forms, wildly fluctuating names, at first plucked, but (from the eleventh century) with a growing disposition to alternate between being plucked and being bowed. The sculptures and the miniatures tell us this much; poetical and other descriptions confirm it, but without enabling us to be in the least precise in our conclusions. The facts themselves were not in the least precise. Fluctuation was the essence of the situation.

We seem to see two general tendencies of construction, each with its own acoustic implications. There are the instruments with flat tables and bowl-shaped backs, having no connecting ribs: the lute itself became the supreme example, but there are bowed instruments like the rebec tending to this form, though narrow enough to allow freedom for the bow, since there are no waisted bouts. Such bowl-shaped bodies have no sound post. And there are the instruments (fiddles on one rather vague modern description) with flat or moderately arched tables and backs, joined by side ribs, and having waisted bouts where necessary to allow freedom for the bow; such box-shaped bodies may have sound posts, but appear often and perhaps normally to have lacked them until the Renaissance began to anticipate the baroque. But the waists were often slight; and indeed, guitar-like instruments with waisted sides appear in ancient Babylonian sculptures long before bowing: just possibly from some symbolical or ritual association with the female form, as we see it stylized in visual representations of that period. Another explanation might just be the more complex vibration.

From the multiform variety of medieval strings, three broad lines evolved using the bow: the lyras, the rebecs and the viols, to which a fourth, the violins, was added a little prior to the baroque period.

LYRA, CRWTH, REBEC

The classical lyre and kithara were plucked instruments with remote descendants like the rotas and the guitars of the intervening centuries, among which the vihuela is as much plucked as bowed, and as much bowed as plucked. But the late medieval and early Renaissance lyre of the arm (*lyra da braccio*) is played against the chest or on the shoulder with a long, soft bow, used with sweeping strokes across the strings. The bridge is nearly flat: the top string carries the melody; perhaps four other strings sound more or less together in the function of drones at the fifth and octave, with an effect somewhat similar to the drones of a bagpipe. In course of the later Renaissance, more arch was given to the bridge; the strings became seven, having their tuning uneven; and genuine harmony was used as well as drone harmony. The two lowest strings are mounted off the side of the fingerboard, and are not intended to be stopped. The five strings over the fingerboard which are intended to be stopped might be tuned: *g*; *g'*; *d'*; *a'*; *d"*. The chords sound very full, the drones add a deep sonority, and the whole effect is ringing and magnificent. It is hard to doubt that there were sound posts here; but we cannot be certain.

The lyra da braccio became symbolically associated during the Renaissance with Apollo in his traditional role of Leader of the Muses (*Musagates*), to which the Neoplatonic philosophers, so influential upon the artistic images of the period, attached high importance. Many pictures of the fifteenth and sixteenth centuries show this connection; the instrument itself was played (above all at Florence), in many interludes and other more or less dramatic musical entertainments of the time. A bass member of the family, called big lyra (*lirone*) or lyre of the leg (*lyra da gamba*), also came into prominence for the most part in Italy, and especially for accompaniment, in which role it continued well into the seventeenth century. It has up to sixteen strings, most stopped but two left as drone harmony; and it, too, is played with long, sweeping strokes of the bow. Its tone is yet more ringing, and it is a very fine instrument of harmony indeed.

The bowed form of the Welsh *crwth* has close resemblances to the lyra da braccio, with which it shares its flat bridge and its drone strings. The fingerboard, however, is supported across an open frame, somewhat reminiscent of the classical kithara. The sound post here is a continuation of the treble foot of the bridge, the table being pierced to let it pass freely through. As a folk instrument, the crwth remained for long in use, and its revival today shows it to have much expressive power in its edgy way.

The *rebecs* differ from the lyres in being usually bowl-shaped (the width being sufficiently narrow to need no waisted bouts); in being without sound posts (which the lyras may or may not have originally included); and in having as a rule three strings for melody only, the tuning of which is not by fourths (like the viols) but by fifths (like the violins). The instrument can be traced elusively through the late Middle Ages under a diversity of names and in a variety of shapes and sizes. By the Renaissance, it had perhaps declined socially and artistically, since its role was chiefly as an instrument of the tavern and the simpler forms of dance, for which, however, its pungent power and fiery colouring give it a remarkable aptitude. It was then a family of several sizes: but only a small rebec of treble register was prominent. For the more robust and popular forms of medieval and Renaissance music, it is a most potent asset, and has been revived for such purposes. In some parts of Europe, particularly the Balkan countries, it has survived throughout the centuries as a folk instrument.

THE FAMILY OF VIOLS

The viols are a most gentle and eloquent family, complementary to the violins, which they outdo in their own special fields as much as they are outdone in the wider applications where the violin family is supreme. The viols can be played robustly and should never be dismissed as unassertive; but their power comes not from the amplitude so much as from the concentration of energy. They need the same focused vibration as a voice produced with the forward Italian placing, not particularly loud under the ear but penetrating impressively to the back of the hall. They are also capable of the crispest possible articulation.

Medieval and Renaissance viols are sometimes pictured played across the knees, and bowed in some strange positions; but the standard baroque position was between the knees or the calves, so that a generic name for them was *viole da gamba*, viols of the leg. The bowing is underhand (i.e. the hand is held, palm upwards, beneath the stick), not overhand as with the violins (though the cello was likewise held on the calves, and bowed underhand, through much of its career). The use of some sort of an end-pin is occasionally shown in late Renaissance and baroque paintings, and is acceptable for modern performance if preferred for comfort, since it is without appreciable effect on technique or acoustics. The position and the bowing must, of course, be retained, since their effect in performance is not merely appreciable but crucial.

The acoustics of the viol and the violin as sound producers are not basically different, depending as they do on strings excited by the friction of the bow and coupled to a resonant body of essentially similar design. There are visible differences: the shoulders of the viol are more often sloping than rounded, the back much more often flat than rounded, the ribs are typically deeper, C holes much commoner than f holes; but none of this is invariable, and none of it is definitive for the characteristic tonal qualities of the viol, except that deeper ribs, by increasing the volume of enclosed air, may give an appreciably lower air-resonance (yet cellos also have fairly deep ribs). There is, however, a characteristic difference in the thicknesses and tensions. The wood is thinner and lighter in the viols; the strings are also thinner and at lower tension: they are more numerous (usually six, sometimes five, or in the later baroque period, quite often seven on the bass viol); but even so, they bear less heavily on the bridge and the soundboard. The result is vibration of greater freedom but lesser amplitude. The sound of the viols is less massive, but also it is more edgy, often with a nutty or even a nasal flavouring which can set off very agreeably its charm and poetry.

It is misleading to describe either family as superior in the absolute. We can only ask, superior for what? The best English fantasies for viols are so intricately contrapuntal, in so low a scoring, that no other instruments can replace their particular balance of warmth with clarity. The most beautiful French solos require a bitter-sweet elegance found only on the bass viol at its most idiomatic. Violins merge too much as harmony and stand out too little as counterpoint for the more complex English fantasies; and even a baroque cello cannot quite match so exquisitely the native mood of French sentiment. We are again reminded of the fundamental importance of giving to any music conceived in distinctive sonorities just those sonorities and no others for its intended effect. It is true that in some instances this factor of an original sonority has more importance, and in others less. Some music is conceived in distinctive sonorities; other music, not least in the baroque period, sounds as well (though differently) in a choice of sonorities. The lighter English fantasies and dances, for example, are apt for viols or recorders or violins or other consorts single (whole consorts) or mixed (broken consorts), and like much other music of the period were regarded then and may be regarded now as adaptable; so too with many solo sonatas of the late baroque, published for flute, violin, oboe, etc. as stated performer's options. The test of the principle is musical suitability; but this principle itself can never be a negligible issue.

The seven gut frets normally tied round the neck of the viol, convenient as they may be as a beginner's aid to intonation, have an acoustic function which is far more significant: if accurately felt by the finger pressed just up to them from behind and a little over, they give the same sharpness as an open string, with no impediment either to fine tuning or to vibrato as described by contemporary authorities (not continuous, and not excessive, but nevertheless discriminatingly available). If the frets are not thus firmly covered from behind, the tone may suffer, and so also may the intonation. Too far behind lacks focus and may become flat or indeterminate; too far across may spoil the note. On the viol, as on the lute, it is often hard to bring all the fingers of a chord precisely up to their frets, and to keep them there so that the sound can go on ringing; but it should be done so far as possible, because this undoubtedly gives the most sonorous quality. On single notes, there should be no difficulty. The firm edge of the finger sounds better than the soft tip, and is more effectually pushed or pulled just enough to get the intonation really good.

There was much discussion for the viols as for the lutes about what temperament should be given to the frets: not so practical an issue as it seemed, however, since all good string players will temper their intonation as they go along, and the frets neither help nor hinder this very much unless a string is badly false or badly out of tune. The thinner covered strings are liable to go badly sharp as temperature goes up, and can pose a problem; but unless circumstances of this kind are too much against him, a good viol player, like a good violinist, makes the necessary adjustments.

There is a very substantial difference between viols of the later Renaissance and viols of the baroque period, not only in outline and general appearance, but in acoustic characteristics. Thus it seems, from a close examination of the rare surviving specimens, that many or all Renaissance viols lacked a sound post, and perhaps a bass-bar. Reproductions of this style yield a somewhat rounder and less forthright tone than standard baroque viols, whose cutting edge is well suited to that assertive period.

The underhand bowing technique contributes to the character of all the viols. Various bow-holds appear in numerous pictures. Some are at the nut, using all the hair for long strokes, to great advantage in slow passages; others are a few inches up the stick, changing the balance and suiting many dances and other quick passages. Since both are authentic, the player can choose or alternate at will; but a firm yet flexible hold at the nut perhaps gives the best all-purpose technique. All viol bows, when screwed to proper playing tension, are in some degree outcurved, which is essential for their characteristic articulation; but their lengths vary between rather longer than our modern violin bow and very much shorter, as do early violin bows (not significantly different from viol bows, and also variable). These bows *must* be well screwed up.

A common fault in modern viol technique is too habitual an audible

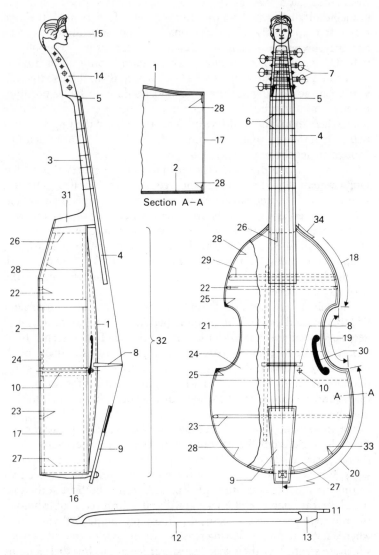

Section A−A

Fig. 24   The viol

1. The belly of the viol
2. The back
3. The neck
4. The fingerboard

5. The nut of the fingerboard
6. The frets
7. The pegs
8. The bridge

9. The tailpiece	22. The upper crossbar
10. The sound post	23. The lower crossbar
11. The bow	24. The cross-strip
12. The hairs of the bow	25. The corner fillet
13. The nut of the bow	26. The upper block
14. The pegbox	27. The lower block
15. The figurehead	28. The linings
16. The hook bar	29. The linen reinforcement strip
17. The ribs	30. The sound hole
18. The upper bouts	31. The neck bracket
19. The middle bouts	32. The length of body
20. The lower bouts	33. The purfling
21. The bass-bar	34. The shoulders

stress between strokes. It should be possible to join strokes with complete smoothness for cantabile phrases, as well as to detach them for any degree of deliberate emphasis or separation. Involuntary sforzandos are merely bad technique, and can be remedied; voluntary articulations can and, of course, should be adequately mastered. The average proportion of separated notes is higher in baroque than in romantic music; but all nuances (except for a few of the most violent) are appropriate in their places, and may be needful for moulding the line. These remarks are equally applicable to violin playing in a baroque idiom.

Strokes in viol bowing, since this is underhand, fall naturally more or less equal for weight in either direction, but if anything, the forward stroke gets a little more impetus, from the effect of gravity upon the arm, than the backward stroke; and it is the forward stroke which most resembles the down bow in violin bowing. The pressure should on the average be very firm. Swift, light bowing can sometimes be musically justified; but broadly, a viol will not speak at its clearest unless it is being played well into the string. Strong finger accents are possible.

The family of viols stood at various actual (as opposed to nominal) pitches at various times and places; but the standard baroque consort might have one (or more likely two) *treble viols* tuned *d*; *g*; *c'*; *e'*; *a'*; *d"*, of which the low *d* is rather too short and tubby-sounding (in fact, rarely used, and then only for a note or two in passing); but the remaining strings are excellent up to about an octave above the top open string. The *alto viol*, tuned a tone lower, was relatively rare and not much needed, though it has a distinctive quality of its own. One or two *tenor viols* are standard, tuned *G*; *c*; *f*; *a*; *d'*; *g'*; the tone is excellent throughout. One or two basses are also standard, tuned an octave below the treble, i.e. *D*; *G*; *c*; *e*; *a*; *d'* (to which a low *A,* might be added, especially in eighteenth-century France and Germany). The *bass viol* is sometimes called *viola da gamba*, or gamba for short, although this name is strictly proper to the whole family of viols. In Germany, tenor gamba may mean what elsewhere is meant by bass, and so commensurately throughout the remainder of the family.

The bass gamba is the prime soloist of the viol family, as the violin is of the violin family. Because of its lighter construction and lower tension, the gamba gives a very fluent and relaxed tone from its upper register (to about an octave and a half above its open top string), where the cello, though magnificent, sounds somewhat special and intense. The low seventh string, when present on the gamba, is not always quite satisfactory except for its open bottom note. The six-string gamba (of which the bottom *D* was often tuned down to *C* at need) is superb throughout, not only as a soloist, but also in its frequent function as a continuo bass. The consort of viols, variously constituted in three to six or more parts, has a glowing ring different from but not (except in range) inferior to a string quartet, and in its own music is one of the most deeply satisfying of chamber sonorities.

An octave below the gamba stands the double bass of the viol family, with a silky texture especially pleasing as a contrabass doubling to the gamba or cello. It was often (and especially in the eighteenth century) called violone; but this word, which literally just means 'big viol', has many meanings in early scores, titles and descriptions, including the gamba or (more specifically) the cello not at contrabass but at normal bass pitch. Of outlying members of the family of viols, the mainly French *pardessus* stands a fourth above the treble, with a sweet and innocent glitter of its own in solo pieces. The division viol is structurally nothing but a rather small gamba, normally tuned, but convenient for the virtuoso variations (divisions) composed and still more improvised for it by Christopher Simpson and others in the seventeenth century. The lyra viol of the same period is a still smaller gamba, variably tuned for solos in which chords are prominent and plucked notes a habitual addition. The *viola d'amore* is in structure like a treble viol but in technique more or less like a violin: its tunings are variable to suit double stoppings in selected tonalities; it has typically though not invariably a set of wire strings added below the fingerboard, not bowed but sounding out sweetly and resonantly by sympathetic vibration; and it will be mentioned again below.

THE FAMILY OF VIOLINS

Without doubt, the violins are the most versatile Western family of bowed string instruments: some might say of any Western instruments, but that depends upon the point of view. The historic rivalry of the viols and the violins is largely historical imagination, since only a few writers like Mace in his *Musick's Monument* or Hubert Le Blanc with his *Defense de la basse de viole contre les entréprises du violon et les prétentions du violoncel* actually saw it in those competitive terms at the time. We might do better to regard it as a change of instrumentation due to a change of requirements. There is no substitute for the viols in an English fantasy of the seventeenth century, but equally there is no substitute for the violins in a concerto by Vivaldi. It was the same sort of causation a little later when the piano took over from the harpsichord because classical idioms have different requirements from baroque, and when the piano itself changed because romantic idioms are different again. The influence of music and instruments upon one another is always mutual.

The violins evolved during the sixteenth century in Italy, under circumstances made very much clearer by the work of David Boyden, for which see my bibliography. They may have owed their form to the lyras, their tuning to the rebecs, their hold, their fingering and their bowing chiefly to the lyras, but in some of their robuster uses, also to the rebecs. Like the rebecs at the time, these very early violins were employed for tavern music and for dance music, in which roles there was no occasion for a sophisticated technique; but the dance music of the Renaissance covers a wide range from the popular to the courtly, and it was in courtly entertainments especially that the violins made their probable entry into good society. The mixed and colourful orchestras which accompanied the ballets, the masquerades and the interludes at the courts of the late Renaissance included violins among much else besides, and by the early baroque they had already entered upon that role as the staple of the orchestra which presently became standard and has not since been basically challenged.

The member of the violin family given, then as now, the unqualified name of *viola* was what we regard as the alto. *Violino* means *little viola*; *violoncello* means, illogically but colourfully, *little big viola*; *violone* means *big viola* (but in various early connotations). As a family, the violins are viols of the arm (*viole da braccio*), in distinction from viols of the leg (*viole da gamba*). There is confusion and inconsistency in all these terms. Viola is merely the Italian word which we translate as viol: what kind of viol has to be discovered as much from the context as from the terminology.

The treble member of the violin family, for which we use the unqualified name of *violin*, has the tuning: g; d'; a'; e". The alto member, for which we use the name of viola, has the tuning: c; g; d'; a'. An always rare and long since obsolete tenor violin lay a fifth below the viola, or alternatively an octave below the violin. The cello now always has the tuning; C; G; d; a; but an alternative tuning one tone lower persisted in the seventeenth and occasionally even into the eighteenth century. The double bass in present use has most commonly the tuning: E_i; A_i; D; G; but most symphonic orchestras now include a proportion of instruments with a device on the pegbox for bringing in an extra playing length on the bottom string, which lowers its open note to C_i.

The sizes in which members of the violin family were made in the late Renaissance and much of the baroque period are more variable than their standard tunings. The reason for this is that gut strings have to be too thick and too slack to sound very easily or very well, in order to give the notes required for the bottom registers. Composers for the violin itself tended very markedly at first to avoid the bottom strings; but this was an undesirable limitation on the higher instruments, and an impossibility on the bass instruments whose function in supporting the harmony does not allow them to avoid their lowest notes. But the longer the string is in relation to its pitch, the thinner and tenser it can be. Hence for brightness and agility, a smaller size of the same instrument was used; and for sonority and depth, a larger size.

It was at least occasional practice to make violins of larger than normal size, so that first violin parts and second violin parts could have a slightly different sonority (i.e. there could be a true second violin). It was common practice to do this with violas, so that the second viola part in Lully's orchestra, for example, lies mainly lower than the first viola part, though never descending below viola c (thus a true tenor violin was evidently not intended here): the size of such instruments differs (as viola sizes still do), but not the tuning.

The cello must in some measure have retained its two tunings even so late as 1741, when the full MS score (Paris, Bibl. Nat. Vm^2 205, p. 138) of Marais' *Alcione* shows *toutes les Basses* (all the Basses) ending on the low B, flat, which some of them at least must presumably have been able to play. And a most tenacious research by Stephen Bonta has established that genuine cellos (i.e. bass violins) were used from the start of the baroque period; a large size (which among a great number of other names might be called violone) for the fullest sonority in continuo accompaniment; and a smaller size, increasingly taken up for its readier agility in concertante parts and presently in solos, which eventually settled for our name of violoncello and which is, in fact, our form and size of cello. From the second half of the seventeenth century, covered bottom strings on the cello made a single size (the smaller) entirely practicable.

The double bass (*contrabasso*) has a yet more complex background. In its present form, it is something of a hybrid development, combining features of the viol and the violin. The shape resembles a viol, of which the flat back, cut away at the top, and the sloping rather than rounded shoulders, make it easier physically to handle so large an instrument. The bowing in a few orchestras still remains overhand, though this is now becoming somewhat obsolete. The tuning is by fourths rather than by fifths; but this is almost a technical necessity to reduce the amount of shifting for the long stretches involved. Nevertheless, for all acoustic purposes the modern double bass is a true suboctave member of the violin family. The thicknesses and the tensions are what count for this: and they are of violin and not of viol proportions. There are chamber instruments of intermediate size; the normal orchestral double bass may have a body length of some forty-four inches, and a height of above six feet. Its tone when well produced is sturdy but sonorous, less silky than the lighter violone which is the true double bass of the viols, but just as expressive in its more powerful fashion.

Unlike the violone, the double bass has no frets. Its technique resembles that of the cello, and is very nearly as agile within a somewhat smaller compass. The effective restriction upon its virtuosity is not so much its awkward size as its depth of pitch, since a string cannot change vibration from one frequency to another so quickly in the very low registers. In the orchestra, the double basses nearly always doubled the cellos at the octave below until more independent parts for them became increasingly usual through the nineteenth century. They can be used as soloists, not entirely with felicitous effect; but in chamber music they can attain to great purity and beauty of warm, deep sonority.

The changes introduced into the violin family since its perfection in the baroque period have not affected its structure, which has neither been improved nor altered. Some intensive modern researches by Carleen Hutchins and colleagues in the 1960s and 1970s have, it is true, encouraged certain very scientific modifications, the results of which are excellent in a somewhat different kind; a family of eight sizes remarkably uniform in tone colouring has been experimentally but successfully built in conformity, but without any prospect of replacing our standard instruments, since they are so distinctive as to be in actuality a separate family. The fittings and the stringing of the violin family, however, have not remained unchanged. The neck has been lengthened by about half an inch beyond the usual baroque average, requiring tighter strings; the angle of the neck to the body has been sharpened, further adding to the total tension; the bridge has been raised, with similar effect, and its arch has been somewhat steepened to allow of more powerful pressure from the bow. The pitch has also been raised above one fairly common baroque standard (no single standard of pitch obtained in the baroque period; and in fact all the features just mentioned were much more liable to variation in baroque than they are in modern times). The purpose of these changing tendencies was to increase the volume as the search for power took increasing prominence through the nineteenth century. To some extent, this purpose was achieved, and Wagner or Strauss came into the genuine advantages of all that surge and momentum of bowed string power. But the price paid in our performances of Bach or Handel has been correspondingly high. Surge and momentum are not what baroque music as a whole requires: transparency and incisiveness are the essentials there.

We are coming to appreciate that these contrasting ideals do not have to be opposed. They are not so much rivals as alternatives for different purposes. It is, of course, possible to use modern violins to very good effect in baroque music, by understanding its styles and its idioms and its appropriate sonorities and pursuing these just so far as the historical differences of acoustic and technical circumstance permit. Nevertheless, it is a much better and more complete solution to use the proper implements: baroque fiddles for baroque music and romantic fiddles for romantic music.

This applies also to the choice of bows. The bow changed through a long transition, which culminated with the Tourte family a little subsequently to the baroque period: basically, from an outcurved stick to an incurved stick. The Tourte type, now habitual, favours a massive articulation, where the earlier type favours an incisive articulation. The difference of implement matters even more where the bow is concerned than where the violin is concerned; and the argument for using outcurved bows for baroque music is still stronger than the argument for using baroque-style violins. Nevertheless, it remains true that the player counts for more than the implement. It is more important to understand the baroque ideal than to have in hand the baroque violin. Both together makes the best work of it.

Even for romantic music, some authentic modifications may be desirable: for example, gut stringing on the violins except that covered bottom strings are appropriate and necessary for any period later than the early baroque.

As to technique, the smaller members of the violin family have always been held up across the arm, and the larger members down on the legs or in front of them. Modern violins are rested on the shoulder and steadied by the chin, for which a chin rest is clamped to the body. Baroque violins used no chin rest, and might rest against the shoulder, which makes shifting down a somewhat delicate movement in order not to lose control of the violin; but it can be done, and was evidently no impediment to the high positions. Nevertheless, pictures and descriptions show that resting the violin on the shoulder and steadying it with the chin was equally authentic, and will certainly be found more convenient and secure by most modern violinists. There are also, as with the viols, variations in the bow-hold shown by baroque pictures and descriptions. The hand can take hold of the stick a short distance away from the nut, which gives a more even balance of the bow, well suited to rapid movements in general and to dance music in particular; or in the modern manner over the nut, which gives a more extended sweep and can be just as delicately controlled with proper skill. Either hold is authentic, but for all-round purposes most modern players may prefer to grip the bow at the nut in our customary manner. There was also a French grip, with the thumb under the hair instead of under the stick; with an exceptionally short bow, it has a certain advantage for crisp dance music.

The early cello was commonly bowed underhand like a gamba, but overhand bowing to match the violin became standard though not invariable in course of the eighteenth century. It was held between the knees until the nineteenth century, when our modern end-pin came in quite late; the acoustic difference, if any, would seem (as on the gamba) to be inappreciable, but historically minded cellists can (although they need not) dispense with that added comfort at no loss to security. The changes in cello fittings resemble those in violin fittings; and a reconstituted baroque cello, used with baroque bow, is just as advantageous for its proper music. It sounds considerably more relaxed, as is to be expected from its lighter tensions. The modern cello is a very magnificent instrument indeed; but there can be no doubt that its tighter tension gives it a somewhat special character as a solo instrument. Its intensity high up is part of its attraction, but it has not quite that universality which makes the violin the prime soloist of the family, both in chamber music and in concertos with orchestra. As an orchestral bass the post-baroque cello is, of course, indispensable, and as a quartet

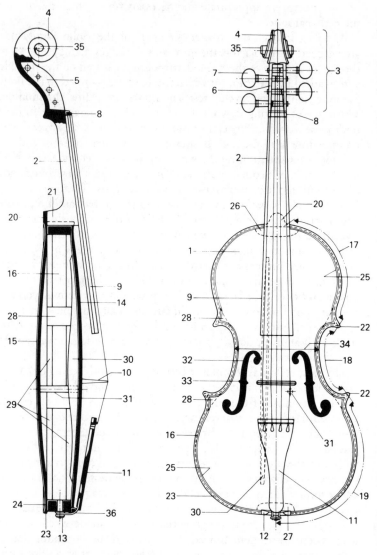

Fig. 25   The violin

1. The body (or sound box)
2. The neck
3. The head
4. The scroll

5. The pegbox
6. The pegbox cheek
7. The tuning peg
8. The nut

9. The fingerboard
10. The bridge
11. The tailpiece
12. The saddle
13. The end-pin (or tail-pin)
14. The belly
15. The back
16. The ribs (or sides)
17. The upper bouts
18. The middle (or centre) bouts
19. The lower bouts
20. The button (or neck plate)
21. The neck bracket
22. The corners

23. The edge
24. The groove
25. The purfling
26. The neck block
27. The end-pin block
28. The corner block
29. The linings
30. The bass-bar
31. The sound post
32. The F hole
33. The F hole notch
34. The waist
35. The scroll eye
36. The tailpiece loop

bass, incomparable. There is no warmer nor nobler sound in the entire range of music.

Certain outlying members of the violin family include the silvery *violino piccolo* a fourth or a minor third above the violin (as used in Brandenburg No. 1 by J. S. Bach); and a still smaller dancing-master's *kit* or *pochette*, about an octave above the violin, and in shape either a diminutive violin or a still more diminutive rebec; it has a small tone, but clear and agreeable. The *viola d'amore* has been mentioned as structurally a viol; but it is played much like a violin, and is variably tuned with six or seven strings of covered or uncovered gut. These are fingered in the usual way, but adding chords like those used by baroque violinists with variable tunings (*scordatura*). When, however, there are wire strings beneath the fingerboard, not bowed or fingered but sounding by sympathetic vibration, the viola d'amore acquires its characteristically ringing sonority, very sweet and sensuous, but perhaps a little cloying when long maintained. However, Vivaldi used it effectively, and so did J. S. Bach for some fine obbligatos; and it has a certain further repertory. (An ordinary violin tuned with wire in place of gut strings might also be called by the same name.) The *baryton* is in effect a bass-sized viola d'amore of considerable charm but limited utility, of which the chief renown rests in the numerous divertimenti and sonatas composed for it by Josef Haydn; its principal tunings resemble those of the gamba on six or seven strings, while the subsidiary tunings for the sympathetic strings, beneath and beside the fingerboard, were extremely various, and ranged in number from a mere further seven to above forty at the outside limit. It was almost entirely a German and especially a Viennese instrument, where it may have had some connection with an odd, more or less guitar-shaped

Viennese invention by J. G. Staufer in 1824, the *arpeggione*. This is a superficially gamba-like, metal-fretted instrument of six strings (tuned mainly by fourths), whose sole claim to fame is a beautiful sonata composed for it in 1824 by Franz Schubert; and that can be quite successfully performed on a cello.

The *quinton* ('five-stringer') has existed as a five-stringed violin: *g*; *d'*; *a'*; *d'*; *g'*; the *viola pomposa* as an alto, probably *c*; *g*; *d'*; *g'*; *c'*. The *viola da spalla* ('of the shoulder') just meant carrying a small cello on a shoulder-strap for processions. But the *violoncello piccolo* (little cello) is a definite instrument, required by J. S. Bach, for example, as an obbligato part to his aria 'Mein gläubiges Herze' (B.W. XVI 258); probably it is identical with the *violoncello alto* (high cello) used by Boccherini and the violoncello 'with five strings' required by J. S. Bach for his sixth unaccompanied cello suite. This is a slightly small or very probably quite normal cello, but given a fifth string at the top: *C*; *G*; *d*; *a*; *e'*. The five-stringed cello sounds very beautiful indeed in Bach's suite, taking out all the strain and replacing it with lightness and glitter, as the delightful *e'* string removes any necessity for climbing high. The instrument may have been in more common use, particularly in France, than has previously been realized.

VIBRATO FOR THE BOWED STRINGS

Vibrato is a natural recourse on bowed strings and some other instruments, the voice especially. The use of it is supported by historical evidence from the sixteenth century onwards. Some baroque authorities recommended, like Jean Rousseau (*Traité de la Viole*, Paris, 1687, pp. 100–01), that vibrato should be 'used in all contexts where the length of the note permits, and should last as long as the note'; others, like Christopher Simpson (*Division-Violist*, London, 1659, I, 16), treated vibrato as an ornament for expressive but intermittent use, or like Leopold Mozart (*Violinschule*, Augsburg, 1756, XI) considered it bad taste 'to give every note' a vibrato, and thereby testified to, while regretting, those 'performers who tremble on every note as if they had the palsy'. Taste still varied through the nineteenth century, and does so today; but our interest here lies in the acoustic circumstances which make vibrato a natural rather than an artificial recourse. We may summarize this point here. The ear has been shown to be appreciably fatigued by any acoustic event which is maintained unaltered through longer than about one-twentieth to one-eighteenth of a second, the shortest time after which a new event can be perceived as such. This constant is not the same in different animals, but in man it represents the reaction time not only for new sounds but for new impressions generally. For sound, the effect of fatigue upon any given group of fibres in the basilar membrane is a temporary deadening, so that colourfulness is lost and loudness reduced subjectively in that area. But the slightest variation in the signal permits normal response to continue.

Vibrato is a frequency modulation, and in some degree an amplitude modulation, of which the most favoured rate of repetition has been found to lie around six repercussions to the second, and not much more nor less. This is heard as if it were an amplitude fluctuation of almost steady pitch, but with a slight ambivalence which both relieves the monotony and prevents the fatigue. We are aware only of a slight enlivening of the tone: what violinists call left-hand colouring. On short notes, it may or may not be desired, but it is certainly not needed. On long notes, it is in general needed to prevent deadness, but may be varied from almost imperceptible to distressingly exaggerated. The historical evidence suggests that it has habitually been thus varied on bowed strings, of which the tone persists, and even on plucked strings such as lutes; but both historical and artistic reasons make it imperative, especially in early music, to use it with every appropriate restraint and judgement. Too fast or too slow, too narrow or too wide, can be equally unpleasant; too much is far worse than too little; but on the other hand, none at all is on acoustic grounds against nature, and on historical grounds against authenticity. The art is to proportion the vibrato to the very various musical demands arising.

10 WIND METHODS

COUPLED ACOUSTICS IN WIND INSTRUMENTS

The vibration of air columns (or other air cavities) contained in pipes, tubes etc. is the source of sound for the second of the great classes of musical instrument to be considered here: the winds. In this case, the direction of oscillation in the source of sound is longitudinal, and in this respect similar to the oscillations which transmit sounds from source to ear through the atmosphere. There are two main methods of exciting such oscillations in an enclosed column of air. Unlike the string whose vibrations condition the pitch, both methods of setting up vibration in wind instruments have it in common that – so far from imposing their own frequencies – they submit substantially to the frequencies imposed by the column of air. The fundamental pitch at which these frequencies are heard depends primarily upon the length of the air column effectively operative; and secondarily upon a variety of other factors to be mentioned below.

The first method of exciting vibration in a column of air is known as edge tone. For a crude visual comparison, watch a flag set in motion by the wind, which in striking its leading edge, forms eddies on alternate sides of it. These eddies cannot be seen in transparent air, though they may be if the air is sufficiently smoky. (Similar eddies can sometimes be seen formed by water moving past a rigid post in the stream.) But the result can be seen in the undulations imparted to the flag as the alternating eddies pass along each side of it. (And similar undulations can be seen imparted by water moving past a flexible reed in the stream.) It may be further noticed that a large flag in a moderate wind receives slower and longer undulations than a small flag in a stronger wind, thus showing that the eddies are of variable speeds and dimensions, corresponding somewhat to variable frequencies and wavelengths in wind instruments.

It is air eddies of this kind by which edge tone is excited, such as in turn excites the columns of air contained in wind instruments of this species, known as flue instruments. Flue is organ builders' terminology for a passageway directing air across an edge. One main category of organ pipes is of this species, which also includes any other wind instrument having such a flue passage built into it (such as recorders) or in effect provided by the pursed lips of the player (such as transverse flutes). As an airflow is thus directed across a fairly sharp edge (which can be called a whistle), eddies are formed on alternate sides of it. The faster the airflow, the smaller and more rapid the eddies, and (subject to certain qualifications) the higher the frequency and the pitch of the edge tone resulting. The chief qualification is that only those frequencies are practicable to which the air column is itself disposed; and although there is a little give and take, the air column and not the edge tone remains basically in control.

Since an airflow loses energy and speed as it moves against frictional resistance (always a factor in ordinary physical conditions), the frequency of the eddies can be slowed, and the edge tone lowered, by withdrawing the edge (as flute players may do to adjust their intonation); or the flow may be slowed by blowing softer. However, this cannot be done to any great extent before the air column takes up its over-riding control again. If the distance is much increased (slowing the speed of the airflow substantially), or again if the speed of the airflow is not lessened but increased by blowing harder, a new situation is liable to supervene. Each eddy breaks into two: the frequency is doubled, while the wavelength is halved; and the edge tone jumps to the second harmonic an octave above, where the air column is under suitable circumstances just as ready to accept it as before. More strongly overblown, each eddy breaks into three, jumping the frequency to the third harmonic a twelfth above: and so on, in theory, up the harmonic series, though scarcely further in practice by this recourse of dividing the eddies.

The second method of exciting vibration in a column of air is known as reed tone. For a crude demonstration, purse your lips and blow a buzzing sound; or more effectively, if you have learnt the trick stretch a coarse blade of grass between the sides of your two thumbs and blow a squawk out of that. The principle of reed tone is that the flow of air first overcomes an initial resistance and forces (for example) your lips apart, until that force is overtaken by the restoring force of elasticity, and the gap is closed again. The reiteration of impulses tends to become periodic, and to set up vibration which may excite an adjacent air column at frequencies within its natural dispositions. A single or double reed of 'cane' (*arundo donax*) or other material thus excited serves in many varieties for reed instruments (such as the clarinet or the oboe). The vocal cords serve the voice likewise; and the lips of the mouth serve brass instruments (such as the horn or the trumpet). The principle of reed tone remains the same in all these variants.

DIMENSIONS AND CONSTRICTIONS IN AIR COLUMNS

It is possible but unusual to employ reed tone without coupling an acoustic resonator: the small, pungent reeds of a harmonium, for example, are tuned to give notes in their own right without further reinforcement to their amplitude and tone colouring other than their mounting on the instrument provides. As a class, however, wind instruments depend upon the more or less periodic vibration of the enclosed column of air, governed in the first instance by its length on the basic formula that wavelength equals four times the distance from node to antinode. The partials, as with strings, follow basically the harmonic series unless otherwise prevented. But whereas either end of a vibrating string must in some manner be attached or supported and must therefore constitute a node, neither end of a vibrating column of air has to be a node, and one end has not to be; for one end at least has to be left open in order to communicate with the surrounding atmosphere.

A closed end prevents oscillation, thereby enforcing a node on all vibration of whatever frequency. An open end encourages oscillation, thereby permitting an antinode for any vibration capable of attaining its maximum displacement at approximately that point. When a cylindrical pipe is open, and therefore least constricted, at either end, the longest complete vibration possible is that which requires an antinode at one end, a node in the middle, and an antinode at the other end. This is called an open cylindrical pipe, and gives a greatest complete wavelength twice the length of the pipe, to produce its first harmonic, i.e. its fundamental. The next longest complete vibration is that which requires an antinode, a node, an antinode, a node, and an antinode: which gives a wavelength half the longest, to produce the second harmonic an octave above. The next is that which requires antinode, node, antinode, node, antinode, node, antinode: which gives a wavelength one third of the longest, to produce the third harmonic a twelfth above. And so it goes potentially up the harmonic series, but actually just in so far as the natural resonances of the exciting tone and of the responding air column (and probably in some measure of the tube itself) combine to build up energy in some harmonics rather than in others. In so far, then, as these more or less harmonic partials are being excited, we hear (unless otherwise prevented) the pitch as that of the fundamental of the note, and its upper partials as the tone colouring.

And in respect of its wavelengths, a conical pipe, whether open (at both ends) or closed (at one end) shows the same basic behaviour as a cylindrical open pipe. But when a cylindrical pipe is closed, and therefore most constricted, at one end, but open, and therefore least constricted, at the other end, the closed end is necessarily a node, while the open end is necessarily an antinode. This is called a closed cylindrical pipe. The longest complete vibration possible is that which requires a node at one end and an antinode at the other end, but neither node nor antinode in the middle; and this gives a greatest complete wavelength four times the length of the pipe, to produce its first harmonic, i.e. its fundamental, an octave lower than an open pipe of the same length. This perfectly natural but rather startling consequence is why, for example, a clarinet (our nearest orchestral approximation to a closed cylinder) looks and is so short for its pitch in comparison with an oboe (approximately a closed cone).

But that is not all the difference. The next longest complete vibration in a closed cylinder cannot be that which would require an antinode at one end, a node in the middle, and an antinode at the other end; for while the open end must be, the closed end cannot be an antinode. Thus a wavelength half the longest, to produce the second harmonic an octave above, is basically missing. The next longest is that which requires a node, an antinode, a node and an antinode, which gives a wavelength one-third of the longest, to produce the third harmonic (properly speaking the second partial) a twelfth above. And so it goes potentially up the harmonic series, of which only the odd numbers are basically available while the even numbers are missing; but actually, these odd-numbered harmonics occur just so far as the natural resonances combine to give them energy. Nor does an actual clarinet lack the even-numbered harmonics altogether, since the exciting reed tone, the formants of the tube, and certain difference tones formed in the ear bring them in to some extent; while the tube itself is not exclusively a cylinder. Low down, however, we scarcely hear them, and the tone colouring is almost literally hollow; nor can they be used for notes in the scale, as the odd-numbered harmonics are.

No wind instrument is so simple in practice as these points of theory suggest. For one thing, there are no quite simple shapes; and every variation in this respect brings its acoustic complications. For another thing, not even the acoustic consequences follow such simple patterns. Thus, for example, the antinode necessarily associated with an open end does not in practice occur exactly at the opening, but at a certain distance beyond it. This is because the contained air constricted within the tube cannot become instantly equalized in pressure with the unconstricted air outside. The difference resulting has to be allowed for, under the name of end-correction. The extent of the end-correction increases with the frequency. This would throw the ascending partials increasingly out of correspondence with the harmonic series, were it not that the first or fundamental harmonic controls the whole vibration, forcing it to remain more or less periodic. But this has also the effect of decreasing the amplitude of the upper partials as they come higher in the series. Again, since end-correction increases with the diameter, the number and strength of the upper partials become less for wide tubes and greater for narrow tubes. And many another complication occurs to influence the actual spectrum of the harmonics. This is, of course, what actually counts. The more attenuated the actual harmonic content, the less colourful the tone; the richer the harmonic content, the more colourful the tone.

Reed tone is an inherently richer source of high harmonics than edge tone, and to this extent is less vulnerable to the effects of end-correction. Again, end-correction is more at openings which do not flare out than at openings which do flare out, so that the shape of any bell or bulb is influential, besides the importance of this flaring section in adding even harmonics where these would otherwise be more or less deficient (a mainly cylindrical trumpet is a case of this). No instrument is ever sharply distinct from its nearest relatives; but the opportunities for merging the outlines are probably greater for the wind instruments than they are for the strings, and are certainly more evident in practice: above all with the brass.

FINDING THE NOTES ON WIND INSTRUMENTS

Notes are found on wind instruments by two basic methods, separately or in combination. One is by altering the length of the air column in operation; the other is by using one of the upper harmonics as the pitch of the note.

The length of the air column in operation can be shortened by uncovering a succession of holes, which when not thus opened are kept closed by the fingers, or by pads worked through keys (there can also be open-standing keys). Now the number of holes required for a diatonic scale does not exceed the fingers available to cover them. On large instruments low in pitch, the stretch between holes may present some difficulties, but not more than can be accommodated by drilling some holes diagonally so that their outer positions on the tube are nearer together than their inner positions where they meet the air column; or by doubling the air column on itself, as in the bassoon; or by fitting one or two simple keys for the most remote of them. Such situations remained very common prior to the eighteenth century; and not before the nineteenth did keys appear in much more numerous and complicated forms.

For a chromatic scale, simple fingerings do not suffice. It is necessary, not only to raise the fingers more or less successively in ascending, and to lower them more or less successively in descending, but also to place them in more complex arrangements. For while opening a hole will cut off the length of the air column on the farther side of it from sharing in the vibration with its previous freedom, it will not deprive it of all its influence. On the contrary, by closing one or more holes beyond the uppermost open hole, the pitch of the note may be sufficiently lowered to give a chromatic alternative in between. This method is known as cross fingering or forked fingering, and on a properly adjusted instrument, aided by a little judicious humouring of individual notes through the player's skill, it will take reasonably good care of a fully chromatic scale. And this, too, was the normal situation for the woodwind until somewhat later than the baroque period. It requires a fine ear and ample experience to perfect the intonation, but these were not lacking, and in practised hands the baroque wind instruments show just the same suitability for their own music as do the baroque string instruments. The tone colouring is apt to be a little more plangent, a little softer, and altogether beautiful in its own characteristically transparent way.

Nevertheless, with few or no keys to assist the fingering, some tonalities are much harder than others, and none can be commanded, perhaps, with absolute security. Partly to extend the range of readily available tonalities, and partly for added ease and assurance, keywork increased through the classical period and attained quite remarkable elaboration in the romantic period. When enough keys are fitted, not only can all holes be placed in their best positions yet kept within comfortable reach; many alternatives can be provided which give a choice of fingerings. There can be greater uniformity of tone colouring throughout the registers, and greater facility for difficult passages, while good enough intonation can be relied upon with much less trouble. Really good intonation, of course, always requires the utmost alertness from the player and all his musicianly co-operation.

Thus there are very admirable advantages brought by extensive key-work; and for their own purposes they have been admirably exploited. But they are not advantages for music composed in other circumstances which did not either offer them or require them. They have been accompanied by changes of technique and tone colouring far too extensive to be ignored by musicians desirous of Renaissance or baroque or classical or even, in some cases, romantic sonorities. So much fairly heavy keywork bolted firmly to the tube has certainly changed its formants, and whatever influence they have on the air column vibrating within (and this is now believed to be quite substantial). So transformed a technique has aided and abetted changes of articulation and phrasing inherent, in any event, through wider changes of taste. These changes were also served by changes of bore and even of material which took modern wind instruments very much farther still from baroque and classical sonority than modern string instruments. Once more, this is not to disparage modern instruments, but merely to question whether we do well to treat them as a great deal more all-purpose implements than in reality they are. For example, contrasts of tone colouring between registers, such as early wind instruments tend to favour, can be a positive asset when deliberately employed. It is ironic, too, that the mechanical elaboration which makes it easier or even possible to perform conventional wind parts of the late nineteenth and early twentieth century can actually make it harder to bring off some of the avant-garde innovations of the present day.

What the woodwind achieves by diminishing the operative length of the air column, the brass achieves, typically, by extending it: either by inserting removable crooks (the older method); or by valves or pistons bringing in added tubing at the touch of a finger (the main present method); or by telescopic tubing (only possible on basically cylindrical tubing of which the trombone is the one modern Western application of this resource). It does not serve very well to cut out lower portions of the sounding length of most brass instruments, because the bell or flare of which it largely consists has too prominent a share in governing the tone. That does affect the woodwind also, mostly on the bottom notes. For this and other reasons, the woodwind makes some use but the brass makes great use of the second basic method of finding the required notes on wind instruments.

This is by inhibiting the fundamental harmonic (and higher harmonics also as required) from sounding, thereby compelling the lowest harmonic then left sounding to take over the pitch. We noticed this as a rare and special effect on some stringed instruments. We have now to notice it as a common and standard effect on all ordinary wind instruments in some degree, and on some brass instruments in extreme degree, either unassisted (the remarkable baroque technique) or with the substantial assistance of valves, pistons or slides (the normal present technique).

In some cases, the upper harmonic required to take over the pitch may be encouraged by a 'speaker' hole which sets up an antinode (just as effective as setting up a node on a vibrating string, since nodes and antinodes are interdependent). Or the exciting tone itself may be forced up by overblowing, and may induce the air column to jump from one harmonic to the next as a result of its natural disposition to fall into quotient parts. This capacity is also conditioned by the design of the mouthpiece, the tube and especially the bell.

Various novel techniques have been developed recently for wind instruments. The horn has long ago been made to yield chords by humming as well as blowing into it and thereby getting combination tones. The woodwind, especially the flute, has now been induced to accept some very unorthodox vibrations, forced on to the air column as simultaneous notes: partly by unusual pressures; partly by setting the lips wider or narrower; and partly, again, by a variety of unusual angles for the airstream and other unconventional recourses, such as partially covering or uncovering a hole. On reed instruments, unusual pressure or lack of pressure of the lips may combine with unusual fingerings to produce strange variants, either in tone colouring, or as chords: and these chords may either be more or less homogeneous, or of remarkably contrasted volume, colouring and character among their notes. It is, finally, possible to produce microtonic intervals such as one-third tones, quarter-tones, or eighth-tones, either melodically or chordally, not to mention the weirdest of glissando effects.

None of these novelties were intended by the designers of such instruments. They have been discovered as by-products, and used for untraditional purposes. That is not an argument against them, or for them. It merely throws the responsibility on the composer, as usual, for seeing to it that they serve his own musical purposes and are therefore music.

11 FLUTES

WHISTLE AND EMBOUCHURE

Flutes as a species have it in common that the air column is excited by
edge tone. This inclines them to a harmonic spectrum of limited content, nearer than other instruments to a simple tone colouring of
acoustic (sinusoidal) purity. Low, soft notes on the flute are simplest;
high, loud notes are least simple, but still remain not very richly compound. There is a feeling of gentleness and an innocence, due to this
relative paucity of upper harmonics, which the ear appreciates all the
better in contrast to more complicated sounds. Though the flutes have
neither the versatility nor the variability of, for example, the violins,
they are indispensable in their own limpid beauty, and are so individual that no other instrument of the orchestra can stand in for
them. They are not acoustically very well suited (except as flue pipes on
the organ) to the lower registers, but are extremely effective in the
higher registers, so that the piccolo yields the highest notes in the
orchestra.

We may distinguish two main classes of edge tone instruments. There
are, on the one hand, whistle (fipple) flutes having a mouthpiece with a
flat passageway or flue directing their airflow across a moderately sharp
edge cut laterally to the tube: in performance, neither the angle nor the
distance can be manipulated; but the speed and the continuity can be
very finely adjusted to the expression desired. There are, on the other
hand, embouchure flutes having no built-in passageway, but depending on the placing of the tongue and lips to direct their airflow across a
side-hole near the end of the tube (or in a few cases, across an open end
of the tube), the angle and the distance being manipulated in performance, as well as the speed and the continuity. The principle is not
different, but the technique is, and so, as a matter of convenience, is the
usual playing position. Whistle flutes, having mouthpieces, are as a rule
held vertically, and played from the top. Embouchure flutes, having

usually side holes, are as a rule held horizontally; but if blown across an open end, they may be held vertically.

The recorder (upright, direct, common, English, soft or echo flute, *flûte à bec*, *flûte douce*, *Blockflöte* etc.), and the transverse flute (orchestral flute, German flute, cross-flute, *Querflöte* etc.), are the chief Western families. *Flauto* etc. in baroque music generally implies a recorder; *traversa* etc. an orchestral flute in our present sense. Both families are of great and indistinguishable antiquity. The recorder was obsolete for over a century before its revival by Arnold Dolmetsch and its subsequent vast popularity; the transverse flute was never obsolete, but has altered very substantially in course of time.

RECORDERS AND OTHER WHISTLES

The recorder is basically a conical tube of slight expansion, having its narrowest end not (like most conical instruments) at its upper, but at its lower end and blown through a mouthpiece at its upper end. Recorders of the Renaissance had a relatively simple bore, were commonly made in one piece, and possess a tone colouring of the most engaging directness and charm: it is important to retain this instrument for its own period, and not to treat it as interchangeable with the quite distinct recorder of the baroque period. The baroque recorder was given a more complex bore, and was commonly made in three pieces having cork-covered joins, friction-tight so as to be readily dismountable; the tone colouring has a little more bite and plasticity, resulting as it does from a slightly more complicated harmonic content.

The technique of the recorder is relatively easy in its elementary stages. The fingering is fairly straightforward, lacking either the assistance or the possible confusion of elaborate keys: only the bottom notes of the larger instruments require keys to bring their holes in closer reach. Chromatic semitones are produced almost entirely by cross-fingering, though a few instruments are made with their two bottom holes divided, so as to be half or fully closed for chromatic shifting. The fine and sensitive control of the flow of air is the chief difficulty of technique. It resembles the breath control of a well-trained singer. It is as if you had to pour your breath into the recorder without frenzy and without faltering, a steady, liquid stream, round and fat, except where considerations of phrasing and of articulation cause you to break it deliberately and unmistakably. Every least nuance of pressure, every poised attack or shapely cantilena is available for expressive use. There cannot be wide dynamic contrasts, since these merely send you sharp or flat; but there need be no limits to the subtlety. It is the shaping of the line at which a good player of the recorder will excel. A breathy tone is of no use for the purpose; for what the recorder player lacks in dramatic effects he must make up in beauty of sound, and herein lies the prime difference between adequate and excellent. In its further reaches recorder technique is no easier than any other, nor is outstanding performance any commoner. Nevertheless, this is the most encouraging of instruments for beginners and children and those who may have neither the wish nor the capacity for arduous accomplishments. The recorder holds plenty to satisfy the virtuoso, but it also holds more than most instruments to content a modest talent.

The entire register of the recorder family lies high, the actual sounds being at the octave above their apparent impact on the ear (probably because of their paucity in high harmonics); and their notation transposes up an octave in actual pitch to correspond. The smallest member is the little sopranino or piccolo recorder used, for example, enchantingly by Handel as an obbligato instrument in his dramatic cantata *Acis and Galatea*, and also appearing in his opera *Rinaldo*, under the name of *flauto piccolo*. It makes other such appearances in baroque scores, though not normally in recorder consorts: high as it soars, it can sound as soft and warbling as a nightingale. In the *Syntagma musicum* of Praetorius (Vol. II, Wolfenbüttel, 1618) eight sizes of recorder are mentioned, down to a rare low bass in F or even D (nearly eight feet in length); but the standard consort in modern times has four members.

The *descant recorder* (in English terminology: but actually the *soprano*, and so called in America) rises from c'' to d^{iv} as a standard range, over which it is of good sonority and melting tone if well managed. The *treble recorder* (actually the *alto*) lies a fifth below, rising from f' to g''' with very full sonority of the utmost flexibility: this is the chief soloist, with a large repertory including sonatas by Handel, Telemann and other German, French and English composers; d' or other tonalities are also encountered. The *tenor recorder* (correctly so called) lies an octave below the descant, from c' to d'''; the tone is a shade more veiled, but excellent up to the top few notes, which can be a little hard to sound agreeably. The *bass recorder*, an octave below the treble, rises from f usually to about d'', higher notes being available on some instruments; the tone in isolation is soft and cooing, but comes across at surprising strength as a consort bass.

Other tonalities are sometimes used for parts requiring them; and a deeper bass in c, not uncommon in the time of Praetorius, is being successfully built again. Allowing for its lower pitch, it sounds very similar to the standard bass in *f*; and it has a glorious bottom. It must not be forgotten that the capacity of all recorders for sounding as if they were playing an octave lower than they actually are is very real, and gives the consort an effect of greater depth and solidity than might be expected. When playing with other instruments, they can achieve a similar illusion, but the scoring has to be appropriately thin and requires a good knowledge of their capabilities.

Quite nearly related to the recorder stands the *flageolet*: the 'French' flageolet of the seventeenth century having four finger holes and two thumb holes; the 'English' flageolet of the early nineteenth having seven finger holes and one thumb hole, variants on which are the double and triple flageolets with their pipes running in parallel from a single mouthpiece. The *penny whistle* is a humble relative, and the *three-holed pipe* a splendid country cousin found in that ancient and honourable partnership, the pipe and tabor, which is a very special sort of one-man band for accompanying folk dances.

You hold and play the pipe with your left hand; you beat the tabor, which is a small two-headed snare drum (hung from your left shoulder or wrist) with your right hand, maybe dancing as you go. Your little finger and the finger next to it suffice to hold the pipe, leaving two more fingers and the thumb for stopping it. But that is enough. For suppose your pipe has a first or fundamental harmonic c'. You ignore this; and indeed it is scarcely to be sounded on so narrow a pipe, designed especially to favour the higher harmonics, while to sound the diatonic scale above, even if you could, would need six holes – in short, two hands. So your scale begins on the second harmonic, c'', reached by overblowing the nominal fundamental c'. No hole is needed. You overblow to the g'' as its third harmonic: still no hole is needed. For the three notes d'', e'', f'' in between you need three holes. And these are all the instrument requires. All higher diatonic notes available can be got as third, fourth or even fifth harmonics of c' or of shorter-length fundamentals established by one or more of these holes; and with sufficient skill you can reach a diatonic compass of fully one and a half octaves, with a few chromatic notes by cross-fingering as well. The tone is clear and pleasing, sharpened by the simultaneous rhythms from the tabor to keep the dancers alert and accurate. A splendid use of simple means to complicated ends.

TRANSVERSE FLUTES

The transverse flute is basically a tube, cylindrical or conical or a combination of both, narrowest (when conical) at its blowing end, where it has a side-hole across which it is blown directly and not through a mouthpiece. This end of the tube is blocked, and what would otherwise be its acoustic functions are taken by the edge-hole. However, the diameter of the hole is less than that of the tube, with consequences which must be corrected in order to prevent them from causing inaccuracy in the harmonic series.

The most elemental flute is basically a cylinder of which the intonation is corrected by the skilful manipulation of the player's breath and the angle to which he turns the instrument. This is the *natural flute* of the Renaissance and the early baroque, a most attractive instrument requiring high technical ability, but entirely satisfactory for its own purposes when this ability is achieved. The *baroque flute* as it was designed from about 1680 was greatly modified by giving it a conical bore with the exception of a cylindrical head-joint. This is known as the *conical flute*, very different from the Renaissance flute, but more different still from the modern flute. Its intonation remains something of a challenge, but can be got very good in ordinary tonalities. It was built as a standard instrument in *d'*, having six fingerholes, and commonly one closed key serving for *e'* flat or *d'* sharp (the one-keyed flute); two keys are a contemporary (even perhaps an earlier) but less typical alternative. The tone has changed (as with the recorder) to the rather more plangent baroque ideal, and it is a very attractive instrument indeed for the music of that period. It is a little too quiet for some of the bigger circumstances of modern concert life, but this is really an argument for reducing those circumstances when it comes to baroque performances, and for giving baroque orchestral music on an orchestra of baroque instruments. Moreover, if the tone of the baroque flute is well enough focused by the player, it does not have to be so very quiet. At the bottom it can be made almost as raw as a properly chested mezzo voice in her low register; at the top, as clear-edged as her head voice; and one of the advantages of the baroque flute is the effectiveness with which its different registers can be distinguished. On the modern flute, as with modern singers, the tendency is for all the compass to sound too much alike.

But if, under appropriate circumstances, the baroque flute is better for baroque music, no transverse flute, new or old, is an equivalent substitute for any recorder. A clear example is Bach's *Fourth Brandenburg Concerto*, with its two well-composed recorder parts. A good and sensitive modern performance, using a small orchestra with two transverse flutes, can of course sound extraordinarily fine: the flutes are like streaks of silver against the background of strings and the virtuoso violin part. But with two recorders, as intended, it is like the gleam of ivory. The colouring is not better in the absolute, but it is not the same; and it is a better match of sound with sense, greatly to be preferred when other considerations are equal.

The conical flute enjoyed great popularity during the eighteenth century with both professional and amateur soloists. From about the last quarter of that century, it was given more keys to facilitate some of the chromatic semitones, and its downward compass became more generally extended to the *c'* below the *d'* in which it stands. This is the instrument needed for the music of the classical composers. Halfway through the nineteenth century, the flute underwent another radical transition. Although the conical flute did not disappear, and is still to be found in a modified pattern with eight keys and six fingerholes, it was in effect replaced by what is now described as the *cylindrical flute* (as distinct from the cylindrical flutes of the Renaissance and the early baroque). This basically reflects a drastic decision by Theobald Boehm to proportion all holes in their best acoustic positions, numbers and sizes, regardless of the limitations of the human fingers needing to reach and cover them; and then to bring them within practicable reach by devising the elaborate system of keys needed for the purpose. This keywork in its essentials is known as the Boehm system, and was also applied to other instruments. The revised fingerings necessitated are sometimes known as Boehm fingerings. More radical still from the acoustic point of view, the bore was redesigned as a cylindrical pipe with a conical head-joint. This is basically the transverse flute as we use it in the orchestra and elsewhere today.

It is not surprising that so greatly modified an instrument has changed its character. With its many large and well-placed holes, almost all of them opened or closed by keys, and its altered bore, the Boehm flute is louder, more even, in many respects easier to control and to finger, and certainly more accessible in the remoter tonalities: evident advantages, although much less relevant to earlier than to more recent music. Some of the flute's pastoral enchantment has waned, its virile assertiveness has waxed a little, and altogether there have been gains and losses in the usual way of such developments. The modern flute, on balance, is a very magnificent instrument indeed at the cooler end of the orchestral spectrum.

The normal compass of the orchestral flute (concert flute, *grande flûte*, *grosse Flöte* etc.) is three complete octaves from *c'* to *c^{iv}*: the basic tonality is *d'*, with a downward extension of two semitones. The *piccolo* (*flauto piccolo*, i.e. little flute) as normally used in the orchestra, stands an octave above the flute, except that it lacks the downward extension to c''. Its range in very expert hands is thus d'' to c^v, the highest notes being quite hard to manage: the orchestra includes none others so high. To diminish an unavoidable shrillness at the top, the Boehm piccolo retains a conical bore. But a sudden figure or scale fragment high up on the piccolo can flash out from the orchestra like the crack of a whip. Another brilliant effect is doubling a flute passage at the octave above. Like all sensational resources, the piccolo is best kept in sparing use, but it is effective indeed on the uppermost boundaries of the orchestral sound.

There is an alto flute (but not so called) a minor third below the regular flute: its bore is proportionately narrow, its tone is silky and intriguing and a little too special for extensive use, and it rejoices in the sentimental name of *flûte d'amour*. The *alto flute* commonly so called (but in England it is called *bass flute* – which it is not) lies a perfect fourth below the regular flute, and though not much used sounds perfectly normal and acceptable. The *bass flute* (or *Albisophon*), generally so called, has in fact a tenor register in *c* with *B* extension; and there are, or have been, genuine bass flutes like the fine instrument produced in 1932 by Rudall Carte, with a lovely tone of true flute quality down to its bottom *C*. Other tonalities and compasses have been used, especially in military bands or drum and fife bands. But for symphonic purposes, the regular flute and the piccolo are the basic representatives; and indeed all edge tone families (except for organ flue pipes) seem to flourish most naturally in the higher regions of our aural range.

MULTIPLE FLUTES

Double flutes and multiple flutes are common folk instruments, of which the *syrinx* or *panpipes* affords a developed example, with its row of stopped cylindrical tubes blown by edge tone across their open ends, and graded by length to give successive pitches. There are, however, no representatives of this class in the familiar Western tradition, except for the double and triple flageolets mentioned earlier in this chapter.

12 REEDS

Reed tone excites the vibrations of the air column or air cavity in all wind instruments other than those excited by edge tone (i.e. the flutes). The brass and the voice use it in principle; but what we mean by reed instruments as a description is those using a slip (single or double) of the reed *arundo donax*, familiarly known as 'cane', or some such alternative as metal or plastic. Reed tone is in general favourable, as edge tone is not, to a complicated harmonic spectrum, far from a simple tone colouring of sinusoidal purity. A reed may beat freely, never quite interrupting the flow of air, or percussively, interrupting the flow of air with substantial completeness: the more abrupt the interruption, the more complex the harmonic spectrum and the more colourful the tone. Where flutes are cool, reeds are pungent, horns are warm and trumpets are brilliant; but in practice these qualities are subject to great variation due to onset transients, dynamic changes, differences of pitch and register, room acoustics, and of course the manifold fluctuations of the player's expressive intentions.

The reed may be taken into the mouth and directly controlled by the lips and the tongue; or it may be set in a cup-shaped mouthpiece called a pirouette, which supports the lips comfortably but still leaves them in direct control. Or there may be a ring on which the lips may rest, but the reed is then merely taken into the mouth without being directly controlled, the cheeks being puffed out; or the reed may actually be mounted under a box or cap which prevents any such direct control. Indirect control by varying the flow of air is available to almost all wind instruments.

Being prone, as they are, to some very distinctive assortments of upper harmonics, the reeds give to the orchestra some of its most individual colourings. There is a certain poignancy, a plaintive ingredient, which characterizes all orchestral reeds, in different shadings, with the sole exception of the clarinet, whose suggestion of hollowness results from its peculiarity of stressing only the odd-numbered partials of the harmonic series. By and large, it is flutes for tranquillity, but reeds for agitation, though there are manners of use, of course, which quite reverse these general tendencies. When heard alone or almost alone, the reeds are strong colouring indeed, particularly if continued for a certain length of time. Blended with other colourings, they pervade such colourings subtly, so that, for example, a single oboe or clarinet may make its presence felt through a large body of strings. Such potent resources require accomplished handling; but their share in the symphonic partnership is very crucial. Both the flutes and the reeds make good soloists in the orchestra, as well as in chamber music; and in an orchestral combination, flutes and reeds blend better than might be expected from their different ways of initiating the tone. The flute may often although not necessarily take the upper part (sometimes a middle part) in such a combination. The bassoon takes commonly the bass; but this instrument (which is akin to but is not strictly of the oboe family) is quite remarkable for its versatility, and may be found in very diverse capacities.

SHAWMS AND POMMERS

The *shawms* are a splendid family of double reeds, capable of some of the most raucous sounds, the stringent refinement of which, in the mid-seventeenth century, led to that much more delicate and sensitive family, the oboes. In the Renaissance, a distinction was drawn between *haut* and *bas*, high and low, not referring to the pitch but to the loudness. Among wind instruments, the recorders, for example, were classed as low (soft) and as suited to the chamber; but the shawms were classed as high (loud) and as suited very largely to the open air. They came in many sizes and under many names (e.g. schalmey, shalmuse, shalmele, chalemie, cialamella, chirimia, etc. – from the Latin *calamus* meaning reed; pommer, bombard, bombart etc. – from the Latin *bombus* meaning a deep or buzzing sound, with especial though not consistent reference to the larger sizes; and in England, wait, wayte, waighte etc., from the town band called the watch or the waits, to which they notably contributed; hautboy, meaning high or loud wood was also common, whence oboe).

The wild grandeur of the shawm is associated with its broad, conical bore, to which the reed acts virtually as a closed end. The taper of the bell may begin almost half way along, and is decidedly flaring at the bottom, while the presence of several vent holes lower than the bottom fingering shows that this portion affects the sound significantly, by encouraging high partials and strong colourings; and so does the large size of the finger holes. The reed helps by being wider and stiffer than any oboe reed; there is normally a pirouette to save the lips from getting too quickly tired, while at the same time permitting as much control as so formidable an implement accepts. No wonder Mersenne (*Harmonie universelle*, Paris, 1636, ii, 303) described the shawms as having 'the most powerful and the most violent tone of all instruments, excepting the trumpet'.

The lowest note on the 'great bass pommer' shown by Praetorius in 1620 is *F*, and the highest on the 'small descant shawm' is *e'''*. Shawms, however, were less commonly used in full consort than mixed with other loud instruments (especially cornetts and trombones) in broken consorts. The shawm is still a vigorous and popular folk instrument in many regions, for example in Spain and more particularly in Barcelona.

THE OBOE

The name *oboe* (hautbois, hoboy etc.) in the early baroque period was used for the shawm, but remained when certain French makers, notably Jean Hotteterre and Michel Philidor, redesigned this robust instrument for indoor use at the court of Louis XIV, probably a little before 1660. Like the baroque recorder, the baroque oboe as it then evolved is made in three sections rather than one. The bore is narrower; the taper is less; the bell is not only shorter but of a smaller flare, though still having vent holes along its length. The finger holes are also smaller. The reed is neither so wide nor so stiff; the pirouette has disappeared. These changes result in a much reduced degree of pungency, though not to the extent of the modern instrument. There is a most agreeable residue of plaintive sound, somewhat resembling the raw chest notes of a mezzo-soprano voice using the true *bel canto* voice production now in course of revival. The tone of a baroque oboe is a little softer and less incisive than any modern school: it has a haunting beauty greatly to be valued for all baroque purposes. It need not be unduly soft when the reed is right and the technique adequate; and it does not have to be out of tune at all.

During the ninenteenth century, keywork of increasing complexity was developed for the oboe, as for other woodwind instruments. Various systems were elaborated, including adaptations of Boehm's brilliantly successful system for the flute, to which, however, it is

evidently better suited. Important as such systems have been in extending the chromatic availability of the oboe, among other instruments,
still more musical significance attaches to certain differences of ideal
with regard to tone colouring. There has been a remarkable French
tradition favouring all that is most poetical and exquisite in the oboe's
potentialities. Expressiveness is at a premium; robustness has a little
suffered; the sound itself could be called relatively pinched or nasal.
The German and above all the Viennese tradition has remained more
faithful to the original qualities: warmer, less cutting, even a little
veiled by comparison with the silvery French sounds. These distinctions
seem to be becoming rather less sharply defined, and the French have
turned again to a somewhat larger bore and fuller tone: perhaps desir-
ably, since at its most extreme the French refinement had moved a little
too far from the highly colourful individuality which is the oboe's
native character. This is always on the side of sensitivity, but a virile
quality should also be at command; and this can be hard to get from
too narrow a bore and too fine a reed, to say nothing of the player's
predilections in the matter. The technical capacities of the best modern
performers on any version of the instrument, including baroque versions, leave nothing to be desired.

We might put it that the standard oboe in *c'*, with a compass from *b*
flat or *b* natural to *a'''* (the top few notes being difficult and uncertain)
has a certain bitter-sweetness inherently, and more so now than in the
baroque period.

Other oboes include a tenor in *f*, called *taille* in Bach's time, and the
elusive *oboe da caccia* which he and others scored for, and which may or
may not be merely another name for the *taille*. There is a distinct
variety of *oboe d'amore*, whose bore is narrow, whose bell is often
bulb-shaped (turned in at the bottom) and whose tone is mysteriously
veiled: it was much favoured by Bach. The standard oboe d'amore is an
alto instrument in *a*. We make far more use today of that very
characteristic and attractive tenor oboe d'amore in *f*, the *cor anglais* or
English horn. The plaintive tone so characteristic of this wonderful
instrument, though limiting the orchestral situations in which it can
best be used, make its entries all the more attractive when they do
occur. There is no woodwind voice more memorable.

A standard *baritone oboe* in *c* is the nearest to a bass instrument
reached by the oboe family proper: it also exists as an oboe d'amore;
but though perfectly practicable in either form, it remains a rarity. The
name of baritone oboe or basset oboe may also sometimes be given to
an early twentieth-century variant, the *heckelphone*, which has a truly

conical bore of exceptionally wide taper and a globular bell with a side outlet, from which emerges a rich and sonorous tone such as Richard Strauss, first and especially, put to admirable use. It is not a very characteristic oboe, but it earns its place.

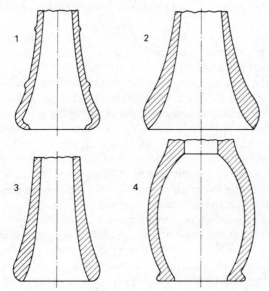

Fig. 26   Oboe bells: old; da caccia; modern; d'amore

CURTAL, SORDUN, RACKET, CRUMHORN

There is one peculiarity of construction which evolved quite variously in the sixteenth century: an air column turned back upon itself so as to be long enough acoustically for a bass register without requiring an instrument really too long overall for practical handling. Bass shawms were indeed in regular use which might be very long and inconvenient indeed, both to hold and to finger, even with the requisite keys. They were sometimes replaced or reinforced by the family of *curtals* (dolcians, etc.), which were made after the usual fashion of the late Renaissance in all sizes, but were particularly useful as double-reed bass instruments turned back at half the overall length of their sounding air column. The curtals are conical; when the tube is cylindrical, the length required for the same pitch is halved again, and such instruments also existed (*sordun, courtaut*). The extreme application of this compact construction is the *racket*, in which many turns of the bore (conical in the sixteenth century, cylindrical in a seventeenth-century variant) produce a register of astounding depth, emerging as it does from a stocky little instrument ranging from a few inches to just over a foot in height: the Renaissance made this, too, in a complete family. The tone colouring is distinctly soft and buzzing, but agreeable in its unexpected manner.

The family of *crumhorns* shares this soft and buzzing quality, with the added peculiarity of enclosing the double reed under a cap, so that it cannot be overblown for higher notes, nor controlled except by the action of the tongue against the slot in the reed-cap, and to a small extent by varying the pressure of the breath (but the scope for this is very limited). A narrow compass of one octave and a note, and a virtual exclusion of dynamic nuance, confine the crumhorns to a certain naive monotony which has its own individual appeal as one more colouring in the rich and varied instrumentation of the late Renaissance, when anything practicable as a family tended to be explored in full. The bore is cylindrical, giving low pitch at short length; the bottom end is curved picturesquely (by steam heating after the bore has been drilled) but without acoustic influence. The crumhorns are mentioned in a number of descriptions of the sixteenth century, including some of the Medici entertainments at Florence; and they retained their popularity well into the baroque period, particularly for stately dances and quiet consorts. A still quieter variant called the *cornamuse* is described as straight but otherwise similar, and there seem to have been such instruments with double bores like the curtals and reed-caps like the crumhorn. It was, indeed, a time of experimentation, and many of the experiments appear to have tailed off into one another.

THE BASSOON

The *bassoon* is a magnificently idiosyncratic double-reed instrument whose relationship to the Renaissance curtal remained closer than that of the oboe to the shawm (the name curtal long continued for the bassoon, together with *basson*, *fagott*, *fagotto* etc.). The bore is conical, but of a very slight taper, with a bell which may actually contract towards its opening: upward-pointing, since the bore has by this time almost turned back to where it started. The double reed is comparatively wide, again nearer to the big shawms than the oboe's reed is to the little shawms. Some of the finger holes on the ascending portion would be out of reach if they were not drilled on a slant, at suitable angles, through the considerable thickness of the wood; and this feature remains through all the nineteenth-century history of added keywork. This keywork never was carried to the same extremes as on most wind instruments; and indeed, the bassoon represents so ingenious a compromise of seeming acoustic impossibilities that attempts to alter it for the better have met only with a limited success. It is something of an instrument-maker's miracle as it stands. Overblowing is available to the second, the third and even occasionally to higher harmonics. Not only is great skill needed, however, to achieve its very extensive range of more than three and a half octaves: no two designs of bassoon (it has sometimes been said, no two bassoons) play alike, and there can be few if any instruments which require quite so much individual humouring. But the rewards of this individuality are very great.

In skilled hands, the agility and the flexibility of bassoon technique fit it for a wide range of purposes. Its lower registers make an admirable melodic bass for baroque continuo accompaniment, and this is a function which in chamber music it frequently fulfilled in place of cello or gamba, or in the orchestra as a doubling for the string basses. The bass parts in baroque orchestral passages can usually be doubled by several bassoons, even when not so marked; if oboes are playing with the violins, it can particularly well be assumed that bassoons should be playing with the cellos. Sometimes instructions such as 'the bassoons silent' may be our first indication that the bassoons are supposed to have been playing previously. The sound of the baroque bassoon is just as excellent in its own proper music as the sound of the baroque oboe and is being cultivated with the same success in course of our experimental reconstruction of the baroque orchestra, than which no step is more advantageous towards giving the music its own natural transparency and incisiveness. Baroque obbligatos and solos for the bassoon exploit the higher registers in addition, though scarcely the highest.

In the classical and still more in the romantic orchestra, the middle registers of the bassoon have often the function of a tenor soloist, in addition to the normal bass functions both in doubling and in holding the bottom part of a woodwind grouping. Only the topmost register needs under any circumstances a certain caution, since it does not always come through very well and can also be something of a strain upon the player's embouchure if too much is asked of him; moreover, a reed well suited to the highest notes cannot also be well suited to the low and middle registers.

Both in and out of the orchestra, the bassoon is something of an individualist. There is, perhaps, a touch of melancholy, open to parody if treated in a comic vein, but essentially noble and even on occasion tragic. The bassoon is not quite the ideal wooodwind bass, standing out a little for its dark colouring low down, in contrast to the plaintive oboes, the translucent flutes and the astringent clarinets; but we are accustomed to the blend, and adept at making the best of it. The bass clarinet is one alternative in this role: but that, too, has a very individual colouring.

The bassoon, like the oboe, has taken two fairly distinct turnings. But whereas the French makers and players of the oboe tended to narrow the bore, thus departing farther from the baroque ideal than the Germans, the bassoon shows an opposite development; for it is the French who retained for longest, and to a lessening extent do still retain, the older bores and tone colourings of the baroque and classical bassoons – not by any means entirely so, but nevertheless appreciably – while the Germans did more to transform the instrument, especially through the radical modifications introduced By Heckel late in the nineteenth century. It must be admitted that the Heckel bassoon, now accepted in most countries and still gaining ground, is a very fine instrument indeed; but it is further from the more robustly reedy ideal which is perhaps nearer to the bassoon's native genius, and the oboe's too. What is chiefly important, however, is not to confuse the modern woodwind with the baroque woodwind: both are excellent, but they are different, and not merely interchangeable. We might say almost as much for the woodwind of the classical orchestra; it still raises technical problems, but they can be perfectly well overcome within the requisite limits of tonality, and the distinction is crucial both for proper balance and for the sheer pleasure of the original sonorities.

The regular bassoon ranges from B, flat, or sometimes A_i, to e'' flat, f'', or on some German instruments a'' flat, though the topmost notes are neither easy nor reliable and are not usually worth the trouble of getting them. Quality does go off above b, flat, which for average purposes makes a good working limit. The *double bassoon* or *contrafagotto* stands an octave lower, with a range commonly from C_i (but in certain German instruments from B_i flat and occasionally from A_i) to f with good effect (but to b flat or even higher with great skill and not very good effect). The value of the instrument lies in its admirable flexibility and grand sonority in carrying the true bassoon quality very low down indeed. There have also been small bassoons: a whole consort early in the baroque period, and various sizes in subsequent, though scarcely in modern, use, including a *tenoroon* at the fourth or the fifth above the regular bassoon, and a monstrous *sub-contrabassoon* with a bottom $B_{\,\prime\prime}$ flat which could only be audible indirectly through its upper partials. In the normal contrabass, bass, baritone and tenor registers, the regular bassoon and the double bassoon between them give everything that the traditional symphonic orchestra requires

THE CLARINET

The *clarinets* are unique in the orchestra for a quite special reason: they are in effect the only representatives of the stopped cylinder, whose basic characteristic it is to accept odd-numbered harmonics but reject even-numbered harmonics. True, this characteristic is by no means unqualified in practice: the clarinet is not quite cylindrical at the mouthpiece, still less so towards and at the bell; and even if it were, onset transients and other considerations would greatly modify the situation. Nevertheless, the clarinet, though it is in reality a very complex acoustic phenomenon, does basically behave as its essential characteristic suggests. The clarinet does sound an octave lower for its length; and the clarinet cannot use its even-numbered harmonics as upper notes, overblowing as it does not to the second harmonic at the octave, but to the third harmonic at the twelfth. More subtly, the clarinet is as a whole far weaker than other instruments in even-numbered harmonics heard as tone colouring. There is certainly more strength than might be expected from the eighth, the tenth and the twelfth harmonics; and in any case, we are dealing with flexible bands of resonance rather than with precisely circumscribed responses. No two notes respond in quite the same way; no two dynamic levels evoke just the same harmonic pattern; no two designs and perhaps no two instruments tally altogether. With all this, the sense persists of something largely absent from the resonance which would ordinarily be present: namely, the expected quotient of even-numbered harmonics. Nothing is lacking artistically, but something is lacking acoustically, and this lack is itself what defines the particular excellence of the instrument. The limitations of artistic material are, as usual, part of the material, and the art consists in turning them to advantage.

It is a possible metaphor, and perhaps rather more than a metaphor, to call clarinet tone in general hollow-sounding. If we add that low clarinet sonority (the chalumeau register) sounds cavernous, that middle clarinet sonority (above the slightly indeterminate throat notes) sounds refined, and that high clarinet sonority sounds disembodied, we are pressing these metaphors, but not necessarily beyond what most people will recognize. Among the many contrasts and associations which give music its power to communicate, this hollowness of the clarinets is one of the most distinctive and inalienable.

The single reed of the clarinet beats in a slot cut along the flat under-side of the mouthpiece, unlike the double reed of most orchestral instruments; this distinction between a double and a single reed is not, however, of much acoustic importance compared with the distinction between a cylindrical and a conical basis to the bore. Reeds as such, indeed, matter very critically, which is why they must be got just right for early wind, and not merely taken for granted in their modern forms. But bore is crucial, and matters most.

The earliest clarinets may have owed something to a previous instru-ment, the chalumeau, basically a stopped cylinder with single reed not capable of extending its limited compass by overblowing, and not at all discarded in the eighteenth century. But around 1700, the flute-maker J. C. Denner either invented or improved a genuine two-keyed clarinet for which (in all probability) a few parts appear in opera scores from the beginning of the eighteenth century. Handel, Vivaldi and Rameau, among others of their generation, employed the clarinet; Mozart formed a very high opinion of its capabilities, and anticipated its later standing in the orchestra. The originally narrow, unexpanding bore grew wider, and keywork increased in line with the common tendency, until by the middle of the nineteenth century there were several systems, including one based on the methods applied by Boehm to the flute. This is known as the Boehm clarinet though not designed by him, but by Klosé and Buffet in France, where it became dominant. Germany, in particular, retained more often what became called the old-system clarinet, perhaps tending to a more covered tone, but so slightly that the player can make very much what he wishes of either. And this exploitation of the clarinet has indeed been very various.

The regular clarinet stands most usually in B flat (now preferred) or in A, with a total compass of almost four octaves; the top octave is how-ever unavoidably somewhat strident. Higher tonalities have been in considerable use, but of these, only the *E flat clarinet*, a fifth above the B flat instrument, is currently of importance in the orchestra. It is not only strident, but harsh and shrill in remarkable degree, and of great value whenever these qualities are desired. Richard Strauss and Mahler are both noted for their admirable use of this excruciating instrument, which must not be heard too often, but is irreplaceable for its own valid purposes. Yet higher clarinets in F, G and A flat are not favoured by symphonists; lower instruments include an unimportant *alto clarinet* in F or E flat. There is, however, a fine orchestral instrument to which

Mozart was much addicted, the so-called *basset horn* in F, having a relatively narrow bore, and thus a relatively veiled but splendidly colourful tone. Considerably more important still, the *bass clarinet* stands most usually in B flat an octave below the regular clarinet. It is an extraordinarily powerful and effective instrument, carrying the regular clarinet quality and flexibility right down through its cadaverous bottom register. The prodigious *contrabass clarinet*, in various tonalities but serving the sub-octave compass, has found no firm footing in the symphonic orchestra.

SAXOPHONE, SARRUSOPHONE

The *saxophone* was introduced by Adolphe Sax in the middle of the nineteenth century, and took its name from its inventor. The bore is conical, like an oboe; but the cone is much wider at the top, tapers less and has almost no flare at the bell. The reed is single, like a clarinet; but it is broader and more massive, requiring a slacker embouchure and a greater volume of breath. The material is metal, like a brass instrument, but there is very little brassy quality to the sound. In short, the saxophone is very much of an instrument in its own right, having the virtues of its own defects as any proper instrument must do.

The broad bore, almost without flare at the bell, discourages high harmonics as tone colouring, and leaves the overall quality somewhat massive, neutral and devoid of that astringent edge which makes for character. The fundamental tends to be strong, the fourth harmonic at the double octave prominent, the fifth and sixth of some intensity, dwindling upwards to about the fifteenth. The large size of the note holes adds some turbulence, the note played and the attack and volume given to it bring the usual variability, the slack embouchure and broad bore allow of considerable adjustments to the pitch and quality, with a looser coupling between the reed and the air cavity. There is thus a great flexibility for expressive nuance and articulation, but also a certain lack of focus and definition, as though the saxophone were a little too ready to be all things to all men.

It is perhaps for these reasons that the saxophone has done best in dance music where its ready appeal is not too severely tested by the more searching profundities of human feeling. Yearning and sentiment, pathos and melancholy can be well evoked, though not the maturest accents of joy or grief, delight or tragedy, of which our lives may be so ambivalent a compound and our great music so healing a reconciliation. It is no shortcoming of the saxophone if it differs from the plaintive oboe or the tender horn, but simply an instance of the usual equation: acoustic behaviour conditions tone colouring, and tone colouring conditions feeling. Musicians have a very sure judgement of what sounds are needed in what contexts, and symphonic music does not appear to be a natural context for the saxophone.

The saxophone, from its flexibility, is a very fine instrument for its own kinds of cantilena melody. Again, the sound warms up very meltingly in a good quartet of saxophones, where the overtones build up to a more complex resonance. There are indeed certain effective passages like the example in Vaughan Williams' Sixth Symphony, but they are not common, and as a whole the saxophones have not found acceptance for symphonic purposes. For their own appropriate purposes, their excellence is not in doubt. There have been a number of sizes in the family, but those generally in current use consist of a soprano in *b* flat; an alto in *e* flat; a tenor in *B* flat or *C*; a baritone in *E* flat; and rather less commonly, a bass in *B,* flat.

The *sarrusophone* was introduced and named by the bandmaster Sarrus in 1856. It is a conical brass instrument of wide taper, played with a double reed; and it bears much the same resemblance to the oboe and the bassoon as the saxophone bears to the clarinet. Of its original eight sizes, only the bass and the contrabass are now much used.

THE BAGPIPES

Bagpipes form a large class of traditional instruments having a bag (still commonly the skin of a sheep or goat or the stomach or bladder of a bigger beast) which contains air replenished intermittently by the mouth or bellows, but supplied continuously by arm pressure to a pipe or pipes. There is a flap or valve to prevent the air from returning while the breath is being taken or the bellows opened. One pipe is a chanter, with finger holes for melody; any other pipes are drones, tuned at the unison, octave or fifth. Single and double reeds, cylindrical and conical bores, are found in various combinations. Except where the chanter is stopped at its lower end and can therefore be silenced by closing all its finger holes, there is no interrupting the sound, and articulation can only be simulated by grace notes; except where the chanter can be overblown by extra pressure on the bag, it can sound only in the fundamental register. Drones, when present, preclude modulation, whence bagpipes have not entered into much ordinary Western music since the Middle Ages. We are not considering here an instrument of ordinary music, but of special character, the most familiar instance today being the wild Highland bagpipes.

The chanter of the *Highland bagpipes* is a shawm-like pipe of wide conical bore and double reed, having a most powerful and barbaric tone colouring to which three drones (two unisons and an octave) with cylindrical bore and single reeds add deep and sonorous support. The tonality is of uncanny strangeness: the chanter is tuned from g' to a'', with an interval of about three-quarters of an ordinary tone between the c'' and the d'', and between the f'' and the g'', sounding by no means out of tune, but rather in tune with some primeval harmony. Two tenor drones of 15-inch length sound a and one bass drone of 30-inch length sounds A, giving strongly the sense of tonic – but tonic to what unformulated mode? No matter what, the heart responds, and is stirred by so fiery a call from so lost a past. If the Highland bagpipe music does not speak to our forgotten depths, it does not speak to us at all; but those whom it touches, it touches with a glorious and eerie satisfaction.

The *Irish union bagpipe* has become a more sophisticated instrument, incorporating as it does, in addition to its relatively mild chanter and drones, a set of pipes, known as regulators, which have keys manipulated by the wrists to add notes of normal harmony and pleasing tone: the chanter overblows to give a second octave for the melody. It is a beautiful instrument, but it is no longer barbaric and it evokes no primeval resonance. The *Northumbrian bagpipe* is an indoor instrument, of which the chanter can be silenced for sharp articulation by closing momentarily all its finger holes. The French *musette* of the later seventeenth and eighteenth centuries is a very sophisticated instrument indeed, having (after Hotteterre remodelled it) two chanters at different pitches, drones which could sound or be silenced at will, and a most sweet and docile tone colouring to which not the smallest exception could be taken in polite society. Other bagpipes of the most varied styles and qualities have existed everywhere and survive in many more or less remote localities.

MULTIPLE REEDS

Double reed-pipes and multiple reed-pipes are found in many folk traditions, but have also taken significant shares in sophisticated traditions, particularly Far Eastern, with a more limited appearance in the modern West.

Chinese and Japanese *mouth-organs* are of great antiquity and beauty, using tiny reeds of bamboo or brass beating freely, but coupled acoustically to wooden pipes of different lengths and harmonic resonance. Examples became known in Europe early in the nineteenth century, and may have suggested a number of experiments in making small instruments using multiple free reeds variously arranged. There is, however, also some resemblance to the regals and more distantly to the reed stops in organs, for which see Chapter 16 below.

In 1844 Charles Wheatstone patented that admirable little instrument, the *concertina*. This is a small bellows of hexagonal or octagonal shape, worked in and out by both hands, the fingers remaining free to press a range of studs which pass air through free metal reeds at different pitches. The air chamber is small enough to be given ample pressure, and the volume and quality of the tone can be varied expressively up to quite a powerful maximum. A fully developed English concertina is chromatic over as much as a four-octave compass (e.g. g to g^{iv}), and is by far the best instrument in this extensive class, versions of which have appeared in many sizes, shapes, complexities and potentialities. They have been taken seriously by some good performers and composers. Behind them lies the simple mouth-organ, a double row of free metal reeds in slots which when held to the mouth, and controlled by the tongue, produce by blowing and sucking a dramatic range susceptible of the utmost virtuosity: its powers were particularly well demonstrated when Vaughan Williams wrote a concerto for Larry Adler to perform on it. *Harmonica* is a dictionary name for mouth-organ. *Accordion* covers larger instruments resembling concertinas of more versatility but less charm, which may have on one side a piano-style keyboard (hence, sometimes, Piano Accordion) of extensive treble register, and on the other side a holding strap for manipulating the bellows and a layout of buttons for bass notes or actual chords. Enormously popular though it became, such an instrument has built-in limitations for musicianly employment – within which it can all the same be brilliantly effective.

13 BRASS

THE ADAPTABILITY OF BRASS INSTRUMENTS

Instruments of which the tone exciting their vibrations is produced by the human lips partake so directly in a bodily action that only of the voice, perhaps, is it more true to say that the player is part of his instrument, and his instrument is part of the player. A horn player, for example, will say that he has to think his note before he makes it, just as a singer will. There is a mental state of being prepared, without which it is too late to prepare the physical state, and though such preparation may or may not literally be deliberate, it had better be habitual. The singer really is his instrument, whereas other musicians use their instruments; but the rapport with which they use them is as much mental as physical, and as much emotional as either. The brass only differs in this respect, that its primary vibrating substance is human tissue; and the singer only in providing in his own person not only the exciting tone but also the resonating cavities. But the state of the lips which the player is bringing to a brass instrument is a physical factor in that instrument so important that no discussion of the acoustic behaviour resulting can be adequate while overlooking it. Reeds are important, but replaceable. The right lips and even the right teeth are among those gifts of nature which must be assumed in brass players before fine training can so much as begin.

There are other reasons, too, why the distinctions between brass instruments are apt to be uncertain at the edges, although impressive at the extremes. The various patterns of the mouthpiece can be shaded off one into another by imperceptible degrees; and mouthpieces not only influence harmonic content by such factors as the angle, if any, at which they meet their throat, but also condition the state of the lips with which it is comfortable or even possible to encounter them. The bore, again, can be graded insensibly from approximately cylindrical through narrowly to widely conical, and through any degree or none of flare or bell towards the bottom end; and if any basic distinction is to be seen among brass instruments, it is almost certainly that between bores which are effectively cylinders and bores which are effectively cones. But since there are no consistently cylindrical bores, and since conical bores may range from quite narrow to very wide indeed, not even this distinction can be taken for absolute.

However, the acoustic consequences of an effective cylinder, substantially closed (as it is in the brass) at the mouthpiece end, and an effective cone tapering out from an end similarly closed, must differ in spite of any approximation of the one to the other produced by partial modifications of the tube. Here, if anywhere, are the two basic classes to which the brass inclines. The trumpet may represent the cylinders, the horn may represent the cones; while on the other hand, both these may represent the narrow bores, and the bugles – but especially that vast and splendid bass-bugle, the tuba – may represent the wide bores. The acoustic range thus variously covered is very ample indeed; the brass species lacks nothing for versatility.

The higher harmonics are intrinsically favoured by small, shallow and angular mouthpieces, by cylindrical, long and narrow bores, and by extensively flaring bells. The lower harmonics are on the contrary favoured by large, deep and tapering mouthpieces, by conical, short and wide bores, and by slightly flaring bells. These tendencies persist through various permutations and combinations. Thus trumpets and horns both have small mouthpieces, narrow bores and flaring bells: but the trumpet mouthpiece is apt to be shallow and somewhat angular, where the horn mouthpiece is more deep and tapering. The trumpet bore is nowadays fairly short and mainly though not altogether cylindrical, whereas the horn bore is decidedly long and mainly conical. The trumpet bell, though it is flaring, is not so extensively flaring in proportion as the horn bell. Even these factors are to some considerable extent variables, but in the result while both trumpet and horn favour the higher harmonics and are rich in tone colouring, trumpet tone is more brilliant and horn tone is more mellow. Then again, the tuba mouthpiece is large, yet tends to be shallow and angular; the bore is mainly conical, yet is very wide even in proportion to its considerable length, the bell is only flaring in relatively slight degree. In the result, tuba tone is not so much colourful as massive, and invaluable at deep pitches to which not every brass family is even capable of descending.

The acoustic influence of the bell, whether flaring extensively or slightly, is likely to be more significant for brass instruments than for the flutes or the reeds. For this and other reasons, that common woodwind recourse of shortening the effective tube length, by opening finger holes, to get higher notes, is less desirable for brass instruments, and has not been greatly used, since to open higher holes inevitably diminishes the influence of lower portions of the tubing. But by a fortunate compensation, that very encouragement which flare and bell afford to higher harmonics as tone colouring, and which makes side holes therefore undesirable for the brass, also encourages higher harmonics heard as separate notes when lower harmonics are being inhibited for the purpose.

This is, indeed, a recourse to which the woodwinds resort; but the brass instruments carry it to much higher levels in the harmonic series. And whereas the woodwind, to make sure of overblowing, may sometimes use small speaker holes to distribute nodes and antinodes at the needful places, brass instruments very seldom do so, relying instead upon the unaided influence of the breath and the lips. On the trumpet and the horn, for example, harmonics very high and close together (up to the twentieth harmonic or higher in some instances) may be picked out by the lips with the most delicate precision. For it has always to be remembered that the selfsame harmonic can make itself felt either, in the ordinary way, as tone colouring, or, if all lower harmonics are temporarily inhibited, as a note complete with upper harmonics of its own for yet other tone colouring. The capability of brass instruments in these respects varies greatly with the design, as well as depending crucially upon the player's skill; but in general, the brass are wonderfully prolific in high harmonics, and the players in professional ability.

This recourse of inhibiting lower harmonics in order to sound higher harmonics as notes is nevertheless itself limited more or less to partials of the harmonic series on the fundamental of the operative length of tubing. The partials of a harmonic series are separated by very wide gaps low down, and by decreasing but still considerable gaps higher up, until they reach levels so high that picking them out by the lips presents technical problems which can only up to a certain point be overcome. Since these problems are not, with the brass, eased by finger holes to shorten the tube, as is customary with woodwind, is there any alternative recourse? Yes, there is an alternative, not by shortening but by lengthening the operative length of tubing. This may be done by either of two available methods.

The first method is that exemplified in the trombone. The trombone, for the greater part of its tubing, is cylindrical. It can therefore be constructed in two portions, one left free to slide along the other, thus telescoping the operative length of tube and air column. At its shortest, called the first position, this yields the highest fundamental and its harmonic series; at its longest, called the seventh position, the theoretically lowest fundamental cannot in practice be sounded on so long and narrow a tube; but the rest of its harmonic series can. Intermediate positions yield intermediate fundamentals at semitone intervals. By changing cunningly from position to position, and choosing an appropriate harmonic, the player can produce his note from the most convenient combination; and he can do this so deftly that the joins can be made imperceptible at will, provided the composer knows the technique well enough to avoid demanding the impossible.

But where this telescopic arrangement cannot be constructed on account of the tubing being mainly conical, the second method can be used, whereby additional lengths of tubing are introduced: either as separate crooks which can be quickly, but not instantly, inserted and removed; or nowadays as permanent sections which can be instantly let in or cut out by valves or pistons. There is a problem here, because the regular expansion of a conical tube has necessarily to be interrupted by such mechanism, with at least some effect on tone colouring; and also because an added section of the right length in proportion to the whole to produce good intonation will not be of the right length when that whole is itself changed by other added sections. Further compensating tubing may then be needed. But the advantages of thus completing the scale are not merely valuable but essential to our modern era. It is only desirable, as usual, to use the contemporary instruments for each period, including baroque brass instruments for the baroque period.

With so many near neighbours in acoustic behaviour, and so many litigious conflicts as resulted in seeking patents for them, it is not surprising that the names employed should also be in a condition of exceptional confusion. Thus what denotes one instrument in England may denote a different instrument in other languages; and indeed many a difference without a distinction has been introduced solely with a view to eluding an existing patent. But when all this is allowed for, the brass species remains rich in genuine diversity.

The strings owe their inexhaustible satisfaction to a wealth of evenly spread harmonics; the flutes owe their limpid fascination to an unusual sparseness; the reeds owe their plangent appeal to certain compact assortments. The brass range from a massive bottom to a sparkling top, rendered exceedingly versatile by the adaptability of the human lips from their most relaxed and ponderous to their most tense and delicate condition. Sombre or radiant, the brass is seldom without a certain sonorous nobility, fit for tragedy or triumph, dignity or splendour, menace or magnificence, candour or mystery: for use it as you will, you cannot easily rob the brass of its inherent grandeur. It is not impossible to caricature the trombone or to vulgarize the trumpet, but only because they have something so vital about which to be sardonic, if that is to the musical purpose intended. For the same reason, muting brass instruments effects a more startling transformation because what is muted is inherently so open. Only the nineteenth-century cornet, perhaps, has from its bore and its tone colouring a name for triviality, perhaps unfair to it since it has its honest uses too. No sound in music is really to be judged except by its fitness to some honest purpose – or dishonest if the artist makes it so.

The brass may float an intricate scoring upon a glow of sustained harmony; it may cut through the orchestra with salient melodies or potent figures; it may be heard in mixed or unmixed families alone. But in any capacity, sonorous nobility is its most characteristic attribute.

ACOUSTIC LIMITS OF BRASS FAMILIES

If a brass instrument is so designed as to excel in its upper register, as a treble instrument should, it will be more or less narrow for its length, since this encourages high harmonics both as notes and as tone colouring. But a narrow air column of more than a certain length is not capable of vibrating as a whole. Thus the fundamental at the bottom, though present in theory, will be virtually or wholly unobtainable in practice. The compass then begins with the half-length vibration giving the second harmonic at the octave above. True, the upwards extension of the compass may with the requisite skill go very high indeed (about four octaves above the theoretical fundamental): but a genuine bass instrument cannot be built for that family; for to widen the bore, thus making the bottom octave available and sonorous, would also limit the top and change the entire tone colouring – and that, of course, is in effect to change the family.

Conversely, if a brass instrument is so designed as to excel in its lower register, as a bass instrument should, it will be more or less wide for its length, since that encourages low harmonics both as notes and as tone colouring. But a short air column of more than a certain width, though readily capable of vibrating as a whole, and therefore of sounding the fundamental at the bottom, is much less capable of vibrating at part-lengths small enough to give high harmonics either as notes or as tone colouring. The upward compass is therefore limited, and so is the brilliance of the sound. And to narrow the bore in order to gain a better top would again be to change the family, since instruments of which the treble size sounds quite different from the bass size do not form one family but different families.

This is only a way of saying that not all brass families are capable acoustically of being made complete in all sizes. Certainly a great deal depends on the mouthpiece, and still more on the player's skill: but there are always acoustic limits to what can be done. Most brass instruments have an upper limit of from three to three and a half octaves above a fundamental which may or may not be obtainable in good or any quality. Some go higher, but with such tension of the lips that the strain is unacceptable. It is normal to use brass instruments basically in the registers where they are best and easiest, rather than push them to unnatural extremes unless for exceptional cause.

We may put it that when an unusually narrow tube is long enough for its fundamental octave to lie in a bass compass, it will be too long to sound there satisfactorily, if at all. It cannot be a bass instrument, but a baritone at lowest. And if we think to remedy this by widening the tube, we shall merely rob it of its highest harmonics both as notes and as tone colouring, which is tantamount to turning it into another instrument.

And on the other hand, when such an unusually narrow tube is long enough to encourage its very high harmonics, it lies too low to be a treble instrument, though it may soar into the treble compass by pressing its technique to virtuoso extremes. It is really an alto at the highest, as was the old natural trumpet, though used also for treble parts by performers specializing in its very highest potentialities. In this long and narrow class, of which the natural horn was another case (and the modern horn is not always shorter although the modern trumpet is), the range of sizes within the family is therefore limited, but the practicable compass of its individual instruments is so extensive that this limitation is effectually disguised; such instruments are sometimes described as four-octave instruments. Other brass instruments, sometimes described as three-octave instruments, have closer limits to their practicable compass, but are less subject to limitations in forming complete families of different sizes but comparable tone. In this way, the scope of the brass overall ranges from very deep to moderately high, with perhaps some general suitability for the low to middle regions, rather than the middle to high regions like the flutes.

THE TRUMPET

The *trumpet* is basically a narrow cylindrical tube substantially closed at the upper end, so that the even-numbered harmonics would be deficient if they were not amply introduced by the somewhat small and angular mouthpiece, by the conical expansion of the lower portion, and by the decidedly flaring bell at the bottom. In the result, the harmonic content could scarcely be richer, and the trumpet tops the orchestra for brilliance.

The trumpets of the late Renaissance and the early baroque were natural trumpets, having tubes of about eight feet for a fundamental *C*, or about seven feet for a fundamental *D*, bent for convenience in the shape of an elongated S or thereabouts, and without assistance from valves or pistons in getting notes not found in the resulting harmonic series. They are therefore restricted to a few notes in the lowest two octaves, and to not many more in the third; but above that they are capable of more notes, closer together, in so far as the player by his unaided lips can pick them out. Trumpeters at those periods were not musicians in quite the ordinary capacity; they were members of a military or courtly or civic corps whose duties were martial, prestigious and ceremonial, though extended to artistic occasions by permission of their patrons, particularly when these occasions were for the entertainment and aggrandizement of the ruling family or municipality. Kettle-drummers were also members, and can be assumed to accompany the trumpeters whether described as doing so or not; they fully expected to improvise their parts, and so in the main did the trumpeters. The Toccata which opens Monteverdi's *Orfeo* (Mantua, 1607) is an early written-out exception, in notated C major for concert D major, since the trumpets are directed to be muted with a resulting rise of a tone in pitch; the drum part is not notated but can reasonably be inferred from the rhythm of one of the middle trumpet parts.

Other tonalities were built, or got by crooks; but D was a standard tonality for the later baroque trumpet. The fundamental is not available, but the upper harmonics of *C* are possible up to about the twenty-first on f'''. No one trumpeter was expected to attempt the changes of embouchure required over this prodigious compass. The top register was called *clarino*, and was given melodic parts only to be performed at all by specialists who cultivated this register to an extraordinary refinement, probably with some slight assistance from a mouthpiece shallower and more angular than the usual. Lower parts, variously known as Quinta, Alto, Principale, Vulgano, Basso, were taken by other players whose embouchure was suitably adapted, using mouthpieces appropriate to these lower registers. But it must be understood that the trumpet itself was not different. A long, natural D trumpet is the standard implement, and the terms Clarino, Principale etc. refer merely to the registers used and the professionals using them.

The *natural trumpet* is an instrument of superb quality, capable as contemporary descriptions inform us of much power but also of delicate restraint, which modern experience fully confirms in the hands of expert performers; indeed, baroque obbligatos for trumpet matching a solo voice on equal terms demand this restraint for the sake of the balance. Professionals of the capability of Don Smithers and Edward Tarr have mastered the baroque trumpet with complete success, and have proved by their performances that no alternative can compare with it for its own baroque parts. Less assertive than might have been expected, but quietly penetrating in its silvery appeal, the natural trumpet has become one of the finer pleasures of the baroque revival.

The difficult art of clarino playing was going rapidly out of use by Mozart's time, towards the latter part of the eighteenth century. Slide trumpets on the same principles as trombones had a considerable history, including some rather uncertain appearances in J. S. Bach and a later vogue in nineteenth-century England, but never became solidly established. The succession to the clarino idiom came partly with the spread of crooks for different tonalities, the orchestral parts for trumpets declining meanwhile to those mainly dominant and tonic progressions in the home key which add grandeur but not much else to Beethoven's orchestra; and partly with an entirely new chapter added when pistons and valves gave the orchestral brass the freedom of completed scales and chromatic modulations. To make the trumpet still easier to play, the length of the tubing was progressively reduced. This enabled the same notes to be found as lower harmonics upon higher fundamentals. Crooks continued to extend the standing tonalities available; but later in the nineteenth century, crooks went out of fashion, and an uncrooked trumpet standing in *F* became the general preference, parts in other tonalities being transposed at sight as necessary. This noble instrument, shorter than the baroque trumpets but longer than the modern trumpets, is even now regretted by those old enough still to remember it.

The fairly long F trumpet (and the E flat trumpet, chiefly used in military bands) in turn gave place to the shorter and higher B flat trumpet now most prevalent, together with a trumpet in A now less often used; the two are sometimes combined by a quick-change valve, but the preference today is emphatically for the B flat trumpet, a very splendid instrument in its own kind, which is, however, at some considerable remove from the older kinds. On such a trumpet, notes in Bach and Handel which can only be found on the long natural trumpet as very high harmonics lie much lower in a higher harmonic series for the same pitch, and are readily available because of the valves or pistons which complete the scale. The length of tubing in the orchestral B flat trumpet is little over half that of the natural D trumpet and the tone colouring is not at all the same. There is also a short c trumpet, less used than previously; a shorter d trumpet (High D) for the higher Bach parts; and a yet shorter f trumpet (High F) for the extremely high Second Brandenburg – makeshifts which can sound very good, but not when compared with a long Bach trumpet properly so called. A piccolo trumpet in b' flat goes higher, but is so short that it can barely exceed a two-octave classification.

The higher trumpets are, of course, valid instruments for their own contexts, as when Rimsky-Korsakov, for example, singled them out with his usual felicity. Like the E flat clarinet, however, they are for special rather than for normal effect. The B flat trumpet now sets our normal standard. It sounds both full and vibrant, especially when not forced unduly high. It has the advantages of very great agility and certainty; but even so, it has of late been subjected to some change, by being given more conical and less cylindrical tubing, rather in the manner of its once fashionable rival, the cornet. Any small gain in flexibility may hardly have been worth the loss of quality.

THE CORNET

The *cornet* (*cornet-à-pistons*, cornopean etc.) of modern usage (not related to the Renaissance and baroque *cornetto* to be described below) has a partly cylindrical but mainly conical, fairly narrow bore; a mouthpiece and a bell of moderate dimensions; a tone colouring of considerable but not of the greatest brilliance; an agility of quite astonishing flexibility over a compass which has been pressed on occasion up to an almost incredible five octaves. The cornet family was developed in the first part of the nineteenth century by adding valves to a variant of the simple French posthorn. It has been made in various tonalities, of which the chief are now b flat and a. It can as well be played with a trumpet mouthpiece, and has sometimes been used as a substitute for the trumpet, but is much more satisfactory when treated as a slightly vulgar, very fluent soloist in its own right.

THE TROMBONE

The *trombone* (sackbut, *posaune* etc.), like its close relative, the trumpet, is basically a narrow cylindrical tube substantially closed at the upper end, and therefore would be deficient in even-numbered harmonics if they were not so amply supplied by a conical expansion of the lower portion and a sufficient though not proportionately very great flare of the bell. The mouthpiece is large though variable, and the way in which it is lipped has much influence upon the harmonic content. In the result, this is rich; and the tone colouring, allowing for differences of register, is nearly as brilliant as a trumpet, but rounder.

The telescopic slide by which the trombone shifts its operative fundamental is the same for all sizes, only the largest needing a jointed handle to help in reaching out the arm to the longest positions. Not all the lowest fundamentals can be sounded in practice. There has been no change in working principle: the bore and the mouthpiece seem always to have been variable; but the flare of the bell is slighter in the earlier examples. Since these took part in chamber music, their tone was certainly capable of being produced quite gently by the appropriate lipping, and it is probable that this was their prevalent manner of handling. The trombone is still beautiful in the pianissimo, just as it can be loud without violence in the forte: a full fortissimo will drown the orchestra, and is very seldom wanted.

Consorts of four or more trombones were available in the late Renaissance and early baroque, on soprano, alto, tenor, bass and contra-bass instruments; the soprano was apparently rare and did not persist. Trombones doubled solo voices and choirs, and took bass parts in support of cornets (old style) and shawms. There was in the Renaissance a symbolical association between the sound of trombones and the sombre mystery of the underworld. We meet it especially in the elaborate interludes and masquerades at Florence and other courts in the sixteenth century; we find a particularly characteristic example for the descent into the underworld in Monteverdi's *Orfeo* at Mantua in 1607, for which the orchestra was of typical late Renaissance variety and colourfulness. The tradition persisted through baroque opera, and comes up magnificently with the statue's trombones in Mozart's *Don Giovanni*; they are used very warmly, too, in *The Magic Flute*. There is an inherent suitability: slow harmony widely spaced on three trombones is a wonderful sound for solemnity. The underworld is by way of being an image for hidden elements in ourselves, and some sense of awe very properly attaches to it, as it does to the priestly initiation which holds the elusive message beneath the fairytale of *The Magic Flute*. Meyerbeer keeps to the traditional scoring in *Robert le Diable*, and Wagner in *Rhinegold* and elsewhere.

The *alto trombone* was taken quite high by Beethoven; but this size is now almost out of use, its parts being played high up on the B flat trombone. The orchestral instrument is commonly built with an F attachment, readily brought into action by a thumb valve; it can be made to take the compass down to the low C through added tubing. There is also a true bass trombone, sometimes in F but now most usually in G. The bore of the trombone may be narrow, medium or wide, according to the quality of sound desired. The lower trombones tend to be the wider; but there is a strong preference in France (and used to be in England) for the narrow bore, with its keener edge to the tone, and in Germany for the wide bore, with its broader quality. More generally, the medium bore has gained the orchestral preference. The flare and bell are proportionately greater when the bore is medium or wide. In dance bands, it is particularly the upper register of the medium-bore tenor trombone which is exploited to such startling effect, not at all for dignity but for a sort of hazardous, out-on-a-limb virtuosity very conducive to the electric tension there desired. The tenor trombone can be taken up to *b'* flat or *c"* with comfort, and at least a fourth higher with increasing strain and difficulty; for ordinary purposes, trumpet sound is much better here.

The true *bass trombone* in F or G has its own solid value, but it is now common to use a medium-bore B flat tenor for the second trombone and a wide-bore B flat tenor for the third trombone, both provided with the F attachment. In its heavier form, this double trombone may have a slide which, when pulled out, will lower the F to E. The F attachment, however, so lengthens the instrument that the seventh and lowest position of the slide cannot then be reached. There is a fine *contra-bass trombone* in C, or B, flat; Wagner used it, and so did Strauss, but it is too rarely required to have become well established. The bass to trombone harmony is often, in fact, supplied by the tuba, with an effect not totally consistent but very satisfactory in practice. Valved trombones are also employed at various sizes but very seldom now in the symphonic orchestra; those of large bore and deep pitch are particularly potent instruments, but altogether the idiom of the trombones depends so much upon their use of the slides that replacing these by valves makes little sense. Wagner's bass trumpet has been called a valved trombone, but misleadingly, since it has in fact the proper trumpet bell and character.

Whatever its varieties of bore, mouthpiece, weight and design, the slide trombone is one of the very few instruments left basically unchanged by the passage of the centuries. Reproductions of early trombones are in successful use, and have their important contribution to make towards our flourishing reconstruction of late Renaissance and baroque sonorities. But there has been no change in their essential nature, generous as this is in any context. They were always valued in opera, but were late to enter the standard symphonic orchestra; from the romantic period they have been an accepted element, as they are today. Except for jazz, they are not particularly versatile. They are an honest voice, both strong and gentle after their historic pattern.

THE HORN

In all the bright splendour of the brass species, the *horns* have an aura peculiarly their own. The trumpets and the trombones hold very much together, and the tuba supports them very appropriately: there is an open quality to all their warmth and colouring, even when the trombones are taking us to the nether regions – daylight can surely be restored! The horns breathe poetry, and this poetry may seem often enough to be symbolically of the night itself, as it is for the lovers when the horns recede at the start of Act II of *Tristan*. No passage has more the essence of the romantic idiom: it is not only the dominant ninths with their yearning harmony; it is the evanescent sound of the horns as they dwindle before the passionate strings break out. The sonority here is the yearning, as much as is the harmony: it is scoring of genius.

The horns can indeed make harsh and brassy sounds, and do not lack for forcefulness; but the poetry is never very far away, and even the brassy sounds of the horn are relatively veiled. The contrast between trumpet sound, carried downwards by trombone sound, on the one hand, and horn sound across an immense range of pitch, on the other hand, is not great, but it is crucial: an aural fact in that vivid legacy we call the orchestra. Like other such facts, it is a combination of harmonic spectrum and variable transients. The horn, with its long and narrow, basically conical bore, its small, more or less tapered mouthpiece and its widely flaring bell, yields ample upper harmonics, and its tone colouring is at the same time keen and mellow.

The horns were familiar on the hunting field, as sophisticated instruments for signalling, long before they entered music through appropriate scenes in baroque opera. Cavalli a little before, and Lully a little after the middle of the seventeenth century found a realistic use for them in fanfares; orchestral parts for horns seem to start at the beginning of the eighteenth century (it is thought with Keiser's *Octavia*, Hamburg, 1705). The natural horn was made or crooked at various lengths and in various tonalities, and in the period of J. S. Bach and Handel had evolved a technique for using high harmonics, close together, on the model of the clarino technique for the trumpet, and with the same concentration of the player's embouchure on one or other register. This lasted a little after the decline in clarino trumpeting, so that Haydn still composed high horn parts of this special character. But Mozart did not; and for a time horn parts in the orchestra tended to become low, simple and mainly on the tonic or dominant harmony of the home keys.

During the second half of the eighteenth century, however, an entirely new technique was developed, based on the discovery that the hand, when pushed well into the bell, will lower the pitch by gradual degrees until, at a certain point, an abrupt rise upwards of a semitone occurs. Horns were redesigned so far as was needed to take advantage of the additional notes thus made available, as well as of a certain softening caused in the tone colouring; and a very sophisticated instrument indeed, the *hand horn* with its attendant technique, resulted. This was mastered by a number of virtuoso soloists, for whom Mozart composed four concertos and Beethoven his Horn Sonata and other chamber works. Notes found by hand stopping (stopped notes) cannot sound so free as notes found on the natural harmonics (open notes); and the art was in part to control this discrepancy, in part to turn it to poetic advantage. To high specialists and low specialists there was added a specialist in the middle register, where the most even distribution could be obtained. And this is what horn playing remained for the finest professionals until gradually the yet newer revolution (early in the nineteenth century) of giving the horn valves and pistons came to seem acceptable. Brahms played the hand horn at the beginning of his career, and his parts for the horn always showed some of the influence of this early training. Another legacy from hand stopping is the use of muted sounds, both in piano (when they sound mysterious) and in forte (when they sound sinister): they are produced by various means, having in common a semitone rise in the pitch which has to be corrected.

The victory of the *valve horn* over the hand horn became fully established only during the second half of the nineteenth century. Piston valves or rotary valves of varying design are arranged to add (or in some instances to subtract) short lengths of tubing. The horn is then fully chromatic on open notes, though hand stopping is still used for idiomatic character. Crooks meanwhile declined, virtually to those in F, E flat and E; and by the end of the nineteenth century the standard instrument of the orchestra was the horn in F, having about 12 feet of tubing. But a higher and shorter horn in B flat was by then coming up; and presently a double horn, having about 3 feet of tubing brought in or cut out to give the choice of F or B flat. The unavoidable difference in tone colouring can be almost completely controlled by skilled playing; and the convenience is so great that the double horn is now standard (except that many first horn players still retain the B flat single horn, often with an added valve to extend down to A).

The trumpet evolved from long to short; the horn is tending, though less radically, in the same direction, as well as to a widened bore and a less funnel-like mouthpiece. So flexible is the instrument for a good player that the resulting change of quality is in part disguised; but the narrow bore historically associated with the French is inherently more veiled and poetic than the wide bore long used by the Germans and now everywhere prevalent. The true, narrow bore French horn is certainly more difficult and less secure, but it is also more beautiful, or at least has more of the refinement appropriate to its own music. Going back to a valve horn with narrow bore is already recovering a wonderful sound; a classical hand horn, or a baroque natural horn, is different again, affording a splendid challenge to modern performers of a specializing disposition.

THE WOODEN CORNET

The *cornet* of the Renaissance and baroque periods (*cornetto*, *zink*, etc.; sometimes spelt 'cornett' in English to distinguish it from the later brass cornet, with which it is not connected) is a narrow, conical tube made of wood or sometimes ivory (straight, or more typically curved), but sounded with the lips in the ordinary manner of a brass instrument: the mouthpiece is cup-shaped and of small to moderate size (detachable except for the mute cornet where the mouthpiece is widely conical and cut into the actual tube, the tone being then more soft and veiled). There being no bell to make it undesirable, notes are found by finger holes very similar to a recorder: six in front and (except in French instruments) a thumb hole at the back. There is a chromatic compass of some two and a half octaves, commonly from g to d''', or a tone higher from a, with smaller instruments (called *cornettino*) in e' or d'. Lower cornets were made but less used, the bass parts being frequently given to a trombone (sackbut).

The conspicuous absence of any bell, besides allowing the finger holes to be used without loss of quality, seems to be responsible for the moderate compass and individual tone quality, which is silvery and ringing enough if well produced, yet with just enough reticence to make it unusually interesting. Perhaps the best word for it might be smoky, rather in the sense in which the best Lapsang Souchong tea is called smoky or tarry: a great attraction for the connoisseur. The technique is very difficult, every note having to be found by the unaided fingers with any cross-fingerings required, and humoured for pitch and quality by the most sensitive lipping. But the agility available to a practised master is quite extraordinary, and the sounds are of an exquisite delicacy and charm, between a soft piano and a respectable though not outstanding forte. Monteverdi's cornetto parts in his *Orfeo* (Mantua, 1607) are a joy; and J. S. Bach used the cornetto in eleven of his cantatas.

BUGLES, SERPENT AND TUBA

The *bugle* clan, of which the most important members symphonically are several varieties of tuba, have the broadest of conical bores, sounded from very large but moderately cup-shaped mouthpieces, and having bells which though imposing in the absolute are relatively modest in proportion to their very ample tubing. Such dimensions are well suited to concentrating most energy in the lower regions of the harmonic series, and producing just that solidity of tone colouring that a proper bass instrument requires.

A fine and early instance of broad, conical scaling is that memorable old-timer the *serpent*, so called from the sinuous tubing by which its six finger holes (subsequently increased by means of keys, though still with no thumb hole) can be reached in fair comfort, if not altogether at their theoretically correct positions, at least near enough for flexible lipping to do the rest. The mouthpiece is cup-shaped and commodious; it is carried by a short length of cylindrical brass tubing before the bore proper begins, where the material becomes wood; there is no bell. Like the curved cornets, the serpent is gouged out in two halves, glued together along their edges and covered with thin leather to prevent leakage. What the cornets, with their narrow bore, are to the horns, the serpent is to the tuba, with its broad bore, and while there is an obvious family relationship, it is not quite correct to call the serpent a bass to the cornet family. It is not such acoustically, nor was it used in that function, apparently, during the period in which the two instruments were co-existent. They are cousins at the closest; and the main original role of the serpent was to support cathedral voices, especially in plainchant. Not until the later eighteenth century was the serpent a popular success (especially in England) as a powerful instrument of the military band, and at times the orchestra. It lingered in country churches to a much later date. 'Old things pass away, 'tis true, but a serpent was a good old note, a deep rich note was the serpent', wrote Thomas Hardy in *Under the Greenwood Tree*. And good it is to hear that deep rich note coming back again in our modern revival.

The usual tonality of the serpent is *C* or *D*, with fully three octaves to be got above the fundamental by clever lipping. The lower register is absurdly adaptable, almost regardless of the fingering used; and if the lips can be sufficiently relaxed, forced or fictitious notes can be coaxed below the fundamental, down to *A*, or thereabouts. The key bugles, in various sizes, and the keyed ophicleides, whose bass member supplanted the serpent in the orchestra, were successors, and the (so-called) Russian bassoon and the bass horn were variants, until valved tubas overtook them all.

Ophicleides are keyed bugles, and *tubas* are substantially ophicleides with valves instead of keys. The highest bugles are most generally known as *flugel horns*, of which the lowest and most important stands in *b* flat. Next down in order of pitch come three instruments, all more or less of baritone range and quality, but varying somewhat in timbre: the most usual names for them are the *tenor horn*, in *E* flat, of which the bore is medium; the *baritone*, in *B* flat, also medium in bore; and the *euphonium* or *tenor tuba*, in *B* flat, but of a wider bore, capable of reaching down chromatically to its fundamental by means of its fourth valve, and sounding nearer to the true bass sonority. Then come two *bombardons* or *bass tubas*, in *F* and *E* flat, and a bombardon in *B,* flat, also known as *contra-bass tuba*. Vaster instruments still have been constructed in *E,* flat, *C,* and *B,,* flat, regions to which our hearing powers do not really descend even though ambitious makers may. The most impressive is the French six-valve C tuba, with all arrangements for a chromatic compass between *C,* and *c″* or higher – phenomenal indeed.

In 1845, Adolphe Sax, the inventor or introducer of the saxophone, patented a complete family of *saxhorns*, of which the lower members are virtually tubas, and valve their fundamental octave, while the upper members are virtually flugel horns, and do not. He had been anticipated by Stölzel with a complete family of valved bugles some years before. Later in the century, Wagner introduced his so-called

Wagner tubas in B flat and F, having the mouthpieces of horns and a bore and tone colouring between the horn and the saxhorn in those tonalities. Only the contra-bass Wagner tuba uses a tuba mouthpiece and plays like a tuba. Others have used them, including Strauss, but they have not really justified their independent value.

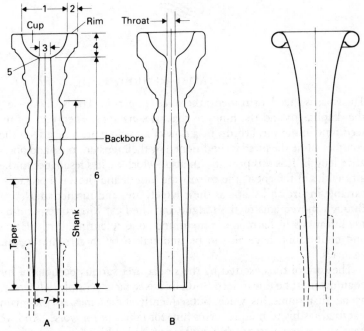

Fig. 27   Trumpet (A, B) and French horn mouthpieces

14 THE VOICE

THE ITALIAN METHOD

The voice is a reed instrument: the voice is a person. The back muscles, the diaphragm and the lungs of that person supply energy to set up reed tone in the vocal cords, by a flow of air whose pressure affects the volume, while the pitch is conditioned by their tension, mass and operative length. It is this primary vibration which excites resonance in the air cavities of the chest, the throat, the mouth and the nasal passages, variable in size and shape as these largely are, and further adjustable through movements of the tongue and the lips, with corresponding modifications of harmonic content and tone colouring. Articulation and enunciation have also to be undertaken by these same organic agencies.

The control thus exerted by the singer over various portions of his anatomy must be fine indeed. Initially it is so far as possible deliberate, as he first trains his voice; subsequently it becomes in the main habitual, as his technique serves him for better or for worse. And we have always to remember that it is his own body which he is controlling. The singer is his own instrument: sometimes in better condition physically and psychologically, and sometimes in worse, but never to be altogether distanced from his own personality. The link between matter and mind is nowhere else in music more immediate than this.

The signals sent by the singer to his own nervous and muscular apparatus need to be coded just in advance. He has to think his note just enough ahead for the necessary mental preparation, or it will be too late to make it with his muscles. We might put it that a good singer has learnt how to focus in his imagination just what he wants to focus in his voice. The acoustic requirements are produced by the musical intention, provided the trained discipline is there; and for most Western purposes, that means *bel canto* voice production on the Italian method. For Monteverdi or Carissimi, for Handel or Bach, for Mozart

or Rossini or Bellini the technique of voice production is the same
although the style is different. Wagner's singers were Italian-trained,
and knew that the voice to penetrate his unprecedented orchestration is
not the forced voice which sounds big under the ear but the focused
voice which cuts through to the back of the auditorium. Caruso began
in *bel canto* but debased it somewhat towards *verismo* (the so-called
realistic style), for Puccini but not at all to Puccini's best interests in the
long run. Frieda Leider and Lauritz Melchior could still make Wagner
big yet effortless; but some of the most favoured German *lied* singers
got so far from Italian technique, and yet so won us by their general
artistry, that the tradition suffered. The voice got ever farther back in
the throat and the brightness and the words ever more covered, until a
reaction set in, and Italian voice production began returning together
with so much else from previous skills now once more coming into
regard.

The basic characteristic of Italian voice production is what singers call
the forward placing of the voice. There is a concentration of the
resonance in the nasal cavities right to the front of the head, rather than
to the back of the mouth or the throat. We are told to bring the voice
right up into the mask. None of the vocal organs being visible, no
advice concerning them can be better than a hint until it is backed by a
demonstration; but the effect when it is produced correctly will be
audible enough. Each note can be taken in the middle with an
absolutely precise attack and accurate intonation, as a distinct event not
marred by any tentative approach or unintended scooping. This can be
done in the fastest scales and arpeggios, both diatonic and chromatic,
which are practised persistently until they are sure and effortless. The
range at first will be kept quite small, but enlarged little by little until
the extreme notes can be taken with as much assurance as the middle
notes. The compass may at this stage become not only extensive, but
distinct in colouring according to the register.

The upper register is the responsibility of the head voice. Nothing
should be more clear and open: it should ring out with a sound neither
forced nor breathy, but so keenly focused that it travels well. The lower
register is the responsibility of the chest voice. The same focused vibration is picked up by the deeper resonance of the chest, which gives it a
raw yet transparent colouring slightly resembling the bottom of a bagpipe chanter. This, too, is an open sound, so that a properly trained
'Italian' mezzo-soprano, for example, will never produce that throaty
hoot associated with the heavier sort of oratorio contralto, but will chest
her bottom notes so that they cut clean and carry easily. It is a sound not

often heard in fairly recent times, and so potent that it has not always been welcomed by the critics, but we are getting it back, and as we become accustomed to it again, so we enjoy it for the glorious character it has always had.

The middle register between the head voice and the chest voice is a transitional register to which great attention was always paid by the teachers of Italianate *bel canto*. Here the problem is to join the two outer registers so skilfully that no break is heard. The head resonance is to be brought down as low as possible, and the chest resonance is to be brought up as high as possible, so that they blend into one another with uninterrupted smoothness across the join. This is what was repeatedly recommended as the union of the head voice and the chest voice. It was not the intention that these opposite resonances should be brought to resemble each other, as is now taught commonly but mistakenly; on the contrary, the contrast should be as extreme as the musical situation justifies, which is often very extreme indeed. But it was the intention that the transition should, wherever desirable, be imperceptible. Thus two notes in succession, but widely separate in pitch, may one of them be a raw chest note and the other a ringing head note; or conversely, an entire passage may blend a little of each without decisively settling for either. It all depends on the music, as tone colouring normally does and should.

This, then, is the basic technique we need for Monteverdi and Carissimi, for Schütz and Purcell, for Bach and Handel, for Gluck and Mozart, for Rossini and Bellini, for Wagner and Verdi, for Bizet and Debussy, for Strauss and Stravinsky, and most certainly for the considerable hazards of modern voice writing. Oriental vocal techniques are different; medieval techniques may have been, but at least since the sixteenth century in Italy that has been the basic method described and practised by generation after generation of vocal giants, not only in Italy but elsewhere. The styles are indeed often very different; but the method is not. Even French baroque opera, so different in artistry, rested on the voice production brought from Italy when Caccini came to Paris early in the seventeenth century and de Nyert returned from Rome a few years afterwards. Neither the eighteenth nor the nineteenth century changed in technique with changing style, as the contemporary textbook descriptions show. Better than that, the primitive but unarguable gramophone recordings, made around the turn into the twentieth century, of the last of the great *bel canto* singers, often at the end of their careers, with the voice almost gone but the vocal magic still glowing through: in these recordings lies the repeated demonstration that their method was supreme, and that it can be recognized as pure *bel canto* in every diversity of individual voices and personalities. Such recordings are preserved in surprisingly large numbers, and may be heard not only in private but also in public collections like the British Institute of Recorded Sound in London, the Historical Sound Recordings Collection at the University of Yale, or the Rodgers and Hammerstein Archives of Recorded Sound in the New York Public Library.

Together with the voice production we hear an artistry in moulding the vocal line which outdoes our own, good as that can indeed be at best. Not only is the *cantilena* sustained and supported without the least involuntary flagging; it is shaped and patterned with inflexions and shadings of the finest imagination, and phrased and articulated with stretchings and separations of the boldest conception. All these are aspects of what was called *portamento di voce*, the carrying of the voice. Every musicianly subtlety is exploited, and every verbal finesse. For, of course, the words are also a fundamental component, so that each consonant can be made to yield its own crispness and each vowel its own colouring. One of the advantages of the *bel canto* voice production is that it allows the words to be heard as they are never to be heard when the forward placing of the sound has not been preserved. How many of the words can you really rely on hearing with most singing today? The standard of clearness in verbal enunciation seems to have declined as much as the standard of exactness in placing the notes: our best is very good; but it is not as good as the height of the *bel canto* achieved. There is a kind of verbal as well as musical imagination to be heard on those old recordings, and together they add up to a specifically vocal art: an art not merely of interpretation but of vocalization. That is the art of fine singing as it has been understood and is now in course of being understood again.

WORDS AND MELODY

Like other instruments, the voice generally has (and voices individually have) bands of natural resonance which act as formants to the harmonic spectrum. The onset transients, the more or less steady state, and the decay or the join as note follows note all have their usual influence; and the harmonic pattern actually occurring reflects the usual complications due to pitch, to dynamics, to acoustic environment and in short to context. But in addition, the singer must control another factor: the words. For song is music and poetry, or sometimes prose, or occasionally verbal sonorities without semantic intention, but nevertheless verbal or at least linguistic.

The sounds of language range from unvocalized consonants providing attack or termination but no steady state, through partly vocalized consonants and semi-vowels, which can be in a manner sustained, to vowels which are necessarily to some extent sustained. For example, D or T bring the tongue behind the teeth, and release it to give a dental start or finish. G or K close the throat to give a guttural. It is also possible to close not the throat but the glottis, the actual opening between the vocal cords, and release it to give a somewhat guttural attack without phonating any particular consonant at all: this is the notorious *coup de glotte* which gives the most explosive attack a vowel can have, and which in its extreme extent had probably no acceptance in true *bel canto*, although it certainly infected its decline (in Caruso's earlier recordings it does not appear, but in his later recordings, it does).

Again, it is possible to vocalize on L or to hum on M or more openly on N, to hiss on S or to buzz on V. But on vowels it is possible to vocalize with or without any consonant at the start or finish. To produce a recognizable vowel requires the voice to yield, in addition to vibration of the frequency from which the note takes its pitch, some further vibration within the bands of resonance from which that vowel results. Thus, for example, the vowel O results basically from a pair of formants at frequencies approximately within the band from 400 Hz to 600 Hz. The lower reaches of a soprano excite them with no difficulty: her bottom c', at around 250 Hz, has upper harmonics to suit; her middle notes actually lie within the formative band for O, and can give it splendidly; but towards her top c''' at around 1000 Hz, she is way above any frequency which could sound an O, and neither skill nor determination will allow her to do so. She must needs thin the vowel sound more and more towards an E as she rises higher; and if she is a coloratura and goes up to f''', there is just no help for it so far as choice of vowels goes, and we must take her vocalization as it comes.

The pairs of frequencies on which vowels seem basically to depend must be differentiated by movements of the tongue and lips which give different shapings to the two main cavities of the mouth and the throat. Pursing the lips inclines to 'oo'; opening them inclines to 'ee' if the tongue is raised, but to 'ah' if the tongue is dropped; and so with the rest of the movements which shape the oral cavities. Words can be thus shaped at a whisper without involving the vocal cords, but spoken or sung only by involving the vocal cords. Since these combinations have also to pitch and colour the melody, they are necessarily complicated, yet can be learnt by imitation and intuition in childhood, as well as educated by training to the limits of human adaptability. But no education, of course, alters the basic disposition by which high notes thin out towards 'ee' while low notes thicken up towards 'ah'; and many other acoustic consequences of this kind occur, especially marked in the female upper registers. The singer may in such circumstances do most to get the words clear by the articulate use of the consonants, always an extremely significant ingredient of *bel canto* voice production, and always subject to the proviso that unless the voice is placed well forward, the words will not be heard in any case.

Put it, then, that certain vowels need formative harmonics not strongly presented by certain notes. It is therefore not always possible to reconcile the enunciation and the melody ideally; the enunciation will be the worse distorted, while remaining recognizable under more adverse harmonic stimulation, than the melody. And it is always part of a vocal composer's skill to join words and notes with a sort of practised tact, so that his line shall be verbally as well as melodically singable. Some compromise is unavoidable in this marriage of the arts, as in other marriages; but where enunciation and melody go well together, as on the whole they do, how splendid a union may result is common knowledge. We sometimes, metaphorically, call music a language; but poetry is literally a language, with all the power of language to describe, to evoke, to unfold before the mind a dramatic situation and a human development. Combine this with music's power to inflect a mood, to touch upon emotion and intuition, to stir our hidden depths, and the potentialities of such an alliance are obvious. Add staging with its visual impact, and opera is in hand to compound both the difficulties and the possibilities of the vocal art.

VARIETIES OF VOICE

The size and condition of the vocal organs vary with age, sex and health. Children of either sex do not basically differ until puberty, when the larynx of a boy grows larger and more massive than that of a girl, and his voice may drop an octave or more in pitch. Before his voice 'breaks' in this fashion, a boy soprano will range about from *a* to *a"*, with a certain cool innocence and agility of his own, capable of virtuoso training for solo work but more usually valued in the male-voice choir. He need not and should not lack for warmth of colouring.

The female soprano has quite a different ring. In the usual chorus of soprano, alto, tenor, bass, she is comfortable from *c'* to *a"* or *b"* flat. A dramatic soprano can take *c'* with fair power if she chests it well, and should reach c''' with full power, as well as with that glitter of high harmonics which marks the best of her kind; a lyric soprano can do as much, but with a lighter timbre making up in elegance what it lacks in force. A mezzo-soprano reaches not quite so high, and colours her tone perhaps a shade more darkly; but it should be just as open and forward, while her chesting at the bottom, where she should go rather lower and more strongly, can be of a very haunting quality indeed. In her own best tessitura, she can and does carry some of the most thrilling of operatic roles. The contralto is of a richer sound and a lower tessitura, including some particularly sombre colourings, also of great effectiveness in opera as well as in oratorio; but she, too, needs to keep her voice well forward to avoid a covered sound which is only agreeable when used for deliberate effect, not too long continued. In the S.A.T.B. chorus, she takes the alto part, and should go very comfortably from about g to e''.

The castrato voice is or was a special case indeed. The male soprano and the male contralto were voices prevented from breaking by castration in childhood, and developed in adulthood to great power and virtuosity at tessituras ordinarily female. They are not currently available or in prospect, and quite right too; but our loss artistically is very real. Most of the heroes in baroque opera are cast as sopranos or altos, occasionally played by female singers, but ordinarily by castratos of some fame and excellence. If a notable castrato was available, he was the best draw; an indifferent castrato was far less popular. More than one castrato was not unusual; on the other hand, female sopranos of comparable glory were also valued very highly, and sought after as opportunity offered. The hero might be a castrato singing higher than his female heroine, all the more confusingly when one or both was for the not uncommon purposes of baroque intrigue disguised on stage as a member of the opposite sex. Heroines might also, though not frequently, be sung by castrato males.

Opera is a convention so stylized already by the mere fact of being sung that one improbability the more was less unsettling than we who have never heard a living castrato might suppose. We can hear the castrato voice on recordings made at Rome in 1904 by Alessandro Moreschi (1856–1922), presumably the last and certainly not the best of his extraordinary species, but quite convincingly powerful and refined enough to prove that there was nothing inherently ridiculous about castrato heroes. His voice, in spite of its feminine tessitura, sounds remarkably masculine – far more so than any boy soprano – and far more dramatically so even than the best of counter-tenors, who can, of course, be perfectly masculine people: natural basses or more or less high tenors using an exceptional register (from about f' to c'' by bringing only a portion of their vocal cords into vibration. Under the alternative name of cathedral altos, they have in England never died out, but have been brought back only recently (first by Alfred Deller) to their pristine virtuosity. They have also been called *falsetti*, though there is nothing false about them to justify the term; or singers of the head (*testo*) as opposed to the chest (*petto*), more reasonably, since that is certainly the register which they so exceptionally exploit.

A castrato part in baroque opera (if it is not too high) can be successfully given to a counter-tenor, provided (which is not always the case) that his voice is big enough and well enough projected. It can also be given to a soprano or a mezzo-soprano of appropriate tessitura, provided that her technique is similarly forward and Italianate. The worst arrangement is to drop the part an octave and give it to a tenor or a baritone, which disturbs the entire balance and scoring of the original, unless the opera is boldly recomposed as Gluck recomposed his Viennese *Orfeo* from that original version (sung with a castrato in the title role) for performance at Paris (where castratos were disliked) with a tenor hero. Many baroque operas are very fine indeed, but it is only fair to hear them in our nearest approach to their intended sonority, with the great preponderance of voices in the higher tessituras.

Tenors in baroque opera were more apt to be sneaky villains than honest heroes (but there were castrato villains too, and bass ones, as well as basses of noble integrity or robust comedy). In the S.A.T.B. chorus, the tenor is comfortable from about c to a'. The real operatic tenor (*tenore robusto*, robust tenor, or *Heldentenor*, hero-tenor) must reach c'' with full power and complete assurance, and his voice must be vibrant with upper harmonics heard as that special shimmering ring which the big roles require for proper effect. A lyric tenor differs only in having, like a lyric soprano, a lighter quality but a more enchanting appeal. A bass should be comfortable in the S.A.T.B. chorus from perhaps F to about e'. A baritone covers from about A flat to perhaps a' flat, with considerable weight and transparency combined. A *basso cantanto* is a bass excelling in his upper register; a bass-baritone unites this fluent top with a very solid bottom, as he is required to do, for example, in the part of Wagner's Wotan. A *basso profundo* is a specialist in the sonorous depths, and there are even deeper Russian-style basses, under the well-deserved name of *contra-basso*, who descend in some fashion to the astonishing pitch of F_1.

It should perhaps be added that with the voice, as with the strings, vibrato is a natural and historical, not an artificial or recent resource. Because the ear loses response on long notes of unduly stable vibration, it is an acoustic as well as an artistic necessity to relieve the monotony by that slight frequency modulation, with a periodicity of some six repetitions per second, which we call vibrato. At this speed, we tend to perceive it as amplitude modulation, sometimes described as tremolo; in some degree, this does normally occur along with vibrato. The speed and width of the vibrato need good control. If it is too fast and narrow, the intensity becomes subliminally agitating or even painful; if too slow and wide, the pitch change becomes obtrusive, and in close harmony confusing. It is unfortunately very easy for a singer to lose control of the vibrato altogether, and to use it involuntarily with horrible effect: a defect very hard to remedy when once ingrained. Vibrato should not always be present, particularly in early music, but requires excellent technique and very great discretion. At no period, however, does the pure and uncoloured voice, without vibrato, and sometimes called *voce bianca*, white voice, appear to have been recommended or tolerated except for rare and special effect.

15 PERCUSSIVE METHODS

SOLIDS AND MEMBRANES

The vibration of solids (which may or may not be in some degree hollow) or of membranes (tensile and coupled to a more or less contained and resonant air cavity) is the source of sound for the third of the great classes of musical instruments to be considered here: the percussion. The directions of oscillation for the whole and the parts may be quite complicated, including both lateral and longitudinal vibration; but the usual relationships of node and antinode condition the partials' spectrum. Where the pattern of vibration is decidedly complex and unstable, unpitched or vaguely pitched sounds result; but where the vibration, or some of it, is sufficiently periodic, both pitch and tone colouring may be beautifully definite and refined.

The method for exciting the vibrations is ordinarily by striking, as the name implies; but rattling, scraping or rubbing, though less obviously percussive, are near enough to pass within the definition for ordinary purposes. Conversely, the clavichord and the piano are both literally percussive instruments, but differ from the percussion so markedly in their other aspects that it is not usual, nor would it be wise, to class them as percussion instruments, in spite of the piano being sometimes used nearly as percussively as a xylophone and quite as percussively as a glockenspiel. Again logic inevitably eludes us: so used, the piano should be classed as an instrument of percussion, were it not that its more important uses are so plainly otherwise.

Organographers (writers on instruments) who distinguish chordophones (string-sounders) from aerophones (air-sounders) divide the percussion into idiophones (self-sounders) and membranophones (skin-sounders). Bars and bells, rattles and tubes rate as self-sounders, but may have any degree or none of coupled resonance from air cavities in or attached to them. Drums are skin-sounders, having much or little coupled resonance from air contained in their shells or frames. These distinctions, then, are relative. Almost any object which can oscillate sonorously when struck may be used for percussion, and a great many have been. The variety is enormous; the distinctions are far from clear, but then they are not very important either. It is the variety which counts – not the classification. In no species of instrument has there been more valuable expansion, whether in the symphonic orchestra, or in the unconventional groupings of the avant-garde. Electronic amplification and modification of percussive sounds which would otherwise hardly be audible have brought further developments.

A REVOLUTION IN PERCUSSION

Most percussion instruments have it in common that they are chiefly valuable for rhythm and for timbre, much less so for melody and scarcely at all for harmony (there are exceptions). The noisier percussion came into symphonic use largely with the fashion for Turkish effects in Mozart's generation; it requires and on the whole it has been given a considerable restraint. Drums (not excluding the beautifully tuned timpani, if vigorously attacked), cymbals, triangle or gongs have tremendous powers of crescendo from very soft to very loud, and of diminuendo back again. They would overwhelm the orchestra if clumsily employed; but they can bring heated emotions to the boil like nothing else. One clash from the cymbals may do so at a moment of climax; or the deep throb of the bass drum, to which our instincts respond no less deeply. Yet barbaric splendour is only one extreme; the other is the lightest of taps or rolls on kettledrums or side drum, pulsing through a delicate passage or even occasionally alone. Traditionally, the main and only regular percussion instruments of the symphonic orchestra have been the timpani (kettledrums); and no wonder, since their notes can be so clear and exquisite.

Where the music is without functional or progressive harmony, as it has always been basically in the East, unpitched instruments of percussion may dominate the ensemble without prejudice to any prevailing tonality. In Hindu orchestras, for example, full sets of drums, bowls, bells, clappers and the like, both pitched and unpitched, may set up a polyphony of rhythms and timbres at least as complicated as any Western counterpoint. These and many other traditions, especially from the Far East, have appealed especially to Western composers of the avant-garde who are themselves not much more interested in functional harmony or tonal progression, or perhaps in tonality at all.

Under such circumstances, nothing is to be lost and much is to be gained by exploiting every subtlety of rhythm and every variety of tone colouring which the most exotic of percussive instruments has to offer, or the most advanced of electronic techniques is able to produce. And in fact there has been something of a revolution where percussion is concerned. No other department of the symphonic orchestra has undergone these fascinating changes and additions; while in avant-garde ensembles, percussion instruments may weave much or all of the entire tapestry. Every sort of bang, thump, clash, tinkle, rattle, scratch, ping or pong that a struck object can emit, with or without electronic manipulation, has been used simply and elaborately, delicately and robustly, separately or together, until our ears are ringing with un-accustomed sonorities and unprecedented convolutions of rhythm, duration, dynamics: the lot. It all seems quite suitable to our complex age, and certainly the revolution in percussion has been among the most enjoyable such development of our times.

VARIETIES OF PERCUSSION

Most solid objects of metal, wood or other more or less resonant materials will vibrate as a whole and in quotient parts, however con-fusedly, when struck. The confusion is never in the least arbitrary; but the vibrations, though always in theory analysable into their partial components, may in practice result in no partial stable enough to take over, in the role of a fundamental which could be heard as definitely a pitch; nor any series of upper harmonics periodic enough to combine in creating that impression. In that event, there may be the most wonder-ful jangling, but there will be no note.

The harder the material with which the object is struck, and the nearer the point of striking to some important node, the more the higher partials will be excited, and the more ringing the tone colouring will sound. The softer the material with which the object is struck, and the nearer to some important antinode, the more the higher partials will be damped (especially if the striking implement is large as well as soft), and the more thudding the tone colouring will sound. There are other variables of construction and of playing technique. But it is only when one partial is able to predominate, as in the double metal bar of the tuning fork, or in the single wooden bars of a xylophone, that a note results, although in such cases it may be a note of singular distinct-ness and simplicity.

So soon as a solid object is at all modified in the direction of becom-ing hollow, its behaviour begins to be that of a coupled acoustic system.

There is air contained, however slightly; there is a mutual feedback, however loosely connected. The more hollow the object, the more close the coupling tends to be, and the more distinctive the effects of the feedback. Tubes contain air almost in the manner of a wind instrument, although with this difference, that the dominant partner, since it is set directly into vibration, is the tube itself. Bells are very complex combinations of a hollow metal object (whose exact shape and mass have crucial consequences) with a more or less contained body of air (having its own natural resonance according to the shape and size given to it by the bell itself). The vibrations resulting are of the greatest irregularity and subtlety; the sounds resulting are so ambivalent both for pitch and for tone colouring, and shift so elusively as one partial or another rings out momentarily above the others, that no imitation or synthesis can quite catch that haunting resonance.

A tensile membrane (vellum, parchment) consisting of the fine skin of an animal, or nowadays of plastic (as polyethylene terephthalate), when stretched under appropriate tension, will vibrate in two dimensions, but without enough regular periodicity of its own to yield a note of definite pitch. If, however, the frame by which it is stretched becomes a shell, normally more or less hemispherical in shape, or if it is more or less cylindrical and closed at the other end by a similar stretched membrane, the coupled acoustic system resulting may well accept periodic vibration such as to yield a note of definite pitch, coloured by upper partials in attractive variety. The note comes from the resonance of the air contained, but its pitch, within the limits of that resonance, can be tuned by altering the tension at which the struck membrane is stretched. These conditions are best fulfilled, in our present Western tradition, by the timpani (kettledrums) with their approximately hemispherical shells, and their varied sizes of head, the smaller of which accept the higher tunings, and the larger the lower tunings.

The point of striking relative to the more important nodes and antinodes affects the volume and the tone colouring resulting: a point somewhat in from the rim is most usual. The volume, however, is chiefly varied by the strength and velocity of the striking. Its range from soft to loud can be very great.

Other techniques, particularly in Eastern traditions, include tapping with the separate fingers, or striking with the palm of the hand, or both in combination. Brushes in place of drumsticks give a swishing effect of no great finesse; but fingering a whole set of tuned drums can be almost like playing on a keyboard for some of the most brilliant of

Oriental drummers, and until recent years no Western drummers could compare with their versatility in such directions.

This sort of accomplishment, too, has become part of our percussive revolution, largely under Oriental influence, and the range of skills now possessed by the best Western percussionists brings us as novel a resource as the traditional skill of our best timpanists has for so long been an ancient one. A modern percussion section in the symphonic orchestra may be numerous, apportioned as it has to be among several virtuoso percussionists, and the effect of it can be like adding a new dimension to the scoring. The effect in music of the avant-garde, again, is particularly arresting, possibly as significant as electronic innovation, and certainly combining with it to open new paths into the future.

16 PERCUSSION

XYLOPHONE AND MARIMBA

Of the many more or less solid instruments of percussion, those with graded bars of wood or metal are among the most adaptable.

The *xylophone* has ordinarily a double row of hardwood bars, uniform in width but graded in length to give successive pitches, and having, like a normal keyboard, a slightly lower level for the diatonic notes than for the chromatic notes. So remarkably brittle, however, is the tone colouring of this simple form of xylophone, and so little regarded in spite of its advantages when such brittle sounds are really wanted, that it is now usually provided with resonators. Metal tubes containing air are fitted beneath the bars, tuned to pick up sympathetic vibrations at suitable frequencies for amplifying and sustaining the sonority. The tone colouring remains very dry by comparison with most, but it is more mellow than it used to be, for better and for worse. To some extent, it can be controlled by the appropriate choice of beaters. As usual, the harder and the narrower the head of the beater, the more it encourages the high harmonics, and the less it damps them out by covering their antinodes, so that the tone rings out more drily; while conversely, the softer and the broader the head of the beater, the less it encourages and the more it damps out the higher harmonics, so that the tone comes over more warmly.

The hardest beaters so favour the higher harmonics at the expense of the lower harmonics that the pitch may be perceived as if it were one octave or even two octaves above the nominal notes, which are already likely to be in a high compass. Xylophones are encountered in many sizes, but in the symphonic orchestra the most usual range is the three and a half octaves from f' to c^v. There is also a four-octave xylophone going down to c'. The part is sometimes notated at sounding pitch, sometimes an octave lower (with or without written indication of the fact – but it is commonly to be assumed). The beaters are normally

15 Full orchestra

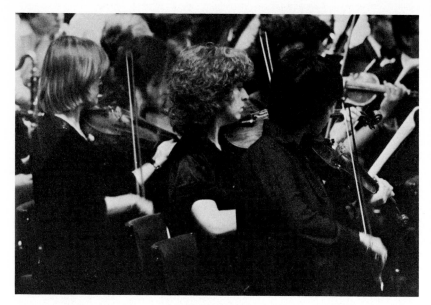

16 Violins in close-up

17 Violas, cellos, double basses

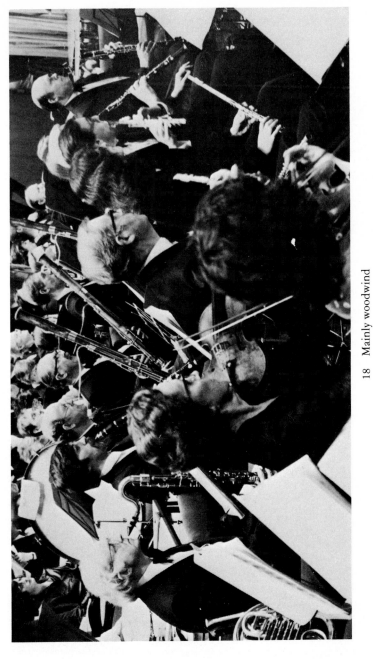

18   Mainly woodwind

19 Flute, oboe, cor anglais

20 Bassoons and double bassoon

21　French horns

22 Mainly brass

23   A pair of orchestral harps

24 The percussion section

held like kettledrum sticks, one to a hand; but two or even (with difficulty) three to a hand can be manipulated for the sake of chords and tremolandos. A proper knowledge of the instrument is needed to compose a virtuoso part for the xylophone which is idiomatic or even possible in performance. One powerful resource is the glissando, in one hand or two, in either direction or both at once, brief or extensive. It can produce some of the hardest and most sudden effects in the percussive repertoire.

The *marimba* is basically a large xylophone one octave below, commonly with four octaves from c to c^{iv} and a notation at written pitch unless otherwise shown. Bars of resonant rosewood are similarly arranged, but usually graduated in width and thickness as well as in length. The tuned metal tubes which stand beneath as coupled resonators are bigger in proportion, and contribute more sonorously to the tone colouring, which becomes louder but gentler. Where the xylophone can give the most glorious clattering, the marimba gives a richer booming, especially in its lower register, where it certainly excels; the beaters are variable, but never altogether hard. Higher up, the marimba has little of the xylophone's aristocratic sharpness. It can, however, sound both soft and loud, with considerable ability to sustain its wooden tones. The name marimba is sometimes misapplied merely to a larger xylophone: the instruments, though related, are not the same. There is also a massive bass marimba covering the octave and a fourth from c, to f, requiring heavy beaters and not responding to them with much agility. Four-beater tremolos are much favoured on the marimba for their strangely poetical and warm sonority.

VIBRAPHONE, GLOCKENSPIEL AND CELESTA

The *vibraphone* is a very different instrument, of fairly recent American origin for jazz use, but now established for symphonic use as well, and adding a sonority to our resources of singular – not to say seductive – attractiveness. The bars are of a plated aluminium alloy, sometimes variable in width as well as in length. A four-beater technique is so common that the diatonic bars (in front) and the chromatic bars (behind) are laid on the same level to make it easier. There are tubular metal resonators, tuned to the bars. A motor can be switched on to revolve, at variable speeds, disks pivoted at the top ends of the resonators; or switched off to leave them stationary but in an open position. When revolving, the disks give a pulsation caused by amplitude and frequency modulations in the resonators, slow or fast according to the speed; when stationary, and open, they leave the resonators to act as a coupled acoustic system in the normal way, somewhat like a louder glockenspiel (which has none). Slow vibrato can be grossly sentimental, and fast vibrato can be grievously agitating; but vibrato of normal and moderate speed, as usual, is genuinely expressive, particularly since it can within limits be brought on and off in course of playing.

Another recourse highly typical of the vibraphone is its damper pedal. This raises the bars from the felts on which they rest, so that they become undamped at will; it is also possible to damp individual notes by cunning placing of the fingers. Since the instrument is extremely resonant when its motor is on, the skilful blending of damped and un-damped is a crucial aspect of its technique. When the motor is off, the tone is less rich and less sustained, but equally excellent, resembling a slightly warmer glockenspiel. Beaters can be varied from soft to hard with great influence on the tone colouring; fairly soft is most typical. Glissandos of many kinds, chords and tremolos are all admirable effects. There are several sizes, but the usual vibraphone range is three octaves from f to f'''.

The *glockenspiel* is older and simpler than the vibraphone, and is a very enchanting little instrument of more power and penetration than might be imagined at close quarters in the orchestra. The bars are of steel, the diatonic notes in front and the chromatic notes slightly higher at the back: there are no resonators, and the tone colouring is clear as a bell is clear, with a certain surrounding ambiguity which haunts the ear. There are no dampers, so that the sound is apt to linger across the harmonies. Beaters of varying material give some choice of quality. The range is most commonly the two and a half octaves from g'' to c'', written two octaves below the sounding pitch. The name glockenspiel, however, is literally no more than the German for 'bell-play', and has also served as a general title for this kind of instrument, including those with actual bells mentioned below. There are or have been other variants, sometimes employing a keyboard to charming but rather limited effect, since the tone is weakened and the dynamics become quite invariable.

The *celesta*, on the other hand, is a modified glockenspiel employing a keyboard to very good effect. Here there are steel bars coupled each to a tuned wooden resonator, and struck with hammers operated through a mechanism which again does not permit of dynamic varia-tion, but does not need it. The tone colouring is soft and innocent, never long sustained (and in addition capable of being gently damped or released at will through a pedal), but making its effect meanwhile like some fleeting pattern on the surface of the music. The size is larger than most glockenspiels, and the compass ranges from c' to c^{iv}, written on two staves at an octave below the sounding pitch. Perhaps the most beautiful part ever given it comes in the Silver Rose scene of Richard Strauss' *Rosenkavalier*, where the celesta, with woodwind doubling, drops into the warm sounds of the orchestra a series of virtually unrelated harmonies; and all the sweet agitation of that totally unprepared young couple drops into our hearts too at the uncanny sound of it. Fitness of scoring could not be carried beyond this point of imagination.

But for wide and complex use, these percussion instruments with solid bars, and often with hollow resonators, have come into their own through some of the most sensitive scorings, as well as some of the most violent ones, of the avant-garde. And broadly this is true for our revolution in the percussion as a whole.

CYMBALS, TRIANGLES, BLOCKS, RATTLES, ETC.

There is a large selection of single or compound objects struck separately or together for their percussive sound, and there is no reason why these should not be increased indefinitely for the sake of noises which had no place in music but may do now. Many objects may also be rubbed or scratched or otherwise excited, with electronic amplification where desired. Objects casually in the room may sometimes be included; but these taper off into 'musique concrète' and do not rate as instruments.

The *cymbals* are brass or bronze plates in many sizes, ranging from a gong-like boom to a searing clash or a smooth tinkling in accordance with their width and thickness, and still more with the choice of beaters and of striking point at various dynamic levels. Small, cup-like cymbals can be tuned to high notes of definite pitch; the large orchestral cymbal is slightly indented at its centre, quite indefinite for pitch, and commonly played in pairs struck or slid or jangled together. Often a single cymbal of variable size, or a pair or a set of them, is suspended for striking: hard beaters excite a clash of high harmonics; soft beaters quieten the effect. One cymbal can be moved above another on a pedal-operated rod (the hi-hat cymbals ubiquitous in jazz); and there are many other cunning techniques and sound effects. The orchestral cymbals are the most impressive, carrying as they do a vibrant power which is used very sparingly but never without climactic possibilities.

The *triangle* is a metal rod open at one corner, and struck or rolled with a beater of the same material. It emits many high partials close in pitch and strength, and has no definite pitch of its own, but always appears to assume the prevailing tonality of the orchestra, to which some of its partials are certain to respond. *Anvils*, real or simulated by a steel bar, were quite a romantic favourite (such as the eighteen demanded but seldom got by Wagner for the cavern scene in *Rhein-gold*; but two tuned a third apart are not uncommon). The *wind machine* is a swishing roll of silk, which got Strauss into hot criticism over *Don Quixote*.

Rattles or *ratchets* can set up a fiendish clattering. *Castanets* are pairs of hollow wooden clackers with a beautifully dry and rhythmic sonority. *Wood blocks* are rectangular with resonant cavities, but not deep enough for a definite pitch, while the quality under wooden beaters is crisp but colourful: though indefinite, the pitch does appreciably conform with the sizes which are commonly arranged in sets of $6\frac{1}{2}$ in., $7\frac{1}{2}$ in. and 8 in. *Temple blocks* are fairly round and quite hollow: they are moderately definite in pitch, are often arranged to be suggestive of the pentatonic scale, and are decidedly sonorous in their chunky way; they are played with wooden beaters or felt-covered beaters of the desired hardness. The *claves* are a pair of short sticks of hardwood, clapped together across the cupped hand for a modicum of resonance: the pitch is indefinite and the timbre sharp. *Maracas* are hollow gourds containing dried seeds which rattle as they are turned or shaken. The *guiro* is a larger gourd with notches across which a stick is scraped. And so it goes on, through many implements and many variations, some of which merge imperceptibly into the bells and gongs next to be considered, and some of them into wooden drums related to the membrane category: log drums and slit drums being the most sonorous of these.

GONGS AND BELLS

The flattest and shallowest *gongs*, having slight rims and no central boss or indentation, are virtually cymbals; but as the rim (and sometimes the boss) takes on acoustic significance, so the behaviour tends towards that particular complexity of which bells offer the fullest and most sophisticated development. Gongs come under this general family name, in all shapes and sizes, tuned and untuned; and sometimes tamtam is used in this same vague sense.

But in orchestral contexts, it is usual to keep the term gong for a massive instrument of varying contours and tone colourings, and *tamtam* for the particular form of gong there more ordinarily used: a moderate to large bronze-alloy plate, flat across, but having a rim (or alternatively with a slight curve increasing to the edge) and of a lesser thickness than most gongs. Tamtams for orchestral use range from some 18 in. or smaller, to 36 in. or larger, and from high sounds resembling cymbals to low sounds resembling nothing else, and of all the more value for that reason. With a soft beater used at the centre, the tamtam will yield a sort of fundamental which can almost be regarded as a note. With a hard beater at the rim, the harshness of the upper partials will confuse any definite sense of pitch, and give a tone colouring of most sinister harshness. With an average beater at a point a little from the centre, the blend of partials will be in smoother proportion, and give a tone colouring as fascinating and almost as complicated as a well-tuned bell.

A tremolo taken quietly on the tamtam builds up a warm pulsation which is effective in accompanying without disturbing an orchestral combination. Louder sounds from a tamtam are too strongly characteristic to blend in such a way; but they are very effectual, especially when built up by reiterated strokes, not heard as separate, but only as a mounting surge of sound. This reiteration is necessary for the loudest volume, which cannot be got by a single stroke however powerful. It is, however, possible to die down from this volume with an effect very appropriate to the nature of the instrument; or again, the full volume can be allowed simply to penetrate the orchestra until it dies away of its own accord. On a very large tamtam, this is an unforgettable experience, and by far the most potent orchestral use to which the tamtam can be put.

Bowls have been much used in the Orient, having sonorities which may be both clear and pitched by reason of the air contained. *Musical glasses* tuned by the amount of water in them, and played by the friction of the wet finger, were once a fashion in Western society. Small *bells* have entered into the orchestra on various occasions; the singularity of their acoustic behaviour fits them rather ill for a symphonic environment, and steel bars or tubular bells (not strictly bells at all) have tended to serve for them instead. Handel in *Saul*, and Mozart in *The Magic Flute* for Papageno's bells used a very small carillon of actual bells with keyboard, then passing by the name of glockenspiel; and certainly bells had quite a considerable place in medieval music. But on the other hand, when Musorgsky wanted the sonority of very large bells in his *Boris Godounov*, he used quite cunning means to imitate it in the orchestra without introducing the confusion which actual bells would have entailed, to say nothing of the impossible size, weight, trouble and expense. The bells cast for Meyerbeer's *Les Huguenots* at the Paris Opéra are neither very big nor very deep, and can only seem so at all by reason of their multiple partials, conflicting as these do with the much more regular partials in the orchestra; and this conflict does not sound at all comfortable itself. Tubular bells, of which the partials are to a normal extent periodic, are very much the preferred solution.

The art of casting well-tuned bells is ancient, traditional, and very largely intuitive, though science has now an exacter part in it. There must be an adequate weight of metal, distributed around the bell in very just proportions. Fine tuning is achieved by skimming (for sharpening) or loading (for flattening) the metal – again at places very nicely determined. When well tuned, a bell actually spans three octaves across its first ten partials: two more than are found within that span of a harmonic series. So far from the lowest partial providing a funda-mental heard as the pitch of the note, this pitch is perceived as being an octave above its first partial, i.e. an octave below its fifth partial, called the strike tone because of this effect of being the perceived pitch. The first partial itself, which is not heard as a fundamental at the perceived pitch of the bell, is called the hum tone; and the art, at least on the English methods of bell founding, is to get it justly to the octave below the strike tone.

The sweetest-tuned bells are got by removing metal so as to bring this inharmonic series of partials into as harmonic a relationship, at least on some of the lower partials, as the acoustic nature of the case allows. Unintentional loading or unevenness in the distribution of the metal sets up nearly but not quite identical series of partials from which unpleasant beats may result. But however set up and adjusted such partials vary in their degree of damping, not only from partial to partial at any given moment, but from moment to moment for any given par-tial. Unlike the harmonic vibrations of a bowed string or a bowed pipe (whose energy keeps them so by being maintained), the vibrations of a bell oscillate more or less independently of one another (so that they do not of their own accord form a harmonic relationship, and can only up to a point be induced to do so by the bell founder).

And that is the basic character of the bell. It is this unusual combina-tion of harmonic and inharmonic partials which adds up to that beauti-ful yet somehow eerie flow. The strange hummings and throbbings of the bells as their pulsations mingle are not quite of our ordinary world of music, which is perhaps why Europe and America have used great carillons with keyboards and pedals for tunes and harmony, but some-how in England we prefer the honourable and complicated skill of change-ringing. It has little to do with the ordinary communications of music; but to hear a fine peal across the fields of an English countryside as the ringers hunt through is a music of its own which we should not willingly abandon.

Tubular bells are not particularly harmonic in their partials either; but they set up enough for the orchestra to reinforce, and blend in reasonably well. They do not in fact sound at all like bells; but they are a very valuable addition to that sort of lightly ringing sonority which is more warmly served by the vibraphone and to some extent by the glockenspiel and (but differently again) by the celesta. Mingling the contrasts between these related sonorities can be remarkably agreeable. Ringing the changes, one might be tempted to put it; but it is a valid contribution. The part of a very large gong or tamtam (as in Mahler's *Lied von der Erde*) has also been given in some orchestras to a tubular instrument of great height and girth, mounted by itself on an upright stand. All the tubular bells are played with a more or less softly covered beater, unless an exceptionally tinny sonority is desired from a metallic beater. The stroke is made at the top edge of the tube, and must be quite accurate, so that the player must memorize enough of his part to watch his tube as it swings in its sling under the impact. The regular set has plated brass tubes of uniform diameter and graded lengths, the diatonic notes to the front and the chromatic notes to the back. There are dampers operated by a pedal. The standard range, notated at sounding pitch, is from c' to f''. Diatonic glissandos and a number of other special effects are possible, but the main value of the instrument lies in its simple chimes.

DRUMS AND TAMBOURINES

Drums with single or double heads of vellum or comparable material remain the most central category of percussion. Whether unpitched or pitched, they carry primeval associations of unsurpassed suggestiveness, and from the symphonic orchestra to the avant-garde retain their ancient power. The best of them combine definite pitch with great charm of tone colouring; the least has some special touch of timbre and of rhythm to contribute. Their contemporary use (including jazz) extends far beyond their traditional use in Western orchestras; but the kettledrums at least have been involved for so long as the trumpets have, and side drums (snare drums) and bass drums are almost equally symphonic. The medieval crusades brought some of our drums to Europe; and there has been a recent invasion of many Oriental or Latin-American forms.

Tom-toms in many sizes, cylindrical, chiefly double-headed but also single-headed, cover a wide range of pitches, generally indefinite; but they can be tuned to sound quite definite with soft beaters, and their relatively neutral colouring can then be matched with kettledrums above the range of those. *Bongos*, also cylindrical, are grouped in pairs or threes, single-headed, small, tightly tensioned, and decidedly aggressive in their tone colouring, unless used with the fingers and palms for delicate effect. *Congas* or *tumbas* share these characteristics in a much deeper shape, the heads being often very tight and thick: the pitch is also deeper and the tone colouring darker; playing with the fingers and palms is particularly favoured. But *timbales* are relatively shallow, with high rims, metal shells and indeed a somewhat metallic tone colouring: they are to be played with light wooden sticks for their sharper sounds, but in different qualities according to the point of contact (including the rims or shells); variety is their speciality, though they may also fit in with bongas and congas as an intermediate pair. In all such drums, the permutations and variations are half the effect, and the subtleties of pitch and timbre are almost unlimited.

The *tambourine* came into quite limited orchestral use along with other 'Turkish music' in the late eighteenth century. It is a little single-headed, open-ended drum with a shallow circular frame, into which small, circular metal jingles are loosely mounted so as to tinkle or clatter when the instrument is struck across the knee, beaten with the knuckles or the palm, tapped with the fingers, rubbed with the moistened thumb, or merely shaken more or less vigorously in the air. There are also variants with no jingles; but it is these which give such surprising diversity and interest to the normal tambourine, which has them.

The *tabor* is a double-ended drum of small to moderate size of which the traditional manner of fastening the skins is by ropes or thongs threaded through the edges, and tightened or slackened to give variable tensions and pitches. There was an ancient association, renewed in our revival of folk dancing, of the pipe and tabor; and altogether, tabors and other fairly small drums (more or less definite in pitch) were necessary for good rhythm in Renaissance dance bands, their parts being improvised along familiar patterns. A single stick is used for the tabor; but *nakers*, which are small kettledrums, and many varieties of side drum, use two sticks and a more versatile technique. Sometimes, but not always, drums of most kinds were fitted with snares: strings or wires stretched across the lower head so as to buzz forcibly against the parchment when the upper or batter head is beaten.

Our orchestral *tenor drum* is a double-ended side drum of moderate diameter but considerable depth, normally used with felt-covered beaters of some firmness, and giving, at a low but indefinite pitch, a tone colouring notable for its sombre suggestiveness, particularly when rolled. Our *side drum*, now going by that name, is similar but less in depth, and it is habitually fitted with snares, from which indeed it derives its characteristic snarl, and its alternative name of snare drum. Its technique is also very characteristic, with two hard, small-headed wooden sticks used for the roll not alternately, but rebounding twice in turn. The skill to do this fast enough and steadily enough can only be acquired by great practice; but it is astonishingly penetrating at loud volume and delicate at soft, the sound of the strokes merging into a curious purring not to be produced by any other means. There are also a number of short, sharp ornaments, in particular the flam (an anticipatory grace-note), the drag (two such), the ruff (three such), and the short roll (or tremolo). These and the paradiddle and reversed paradiddle (rebounding strokes) give a stylishness to the technique which immeasurably enhances its effectiveness, as the performer knows well even if the composer does not (but of course he most certainly should). They are not by any means confined to the side drums, but have a very wide application to the percussion generally. Only the kettledrums keep their own technique somewhat apart, and their own idioms, to which a pecular dignity and restraint is apposite.

The *kettledrums* are enlarged and refined representatives of the ancient nakers, always warlike and aristocratic in their connections, and by the Renaissance the privileged instruments of courtly drummers. Lesser musicians had no right to them; for the kettledrummers were members of the same guilds as the trumpeters, and shared their special conditions of apprenticeship and employment. Their skills, too, were not public knowledge, but secretly and solemnly imparted. Like the trumpeters, they did their work for the most part improvising, within conventions strictly established but flexible in detail. So beautifully tuneful are the kettledrums that the bass line of the trumpet harmony could safely be entrusted to them. Their position in the symphonic orchestra became more intimate than that of any other percussion, and they justify this position by their extraordinary power of suffusing the orchestra as much with pulsing colour as with rhythmic impetus. Their loud is forceful enough to need considerable discretion, their soft is gentle enough for the quietest passages, and their crescendo and diminuendo can match to any gradient, both in their separate strokes and still more in the roll. They can sound as well alone as in combination, and within their limits of range and idiom are as expressive as a composer knows how to require of them.

In construction, the kettledrums (timpani) are large, single-head drums of variable but considerable diameter, having almost hemispherical shells of brass or copper, and possessing since the seventeenth century screws or other accurate devices for altering the tension of the vellum to different pitches. Fine calf skins are traditional, but generally replaced now, as with most other drums, by very reliable plastic material. The sizes may range from 32 in. upwards: the full standard complement, however, runs 30 in. (*E* flat to *A*), 28 in. (*F* to *c*), 25 in. (*B* flat to *f*), 23 in. (*d* to *g* sharp), with a note or two more at either extreme if required, and sometimes a small drum (piccolo timpano) for *f* to *c'*, though if such high notes are really needed, tomtoms will do them better. No one kettledrum sounds well over more different pitches than those a fifth apart. Two at 28 in. and 25 in. (in all *F* to *f*) will commonly suffice, or three of which the third may be either 30 in. or 23 in. Four are not very often essential, but can ordinarily be relied upon if required.

Setting up the timpani before the music starts is no great problem; but when it modulates, the timpanist may have to modulate as well, re-tuning one or more of his drums to the note next required. With hand-screws standing at intervals around the rim, this took, with the greatest skill, a certain time, being done as silently as possible against the orchestra – perhaps ten seconds if the new pitch was far removed; and the composer had to allow sufficiently for this situation, which may still occur in amateur conditions. Professional timpanists nowadays will expect to be provided with machine drums, on which either one master-screw (sometimes by turning the drum itself) or a pedal-operated mechanism (pedal drum) will do the work immediately, often with a tuning-gauge to show when the required new pitch is reached. With machine drums, continuous chromatic passages are possible, and also glissandos with or without a roll to keep up the sound. Yet with all these modern conveniences, it still remains true that the most effective passages are those composed with something of the older technique in mind, since notes well placed at a certain distance apart will sound much more distinct and natural on the timps than rapid progressions of a close or chromatic succession. Clear as they are for pitch (excepting in the lower registers) the notes stand out much more clearly if they are not set too closely upon one another. Kettledrum sticks are covered with piano felt varying from soft through medium to hard for different qualities of tone, but wooden sticks are occasionally requested. A bigger, slacker head sounds different from a smaller, tighter head for the same note; the point of contact (normally some three to four inches in from the rim) has some useful influence; the player's practised skill by far the most.

The *bass drum* is the remaining percussive element on a regular footing in the symphonic orchestra. It is a very wide and moderately deep cylinder of varying proportions, commonly with a double head, less often with a single head. Single or reiterated strokes at one or either end have an explosive violence not often required in any great loudness; but tremolandos with one kettledrum or similarly felted stick at either end at once can be quite phenomenally disturbing, at a level of perception which seems somehow almost more subliminal than aural. You become aware of a vibrant power seeming to be more in your bones than in your ears; and so indeed perhaps it really is. No scoring gives a greater feeling of finality, as if the ultimate is happening and there is nothing you can do but submit to it. The timps for beauty and precision, indeed; but the bass drum for the last deep thrill among all instruments of percussion.

17 THE ORGAN

THE ORGAN AS MACHINE AND INSTRUMENT

The organ is an instrument capable of such different forms that we have first to ask what is common to them, and next to take a sampling from the many variations.

What is common to any organ is that it is a means of sustaining a pressure of air beyond the capacity of the human lungs, and of directing it selectively by keyboard and other mechanisms towards an array of pipes ranging from few and simple to many and complicated. Thus even a small organ has to some extent, and a big organ has to a great extent, the character of a machine: more so than any other means of organizing musical sounds with the exception of electronic apparatus. Yet the ends to which such mechanical means are directed remain human ends. The organ is the servant, the organist the master; and a very expressive relationship he can make of it when the cirumstances are favourable.

It is part of the organ's variability that it can use both the two basic methods of exciting vibrations in a resonant air column: edge tone, for flue pipes; and reed tone, for reed pipes. Small or moderate organs may have only flue pipes or only (less often) reed pipes; reeds may sometimes have curtailed or miniature pipes (as in the regals or in certain organ stops) or even none (as in the harmonium). But some small organs, many moderate organs and all large organs have both flues and reeds of varied scale and voicing, giving different tone qualities and attacks, these resources usually being available both separately and combined.

Different ranks may also stand at different registers of pitch. The standard register is the 8-foot, so called from the length of pipe basically required to sound its bottom *C*. One octave down requires the 16-foot; two octaves down requires the 32-foot (not unusual though less frequent); three octaves down requires the 64-foot (very unusual indeed and of very doubtful value acoustically). One octave up requires the 4-foot; two octaves up requires the 2-foot; and there are fractions such as 5$\frac{1}{3}$-foot for a fifth up, 3$\frac{1}{5}$-foot for a tenth up, 2$\frac{2}{3}$-foot for a twelfth up or 1$\frac{1}{3}$-foot for a nineteenth up, valuable in particular to reinforce selected harmonics as tone colouring in mixtures which may often be very striking and indeed conspicuous. It is also not unusual to simulate the sounds of very long pipes by using the difference tones between two ranks of shorter pipes. Those stops of which the pitch does not accord with the note whose key is pressed, but sounds at a fifth, a third or other interval, may be called mutation stops. And those stops which sound one or more pitches in addition to that which accords with the note whose key is pressed, are known as mixture stops.

Pipes narrow in proportion to their length favour higher harmonics, for a brilliant colouring; pipes wide in proportion to their length favour lower harmonics, for a sober colouring. Edge tone gives to flue pipes less tendency towards higher harmonics and brighter colouring than reed tone gives to reed pipes. A stopped end may drop the pitch an octave. Open pipes may sound an octave up, at the second harmonic, if the exciting tone is caused to overblow; and stopped pipes may sound a twelfth up, at the third harmonic. Reed pipes are mostly conical; if they are made cylindrical, the pitch may drop an octave. The voicing of the exciting tone can be made more forward, for a keener attack favouring higher harmonics and a more fiery colouring; or less forward, for a smoother attack favouring lower harmonics and a milder colouring.

Again, different organs work on different pressures of wind, ranging from low to moderate (in all ordinary conditions) if the pumping is by manpower, as once used to be the case; but frequently (though not necessarily) reaching much higher if the pumping is by machine-power, as is now ordinarily to be expected. The effect of different air pressures upon the attack, the tone colouring, the volume and even the pitch can be absolutely crucial; and it is one of the main distinctions between the classical organ and the romantic organ that wind is supplied basically at so much lower pressures to the classical pipework, and at so much higher pressures to the romantic. This became possible not only through the powered supply of air, but also through powered aids to bringing down the keys against the resistance built up by wind going at high pressures to numerous pipes.

There are many further recourses for modifying the behaviour either of the exciting tone which initiates vibration in the pipes, or of the resonant tone with which the pipes respond; and in effect that always involves both, since there is invariably feedback in some manner and degree between both these partners in the coupled acoustic system, to say nothing of the acoustics of the building and of the ear itself. Even the material used for pipes possibly affects the harmonic spectrum: wood or metal of varying hardness and smoothness and at varying thickness, including the different alloys into which metals can be fused in varying proportions. Every factor, in every combination, which affects the acoustic consequences, adds to the variability of which the organ is capable.

To bring such diversity of resources within the organist's control requires machinery of corresponding complexity; and this is a factor in the development of the organ which has both positive and negative implications. It is in itself a gain to increase the choice of suitable effects; but it is a loss to do so at the cost of putting a greater barrier between the player and the sound. An organist cannot ever make his sound with quite that sense of immediacy which most instrumentalists enjoy in some degree, and singers in the highest degree. The simple, unassisted tracker actions found in early organs certainly let him feel that he is opening the pipes himself, though his physical influence on the way they open may not be very great. Power-assisted actions remove that influence entirely: the organist may feel that he is telling the machinery to open the pipes rather than opening them himself. The link is just that much more impersonal.

Any subsidiary machinery by which stops are operated and colourings are selected adds to this impediment, not seriously in relatively simple organs, but increasingly as mechanical devices multiply. Particularly is this the case with devices for making dynamic accents and fluctuation of volume such as do not arise from the basic nature of the organ. But in truth there have been very different ideals of what organs and organ music should be; and for this reason it becomes correspondingly important to suit the choice of instrument to the music, and not the music to the instrument. In any event, no organ can be better than its organist. The manner in which an organist approaches his formidable partner affects his expression all the more because it must be transmitted through so much machinery. Our revival of baroque-style organ building and restoration would have had no success if we did not have the organists with the baroque technique and understanding to insist on it. Bless them, they do.

The basis of any organ technique concerns the joining and separation of notes. There is no equivalent on the organ to the damper-raising or sustaining pedal on the piano. If notes are to be joined or to overlap, it is the organist who must hold them down by touch, and much of his training is directed to a fine skill in doing so. But conversely, there is little or no direct equivalent on the organ to the dynamic accents and nuances of volume which the piano can produce by touch alone, and most other instruments by some form of expressive manipulation within reach of muscular as opposed to mechanical control. If notes are to be articulated and phrased on the organ, it is the separations between them which must suggest whatever is lacking in the way of dynamic accents and nuances.

The entire individuality of the organ as an instrument is linked with its distinctive character as a machine. It derives from this character a certain steadiness not obtainable elsewhere, except electronically, and only approached to some extent by the harpsichord. The steadiness of organ sound may come across to us as tranquillity, or as forcefulness, or even, if that is the prevailing mood of composer or performer, as ruthlessness. The flow of organ sound is potentially unceasing, and it is for the organist to relieve and to mould that flow by his phrasing and his articulation. Nevertheless it is in the nature of organ sound to flow. That is why the devices of the romantic organ for producing flexible dynamics indirectly may represent in some measure a denaturing of this noble instrument. They are certainly impressive, but it is less certain that they are genuinely expressive. Perhaps they are so, however, for their own music; and that is, after all, the only relevant point at issue.

If an organist, either lacking such devices for dynamic flexibility or choosing to ignore them, relies on his own phrasing and articulation to shape the line, and if he changes his stops and his registration pretty much in the old baroque way where breaks of sense in the music itself make it convenient and convincing, then he is doing what the basic nature of the organ most invites. The line is patterned and divided: we are not just being drowned (as we all too easily can be) in an unremitting flood of sound; but we are being carried forward very firmly, and without arbitrary distraction, from landmark to landmark, so that when we do arrive at a change of volume or of colouring, it is all the more telling for not having happened too soon.

The same considerations apply in some degree to the harpsichord, which unlike the organ has an evanescent tone, but is scarcely more responsive dynamically to the touch. It can have that same fine effect of carrying us along reliably, changing registration not just for the sake of surprising us but rather for genuine reasons in the structure of the music. Of course the music should always be the deciding factor, and there are good as well as bad uses for clever registration. But the finest of all harpsichord music is probably that which plots itself into contiguous areas of sound and does not call for or tolerate too many or too wayward contrasts. And still more so may this be the case with the earlier schools of organ music.

The romantic schools of organ music have their own different requirements, and entail different machinery for effecting them. Showmanship is often the better part of musicianship here; and even in baroque organ music, showmanship has its due and proper place. J. S. Bach putting a big baroque church organ through its paces was not reticent; both as composer and as performer, he knew how to carry virtuosity to the limit. Any but a very small organ, whose charm lies rather in its elegance and its piquancy, gives something of the authentic thrill of power that machinery suggests; and there is in general no reason to refrain from using the full resources of a big organ. It is only important to use them appropriately for the music in hand.

Certain departments of a big organ will be designed to resemble solo and orchestral instruments, and be labelled correspondingly. Narrow pipes can be given a harmonic spectrum resembling the strings; broad pipes can be given a harmonic spectrum resembling the heavy brass; and many other such resemblances can be established by various recourses. But the ear, though it may be very well satisfied, cannot be deceived. The onset transients would alone be sufficient to make clear the difference; the steady state, though similar, cannot be the same; the decay is again unmistakably distinct. So wide and so eloquent is the range of actual organ attacks and colourings that no such comparison can do them any flattery. And always it is the steady state at which the organ excels. It is that characteristic impression of steadiness which does most to give the organ its distinction and its individuality.

ORGANS DOWN TO THE BAROQUE

Big organs include great variety within themselves; but also there are many varieties of organ big and small.

The organs of Greek and Roman and also of Byzantine antiquity included a variety called *hydraulis*, *water organ*, from a device for steadying the air pressure by means of water pressure maintained by gravity. There might be different ranks of pipes, and a probably very efficient keyboard action. The keyboard was subsequently lost, being replaced by a much less delicate system of sliders. By the twelfth century, the keyboard reappeared, but in a large and relatively crude design for big church organs intended to be powerful rather than refined.

The big *church organs* of the middle ages may have had multiple ranks of pipes, but no devices for separating the ranks in order to play on them individually. When a slider was pulled or a note of the keyboard was pressed down, all pipes relating to that note came into play together. The air pressure thereby supplied to them (by the muscles of as many men as were needed) added up to so heavy a resistance to be overcome in order to get the key down, that no delicacy of action was possible. The full force of the fist might have to strike down, though this like other technical details remains quite problematical. The noise of such multiple ranks sounding together could not be subtle, but it may well have been loud and is likely to have been highly colourful.

The pipes thus jointly brought into operation might be of varied scaling and voicing, perhaps of different materials and probably of different proportions. They might include not only unisons but mixtures; and not only at the octave or the double-octave but also, for example, at the fifth plus one or more octaves (quint), or the third plus one or more octaves (tierce). A quint rank will reinforce the third harmonic and a tierce rank will reinforce the fifth harmonic, with potent enrichment of the colouring: the stronger the mixture, the richer the colouring, until it may become really fiery. Beyond a certain strength, however, the mixture will not be heard just as colouring, but as notes (for example, fifths) moving in parallel: an effect valued for its own sake in certain forms of medieval counterpoint and perhaps appreciated from the church organ as accompaniment or otherwise. Contemporary descriptions are unclear and prone to palpable exaggeration, but the celebrated tenth-century organ at Winchester was credited with 400 pipes, 10 to a note; with a team of 70 to blow the 26 bellows; and with a sound scarcely endurable close at hand and audible all through the town.

That would have been at the largest and noisiest extreme; but small or moderate organs might well be movable, though left normally in position (*positive organ*); while very small organs were easily carried by a strap across the shoulder, and played with one hand on a miniature keyboard while the other hand worked a tiny bellows at the back (*portative organ*). Such small organs, including the little portative, have been reconstructed in course of our medieval revival, and lack nothing for delicacy or sweetness.

The Renaissance brought development both in the use and in the mechanism of organs. At least one church organ surviving from the late Renaissance in Italy shows the medieval predilection for fiery power retained in remarkable force, the voicing being so forward as almost to blow you away; but the general disposition was already tending towards the smoother colourings and neater actions of most baroque church organs. The portative organ remained in fashion; the positive organ by then may even have exceeded it in popularity; and during the transition from medieval towards Renaissance idioms (with Landini, for example, or Dunstable or Dufay) this splendid little instrument contributed a melodic line (rather than chords) to many chamber groupings.

By the full Renaissance, we find one form of small chamber organ, the *regal* or *regals*, whose characteristic feature is having for its exciting tone a set or sets of beating reeds (i.e. as in the clarinet) to which resonating pipes, when added at all, only contribute in secondary degree, being commonly so small in proportion that they barely modify the wonderfully snarling tone of the reeds themselves by helping to pick out some of the upper harmonics. However, many sizes and modifications existed, some having pipes (wooden or metal) of more conventional proportions; and some having more stops than one. A late Renaissance and baroque variety is the *Bible Regal*, so-called from being made in the outward shape of a large book, which when unfolded reveals the hinged keyboard and tiny pipes of a true regal: looking like a toy, but sounding uncommonly assertive. Regals are among the reedy and brassy sounds used by Monteverdi for his underworld scenes in *Orfeo* (Mantua, 1607); and both in church and in the theatre, that snarl was heard. The church organ itself was given reed stops based upon and named after the regals, and this may have provided a historical impetus to the organ reeds.

Larger organs in the late Renaissance inherited or evolved a number of important modifications, which include a fully chromatic compass, multiple keyboards both manual and pedalboard; multiple ranks of pipes capable of sounding separately as well as together; couplers for joining or unjoining different keyboards (including the pedals); more varied scalings, voicings and other features of acoustic design; and with all this, actions of an excellence and delicacy quite unlike the frequent medieval grossness. The lead in these improvements was taken in North Germany, where by the late fifteenth century all the essential features found subsequently in the baroque organ were already emerging; but elsewhere, the Renaissance organ still remained relatively simple, though not for the most part so ferocious as the Italian survival mentioned above.

The baroque period was greatly attached to small and moderate organs for many chamber purposes (*chamber organ*). Throughout the seventeenth century and afterwards, a chamber organ stood in many houses of quite ordinary status and prosperity. In England, at any rate, a chamber organ was almost as common for keyboard solos and accompaniment as the small harpsichord or spinet. Much of Farnaby, Orlando Gibbons or John Bull sounds well either way; while the great English fantasies for viols often invite the chamber organ as support, and not (though the lighter consorts do) the harpsichord. There may be no more than one or perhaps two ranks of stopped wooden pipes, sweet in tone and quite appreciably responsive to fluctuations of touch, because of the simple tracker action and very light air pressure. Or several ranks of different colourings may be included. Larger specimens, while still with a certain effort portable, may be quite elaborate, resembling those admirable instruments sometimes built into the great hall of seventeenth- or eighteenth-century mansions (a few of which survive more or less intact). Handel's fine concertos for the organ are quite well served by these larger chamber organs, or equally by a small baroque church organ, such as may be found surviving in considerable numbers and in a state which if not satisfactory can be successfully restored.

The great church organs of the baroque period are now valued to the full, and where necessary are lovingly restored. There were various improvements in the apparatus for supplying the wind in sufficient strength and steadiness, always a crucial issue where the demands on air pressure are increased. Very many new variants were added to the basic open and stopped diapasons, flutes and reeds. Those unusually narrow, open flue pipes which come nearest to simulating string tone made a conspicuous appearance in the eighteenth century. A tremolo stop, agitating the wind supply with quavering effect, was a not so desirable invention, being highly liable to abuse at best: a much more satisfactory way of giving an effect of vibrato is by slightly mistuning two similar ranks of pipes to beat together; but basically any such deliberate unsteadiness seems foreign to the organ's nature. Normal beating will give quite enough of a shimmer to keep the sound alive.

Wind pressures remained on the average very low by later standards, thereby allowing quite extensive tracker actions to work as well as could be expected against the quite considerable pressure built up by any unusually full registration, and very well indeed under average conditions. Since the fingers depress the keys unaided, some stiffness is unavoidable when stops build up; but there is no substitute to equal tracker action as a means to baroque expression on the organ. Mixture stops remained extremely popular, often with decidedly raw effects of colouring, much more to our present liking than to that of a generation ago. The voicing on the whole is quite forward, less fierce than may have been favoured in previous periods, but decidedly keen to our later ears. This, too, is a baroque virtue now cordially appreciated.

The above considerations must be taken quite generally. There were many traditions in baroque organ building, as in baroque organ playing. Bach on the one hand, let us say, and Couperin on the other hand, had different styles and different expectations, yet their common ground is very apparent by contrast with the romantic organs (themselves diverse) of the nineteenth century. The baroque ideal always tended towards clarity and contrast. The basic sound is both ringing and distinctive; the colours are rather opposed than blended; the attack is positive; the dynamics are mostly maintained on well defined levels, and although the Swell box, enclosing part of the organ with movable shutters allowing moderate crescendos and diminuendos, was a baroque development, it probably took a very subsidiary role in any typically baroque situation (even some harpsichords were given a ridiculous Venetian swell – opening and shutting like a Venetian blind – in a vain attempt to keep up with that formidable rival, the early piano).

There is of course no one baroque style: there are only baroque styles. Yet all baroque styles have a common leaning towards transparency and incisiveness. The baroque organ is never an exception to that prime necessity.

THE ROMANTIC ORGAN AND SINCE

The organ of the classical period, for which Haydn wrote a concerto and Mozart seventeen sonatas, passed by stages – including the transitional excellence of Samuel Wesley and of Mendelssohn – to that very different and imposing variety, the full nineteenth-century or romantic organ.

The development of the nineteenth-century organ centred upon two tendencies closely related to one another. The first of these tendencies was to reduce the stark contrasts between one stop and another, and to multiply stops intended rather to merge imperceptibly than to stand out decisively. The second tendency was to increase air pressures to meet new demands upon the wind supply, caused by many stops of demanding capacity, working at high pressure for massive volume and opaque colouring. The heavy and laborious actions thereby resulting were by then a problem, since the valve which lets air into the pipe must be pushed open against the pressure within; and the greater that pressure, the greater the resistance to be overcome. But this problem in turn called up its own solutions, appropriate enough to the age of the industrial revolution. Pneumatic actions were devised, by which air itself under pressure was enlisted to oppose the air pressure needing to be overcome; or electric actions were later devised which supplied most of the necessary force; or some combination of the two was contrived. Unreliability was something of an obstacle, and left many nineteenth-century organists still attached to tracker action; but the designs improved and the advantages, for such organs, were decisive. The most successful actions for the purpose are very possibly electric actions, which can be very light, work instantaneously, and can be situated apart from the organ at any convenient position, including a place in the orchestra for concerted playing. The only connection needed between console and organ is a multiple electric cable.

An electric action is sometimes constructed with a double touch, so that light pressure opens a somewhat reticent stop, but firm pressure brings in another stop of stronger character: dynamic accents can thus be made, and various other special effects obtained. By a system of combination pistons, again, not only can advance preparations be made for bringing in or taking out selected stops on the instant, but sforzandos, crescendos and diminuendos can be arranged by the sudden or gradual manipulation of graded stops (rather as a harpsichordist gives an effect of louder or softer volume by increasing or decreasing the stops in operation, though the modern inclusion of pedals for that purpose is not really at all suited to the baroque harpsichord).

The lack of a sustaining pedal on the organ comparable to the damper-raising pedal on the piano is no disadvantage, since the feet can readily be used on the pedalboard to sustain a note at will (hence the terms pedal point or organ point) and other kinds of legato can be maintained by clever fingering: if anything, the fault is likely to be an excess rather than a deficiency of sostenuto. But it is remarkable how convincingly an organist can give an illusion of dynamic accentuation by the traditional recourse of taking a silence of articulation out of the note before, thus drawing attention to the note after. So long as organ keys were not and did not need to be power-assisted because wind pressures were moderate, the player might in favourable circumstances still hope to open the pallet or valve more promptly by depressing the key more smartly, thus effecting a very slight but not inappreciable accent if not too many stops were drawn. This slight recourse was lost when power-assisted action, and especially electric action, became standard. Thus a modern organ, even when it has some suitable stops and tone colourings, cannot quite do duty for a baroque organ, unless parts of it are equipped with tracker action. Completely baroque organs are, indeed, being built again: it is only necessary to keep the distinctions clear. The most radical reproductions are the most successful.

The finest achievements of the romantic organ came with the French developments throughout the nineteenth century and a little afterwards. French organ builders and French organists have tended to subordinate those solid, plain diapasons which have elsewhere been the preferred foundation, in favour of much more colourful stops of greater dramatic capabilities. There is really no musical experience quite like a brilliant organist launching himself into Widor's celebrated Toccata on an instrument fully empowered to do that masterpiece of inspired bravado justice. There is a whole school and tradition of such music and such performance: it may not be very profound but it is wonderfully exciting. There is a brazen triumph about these very large, very complicated and very mechanized romantic organs, not of course confined to the French, but representing a world apart from the average non-organist. Not until the baroque revival, perhaps, did organists and other musicians quite stand together again in mutual regard, and on the crest of that regard the romantic organ too also benefits, with the exquisite work of Messiaen doing as much as anything to bridge the gap. So treated, the organ is a humane instrument indeed.

The *harmonium*, arguably a remote or indirect descendant of the regals, is a sort of pipeless chamber organ of which the reeds are not beating but free: they do not meet a platform to close their flow of air intermittently but completely, like a clarinet, but vibrate on their own without constraint. The harmonium blows air out across its reeds. Its close relative, the *American organ*, sucks air in, and has in general a milder quality. Some variety of stops may be introduced into either of these; and in particular, there is an improved harmonium first exhibited at Paris in 1855 by Victor Mustel, and known as the *Mustel organ*, with several stops for special expression, including a tremolo produced by the beating of two slightly mistuned 2-foot ranks, one above and one below the fundamental pitch – altogether an instrument of considerable quality. The accordion, the concertina and the mouth-organ, already mentioned, are further relatives. The electronic organ will be considered in the following chapter.

18 ELECTRONICS

INTERCHANGING ELECTRIC AND ACOUSTIC SIGNALS

The flow of electrons which constitutes an electric current can serve music in various ways, all dependent upon one basic principle: the close equivalence which can be set up between electric signals and acoustic signals. An electric current can oscillate, and this is vibration. It cannot be heard; but it can be converted into acoustic vibration which can be heard. The wave forms assumed by electric oscillation can reappear as acoustic oscillation; and the wave forms assumed by acoustic oscillation can reappear as electric oscillation. It is this equivalence which permits not only the secondary uses of electricity in music, such as transmission and recording, but also the primary uses, as in the new species broadly called electrophones, and in various more or less elaborate music generators and music synthesizers.

Since conversion between electrical wave forms and acoustic wave forms can go in either direction, the initial vibration can be either. But the operative vibration, to be heard, must be acoustic, at which stage the ordinary behaviour of sound vibration in general, and of these sound vibrations in particular, must needs apply. There are no special sound waves for electronic music; there are only normal sound waves set up by electronic means. Electronic sounds, when used for the purposes of music, are musical sounds: as usual, there is no other test.

It is a secondary use of electricity in music when the initial vibration is acoustic. The source may be a traditional performance broadcast or recorded live: in this case, the closest practicable fidelity to the original is the usual intention. Neither the acoustic nor the psychological circumstances can be altogether reproduced; but nevertheless, the value of hi-fi listening can be so very great as a deliberate musical experience that it far outweighs the limitations. It also outweighs the disadvantages of not always being able to escape canned music which you do not want to hear, and of which the drug-like background influence is one of the minor irritations of modern life, as well as one of the more disquieting symptoms.

Or again the source may be more or less traditional in part, but electronic in part, as when the electric piano or the electric guitar excites vibrations in much the usual way, but gives them their resonance and amplitude not at all in the usual way. Or yet again, the source may be quite untraditional, as when random objects are explored for their sonorous potentialities with a microphone. The resulting wave forms in all these cases can be picked up, amplified, modulated, combined, stored, transmitted and in any such ways manipulated electrically, before being reproduced acoustically in the sounding cones or diaphragms of loudspeakers or headphones; and this reproduction, with or without modification, of sounds previously existing, is one of the two directions in which electricity can be used in music.

The other direction in which electricity can be used in music is not secondary, but primary, and occurs not by reproducing but by producing sounds. Here the source is not acoustic but electric. It consists of wave form oscillation generated in a considerable variety of electromagnetic, electrostatic or electronic circuits, singly or in combination, and controlled either by hand or by previously prepared instructions, such as the perforated paper rolls in one elaborate form of music synthesizer, or various codes of computer programming, some of which may further include an element of partially random selection. All manner of processing can again be applied at will; and the end product can again only appear when electrical oscillation is converted to acoustic oscillation – at which stage sound vibrations result (and can themselves provide acoustic material for further electrical processing if so desired).

It is possible to bring electrically produced or reproduced sounds into a combined texture with traditional instruments, the voice included. This can sometimes be a rather uneasy alliance; but the contrast of natural and electronic sounds can itself be made very suggestive – hinting, for example, at different planes of simultaneous experience. Electrically produced or reproduced sounds can, again, be electronically manipulated on stage as a form of live performance, with or without the presence of traditional instruments modified or unmodified. The electronic presence, however, may often be supplied on tape, and the natural presence may also be introduced by way of tape; indeed, the permutations and combinations are very considerable as between taped and live, and as between sounds modified and unmodified. The dimensions of space may sometimes be emphasized as a sort of side-commentary upon the ordinary musical dimension of time. This is commonly done by multiplying loudspeakers with different channels around the room. Moreover, some physical movement across the stage, or even around the auditorium, may sometimes be introduced; and so, too, may some divided spacings, or grouping, of live performers. Yet sound, however disposed, diversified, transformed, divided and reunited, sound is always sound, and what signifies from the point of view of music is never the sound alone, but the human communication utilizing the sound. Not just the sound and the sense: the sense in the sound.

GENERATING ELECTRONIC WAVE FORMS

Devices which generate electronic oscillation do so in a useful variety of wave forms. The simplest is substantially a sine wave, by definition a single frequency to which the response of the ear-brain system is a simple tone. Compound tones can be built up by adding simple tones, each of a single frequency: this is an additive method of obtaining complex sounds. But other oscillators are not sinusoidal: for example the type known as relaxation oscillators, which charge and discharge a capacitor or an inductor through a resistor (but this method, by charging and discharging capacitors, is itself becoming rare in oscillator design, having been largely superseded by the so-called 'chip' technology using integrators). Wave forms which are not sinusoidal may be of the form called sawtooth, producing all harmonics, but at amplitudes decreasing up the series in the ratios of $1, \frac{1}{2}, \frac{1}{3} \ldots$. Or the wave form may be triangular, producing only harmonics of odd numbering, their amplitudes decreasing as $1, \frac{1}{9}, \frac{1}{25} \ldots$; or square, with the same spectrum but more amplitude in the harmonics and therefore more brilliance of tone colouring. Other shapes yield other harmonic contents. Furthermore, there are devices which can strengthen some of the harmonics present and weaken others, either steadily or with fluctuation.

If a dense but random series of unharmonic vibrations is generated over the entire audible range, a strange, roaring hiss is produced, like the sound of a strong wind rustling through the many leaves and twigs of a dense forest. The name for this is white noise, on the analogy of white light, the components of which are all the colours of the visible spectrum combined. By means of band-pass filters, white noise can be obtained in selected bands of vibration, which are recognizably higher or lower in pitch, and when very narrow are definitely assignable to a single pitch: if low, like thunder; if high, like escaping steam; and always a little uncanny. These bands, too, can be used for tone colouring when blended with other vibrations; or they can be heard alone. The same use of filters can be applied to any compound tone, and if this is harmonic, definite frequencies can be derived from it in any desired selection which that tone includes. Low-pass filters cut off high harmonics; high-pass filters cut off low harmonics: either by rejecting or diminishing vibrations at other than the desired frequencies (band-reject filter); or by passing or favouring vibrations only at the desired frequencies (band-pass filter). In any such case, an originally wider selection of partials (harmonic or inharmonic) is reduced to a narrower selection. This type of processing to get selected frequencies is called subtractive.

There are frequency dividers for producing lower frequencies from one or more master frequencies of higher pitch, as multipliers for producing higher frequencies from master frequencies of lower pitch. Selective reinforcement can bring out certain harmonics, just as selective filtering can reduce or remove them. Octave doubling can be effected on either side of the fundamental pitch or both. Effects of echo (distinct resonance) or of reverberation (merging resonance) can be added in any desired degree. Fluctuations of pitch (frequency modulation) or of loudness (amplitude modulation) can relieve any undue tendency to monotony or to fatigue of the ear, for which purpose some form of vibrato at around 6 Hz or so is commonly desirable on notes of fair length. Both pitch and tone colouring may also be changed by a remarkable device known as a ring modulator, which accepts oscillations of two different frequencies, and produces summation and difference tones generated between them (which may be used with or without the input tones, depending on the nature of the circuits).

The very important variant factors of the envelopes surrounding steady states are the subject of further devices for controlling the rapidity and the dynamic curves of attack and decay. Stereo effects can be introduced and controlled by varying the amplitudes going to different loudspeakers on different channels. Mixers can combine two or more input signals into a single output signal. Sequencers can repeat controlling instructions in a selected order, and pass them on to further devices. In these and other ways, the choice of pitches, tone colourings, dynamics and other expressive elements can be widened to the very limits of the practicable, which in effect probably means above all the limits of the controllable. And all this has been and is being achieved within quite recent history, at a rate of change which is accelerating all the time.

ELECTRIC INSTRUMENTS

The basic principle of interchanging electric and acoustic signals was already established with Bell's invention of the electric telephone in 1876: exactly contemporaneous with Edison's invention of the acoustic gramophone, which established the possibility of storing acoustic signals for subsequent reproduction. In 1906 Cahill's *dynamophone* (also called *telharmonium*, and already patented by 1897) pioneered electronic music: it was essentially a modified (and extremely heavy) dynamo, generating sine waves by a series of toothed wheels rotated near to the poles of matching electro-magnets, to act as inductors; multiple keyboards accommodated different players, while banks of switches added harmonic generators to the fundamental note for controlling the tone colouring; and the output of all this was fed over telephone wires to receivers in a neighbouring room. An even more elaborate version was completed by 1914; but by 1915, a far simpler invention suitable for instituting electrical wave forms was in practical availability, the *valve oscillator*. For long this remained the most useful source, from which oscillations too rapid for audible frequencies might be paired to give heterodyne frequencies at the difference between the two several frequencies, these being adjustable to any desired point within the audible range.

Several instruments on this method were made between the wars, including the *keyboard-operated dynophone* which so interested Varèse during the 1930s, and the *thérémin* of which the pitch responds to the variable capacitance set up between a metal rod and the hand moving nearer or farther away. The *ondes martenot* can be played from a keyboard giving definite notes for melody (not chords); or alternatively by sliding a metal ring, worn on the right hand, along a carbon track, giving continuous pitch changes, while the left hand works switches for subsidiary filter and timbre circuits changing the tone colouring and volume; and this instrument, scored for among other composers by Messiaen, is still in current use by some active performers such as John Morton. The *trautonium* works differently, producing sawtooth waves at continuously variable pitch by feeding the output of a sweep generator directly to a thyratron, the pitch being varied by varying the resistance.

The *Hammond solovox*, though now obsolete, had a great run of popularity. It had a three-octave keyboard deriving vibrations from one master oscillator synchronized with frequency dividers, and it could be clamped to a piano on which an accompaniment could be played. The

Hammond organ, on the other hand, is a complete and very effective keyboard instrument for normal chord playing, mentioned below.

Chord-playing electrophones can have multiple oscillators or other generators, with any desired auxiliary circuits. When the electrophone is electronic, valves were common sources, now almost entirely replaced by transistors; but there can also be electro-magnetic, electrostatic and even (as in film soundtracks) photo-electric sources. A separate oscillator may serve each note separately, or twelve oscillators may serve semitone intervals with frequency dividers (or subsidiary synchronized oscillators) for octave transpositions. Further circuits may control volume, envelope or tone colouring; and there may be devices for coupling and for pre-setting. The term electronic organ should strictly imply electronic sources; but all the methods mentioned here can properly be called electric organ, and are in loose terms called electronic organ. There is generally speaking the intention to provide a close and practicable alternative to the pipe organ, cheaper to build, easier to maintain, and entirely serviceable for most or all the purposes ordinarily required.

The *electronic organ* so described is the most successful instance of imitating an existing instrument of traditional design; perhaps because the pipe organ itself is very much of a machine as well as of an instrument. Yet imitating traditional instruments is in itself a limited ambition which the electronic organ may well be thought to surpass, and which other electronic sources of sound have for the most part long ago left behind them. The virtues of electronic music as a whole lie in creating effects not available to traditional instruments. It is not that the range of basic tone colourings has been so greatly extended, since most varieties of harmonic spectrum are covered in some manner by existing instruments. But the manner of their production and combination, their envelopes, their volumes and their rapidities in performance: all this and much else has been very greatly extended.

The electronic organ is exceptional in staying (artistically although not technically) so close to tradition: but it does so with fine results, and at its best is a valuable instrument whether viewed as an ingenious substitute or as an independent creation. It has, perhaps, some qualities of both. And, of course, the pipe organ remains what it always was, a noble instrument in no way diminished by having been up to a point electronically imitated. Beyond that point, no imitation can be the same, but must justify its existence in its own right, as at best the electronic organ does.

The *Hammond electric organ* was an early instance, generating tone magnetically. A series of metal wheels, having octagonal outlines, revolve at constant but different speeds, so that their protuberances approach a permanent wound magnet the requisite number of times per second to induce electric impulses at the frequency for each note desired. Normal keyboards make the necessary contacts. Tone colouring is additive, by borrowing a variable selection out of a choice of eight partials from other notes of the scale: these partials are nearly but not quite harmonic, since the scale is set to equal temperament. In practice, the effect, though not ideal, is remarkably varied and within its built-in limitations acceptable.

The *Compton electric organ* had a much subtler method of generating wave forms electrostatically. The forms are calculated to include an unrestricted selection of accurate harmonics, and engraved physically on fixed metal disks which are scanned by rotating disks with corrugations designed to pick up electric potentials from the varied engravings facing them. Normal keyboards again make the necessary contacts. The choice of tone colourings, as on the Hammond, is controlled by stops, but is greater both for range and harmonic accuracy.

The *Baldwin organ* was strictly electronic, with transistors replacing the earlier vacuum tubes, and with frequency-dividers, tone colourings being supplied by subtraction from sawtooth waves (giving diapason quality) by means of selectable frequency filters; square waves (giving stopped-pipe quality) are also derived through further circuits. The *Allen organ* at its biggest used an individual transistor oscillator for each note of each register, very much like an individual pipe; on most models, however, some borrowing has been admitted, as it is on pipe organs. On this splendid instrument, both attack and decay are controlled to give a convincing envelope; even the pipe organ's familiar chiff can be introduced, and that slight disparity in phase and in pitch which gives such life to multiple sounds whether on the organ or in an orchestra or a choir (but see below for more recent developments). The *Conn organ* shared some of these methods on a somewhat simpler scale; and there are others such. The electronic or pipeless organ is a large and above all an evolving species, but geared now increasingly to newer ways of synthesizing music. Much of the above has been overtaken by these newer developments and is rather of historical than of topical relevance; but it is interesting how various the methods and the mechanisms are which can result more or less satisfactorily in electric instruments (electrophones).

PARTLY ELECTRIC INSTRUMENTS

Instruments of which the structure and the exciting tone are more or less traditional, but the coupled resonance is not, may often belong rather more to electronics than to acoustics. The vibrations, instead of passing to the normal bodies and cavities for gaining amplitude and tone colouring suitable for passing to the air, may be picked up electro-magnetically or electrostatically, and amplified electronically with or without modifications to the harmonic spectrum, the envelope or other characteristics.

Metal strings on pianos, guitars or (less commonly) on other string instruments can have their vibrations directly converted into electric signals. Thus the *electric piano* may have electromagnetic pick-ups over its strings, the electronic output being amplified, and modified if desired, but allowed to blend with the usual acoustic output of the frame and soundboard; or this acoustic output may more probably be suppressed by removing or damping the soundboard. The point along the string at which the pick-ups are mounted (whether by a node, by an antinode or intermediately) will affect the harmonic content just as the point at which the hammers strike affects it. Moreover, the piano may be 'prepared' by interposing screws, etc., between the strings, with dis-turbances also transmitted to the electronic pick-up; or strings with their dampers raised may be rubbed or scratched or plucked, these small sounds being likewise amplified. The *electric harpsichord* can be similarly set up and prepared, but not directly manipulated on its strings because it has (normally) no damper-raising pedal: what is usually meant is simply a small but normal harpsichord intended for electronic amplification and processing. There are also electronic simulations of the piano and the harpsichord; but these do not process any acoustic ingredient, and are in fact fully electronic.

One version of *Wurlitzer electric organ* was electronic in all respects except in having for its source of exciting tone brass reeds kept in con-tinuous vibration at low wind-pressure, but contained in soundproof material from which no sound is heard directly: each reed forms a capacitor plate of which the paired capacitor can be selected from a choice of metal screws or strips placed differently in relation to the reed, thus giving different harmonic contents including mixtures; vibrato is by phase-modulation giving fluctuations of frequency, whereas vibrato on the Allen organ might be by Doppler effect: a fluctuation of effective wavelength by turning the speakers towards and away from the listener's ear.

The *electric bass* (double-bass) can have a vestigial body with metal strings of normal length, but produces far better sounds when left com-plete with its own fine and resonant body; the lightest of fingered harmonics can come through beautifully. The *electric guitar* has achieved enormous popularity in pop and rock bands and substantial use in ensembles of the avant-garde. This, too, may appear with a vestigial body, or more satisfactorily with a normal body. As usual, the point along the string by which a pick-up is placed affects the harmonic content, on the whole harshening it if near the end and mellowing it if near the middle, but always subject to the nodes and antinodes adjacent. Sometimes a choice of pick-ups allows instant changes of tone colouring. The plucking point also retains its habitual influence.

Similar devices can pick up vibrations from the reeds of wind instruments, as in the *electric clarinet*. There are many other possibilities; but the method is perhaps yielding ground now in competition with music synthesizers or computer-controlled systems, where the sound is generated by fully electronic sources.

ELECTRONIC MUSIC

Electronics is the science and art of putting electrons into motion. The sophistication with which this can be done grows continually more remarkable, but the applications to music are not all of equal interest. There are transcriptions of traditional music for electronic sound, and there are electronic imitations of traditional sound; but these always lose something of the original individuality and usually show very doubtful compensating advantages. There are wave forms picked up from natural sources, including traditional instruments with or without electronic modification. There are electronically synthesized sounds, alone or blended with acoustic sources; but purely electronic sounds seem to hold most achievement and promise, under two distinct though potentially related categories which are now tending to merge into one: music synthesizers, and computer music.

A very celebrated instance of electronic transcription was the recording marketed as Switched-on Bach, and prepared by Walter Carlos on a Moog synthesizer in 1968. 'No combination of live instruments could achieve the clarity of texture of this recording', claims Benjamin Folkman on the record sleeve: 'at last, every note and line can be heard'. True: every background counterpoint comes into the foreground where it does not belong; and there is consequently no depth at all. Bach, being Bach, survives even this well-meant masterpiece of misplaced ingenuity; but, of course, such a method ignores the principle so often stated in this book, that in music the sound is the sense and the sense is in the sound. Meaningful transcription within compatible boundaries is not impossible, but nowhere within the boundaries of baroque music does there lie any natural compatibility with electronic sound. Only the electronic organ, in so far as it imitates the pipe organ in general and the baroque organ in particular, may come up with compatible sounds, and then only if it is a good specimen of its kind.

The success of a good electronic organ in imitating the pipe organ is not absolute, nor does this imitation represent the total achievement of the electronic organ; nevertheless, it is a valid achievement so far as it goes. Elsewhere, imitating traditional instruments electronically is not by any means the best use to which this relatively new and very powerful technology can be put. It is not very difficult to match the basic harmonic spectrum of a steady state; rather more difficult to match the envelope with its crucial variables of attack and decay. This needs elaborate auxiliary circuits to simulate at all, and then not with that unpredictable waywardness and imperfection pertaining to all traditional instruments, to say nothing of all human performers. No two notes running on traditional instruments are likely to sound just the same. The actual instrument; the pitch of the note and the register in which it lies; temperature and the humidity; the room acoustics; the player's mood – all these contribute to the variability. The relative exactness of an electronic substitute will not catch this characterful fallibility, of which the essence is that it feels natural and true to life. The imperfections are part of the character, and trying to improve them is apt to be rather a self-defeating enterprise: the more it succeeds, the more disappointing it sounds, as experience with electronic simulation has long since shown.

We neither hear nor apparently do we wish to hear perfect sounds. Mersenne in the early seventeenth century, Tartini in the eighteenth century and Helmholtz in the nineteenth century explored the unlinear or unsymmetrical responses in our ears, to which we now add the selective codings in our nervous systems. Lloyd suspected and Boyle and Taylor, Winkel, Benade and other leading acousticians confirm that not only our physiology but our psychology conditions what we experience as sound. The links of such bio-feedback are so complex and incalculable that in some measure we hear not only what we expect to hear, but what we want to hear. We have not only a margin of tolerance but a margin of preference. We can redress subjectively quite gross deficiencies and inconsistencies in the objective vibrations, hearing as complete and satisfying some incomplete and unperiodic approximation that would never pass the test under scientific measurement. Even when the sampling is further reduced by grossly inadequate transmission or reproduction, we supply for ourselves enough of what is missing to recognize and perhaps enjoy the sketchy signals. But that unintentional reduction, of course, is in no way an advantage. What does seem to be advantageous is our native ability to allow for some element of unforeseen spontaneity; and it is, of course, just here that electronic simulation is most at a loss. It is as if the psyche actually prefers its artefacts to be just that much incalculable, idiosyncratic and in a word, human.

Electronic music is far more convincing when it attempts no competition with traditional music, but finds its own idioms and its own sonorities. There is nothing that is rigid and much that is impulsive about that picking up of acoustic vibrations electronically from natural sources which next brought a historic breakthrough into electronic music. Disk recordings, blended together from variable-speed turntables into a superimposed sound, provided a method which interested Milhaud, Varèse and Hindemith; but this method could not by itself lead very far. Photo-electric sources were also tried (by Milton Babbitt, for example, as early as 1940), where acoustic vibration records corresponding patterns, of variable area or density, visually on a soundtrack. This is then run at constant speed, so that light passing through it will cause matching responses in photo-electric cells.

The electrical signals resulting can generate wave forms for direct amplification or for further processing, convertible in the usual ways to sound. Alternatively, visual patterns can be drawn by hand, without acoustic source but with acoustic output when similarly converted to sound. This photo-electric method is well exemplified in the system devised by Daphne Oram and called ORAMICS, which has the merit of offering with modest resources a freedom of control unattainable from any but the largest of voltage-controlled synthesizers; the principle of graphical input has, however, received fuller consideration only with the newer digital synthesizers, mentioned below.

Disk recordings from natural sources, including and combining casual sounds (e.g. from a railway train) and traditional instruments (e.g. a piano) were at first used for the sounds called *musique concrète* launched by Pierre Schaeffer at the Radio-diffusion-Télévision Française in 1948. The sounds were disguised (e.g. by making changes of speed and therefore of pitch, or by cutting out the onset transients) and treated as material for electronic compositions – but not entirely electronic, since the source of vibration remained acoustic. Messiaen, Boulez and Stockhausen took some passing interest, but concluded that the sources used were too restricted. Another school, started by

Herbert Eimert for the Cologne studio of the Nordwestdeutscher Rundfunk (which became the Westdeutscher Rundfunk), insisted, on the contrary, upon restricting their material to electronically generated wave forms. The rivalry was keen for some time; but the strictly electronic school, to which Stockhausen soon attached himself as something of a leader by right of talent, and to which he introduced certain severely serial procedures of composition, became gradually dominant. Rivalry has declined since some elements of *musique concrète* as well as strictly electronic material became acceptable to most composers of electronic music. The movement is very broadly based at present.

By about 1950, the tape recorder (invented in 1935 but not then generally released) provided a technique of far wider scope and versatility. Every desired source (acoustic, electronic or both) can be recorded, blended, physically cut up and spliced on sections of tape; speeded up, slowed down, reversed, electronically modified in any desired degree; and finally assembled on the single or multiple channels of a master tape. The tape, coated with minute particles of magnetic material, is given patterns by electro-magnetism from a recording head across which it is wound at constant speed; and it returns them by reverse process, through the same head, or a different head for greater fidelity and certain special effects such as synthetic echoes. The speed on replay is variable, changing both pitch and tone colouring. A single tape recorder, or better two, can produce electronic music within limits; and an American school of music for magnetic tape had some brief success with John Cage, Morton Feldman and others, followed by the tape music of Luening and Ussachevsky.

From 1955 the more elaborate equipment needed for extending the various methods of assembling electronic music was provided by a rise of studios in many countries of the world. Luciano Berio and Bruno Maderna started their Studio di Fonologia under the auspices of the Italian Radio at Milan (used by John Cage) in 1955; Tokyo, Warsaw, Munich, Eindhoven, London and Stockholm followed; Paris and Cologne continued actively; the Americans came in strongly at several centres, including the famous Columbia-Princeton Electronic Music Center at New York (used by Varèse) and others at Ann Arbor, San Francisco and the University of Illinois at Urbana. But the techniques remained laborious, depending as they did upon the painstaking recording and splicing together of very large numbers of short pieces of magnetic tape, with many problems for the composer in envisaging results only partially audible during the intermediate stages.

It was at this point that two further techniques began to become more important, and soon to dominate the electronic scene: music synthesizers and computer music. By a music synthesizer is meant an assembly of electronic components together capable of generating wave forms and processing them, on their way to amplification and eventual dissemination as acoustic vibration. The first appliance of major importance for synthesizing music was acquired in 1959 by Columbia University, New York: the R.C.A synthesizer, Mark II (in essentials the same machine as the experimental Mark I of 1955). This had been developed by Harry Olsen and Herbert Belar, and further researched, modified and expanded by Otto Luening, Vladimir Ussachevsky and Milton Babbitt, of whom Babbitt has been the most adventurous. The R.C.A. synthesizer is a room-sized appliance of great historical significance, later succeeded rather than superseded by smaller and more accessible appliances. Instructions are imparted to the R.C.A. synthesizer by perforations punched in a continuous roll of paper (shades of the player-piano!) and executed by circuits generating oscillations within the audible range of frequencies. These circuits are geared to the chromatic scale in equal temperament; but there is also control of a vast range of auxiliary characteristics which include volumes, durations, tone colourings and envelopes.

Since 1966 small but potent music synthesizers have been available commercially. The Moog and the Buchla set two practicable patterns. These were designed for producing tapes, to be built up by stages, and performed on tape recorders; but later developments have put the music synthesizer itself on to the concert platform as a chordal instrument for live performance. Rock ensembles have fastened on to this in a big way, and avant-garde ensembles have found a place for it. But there are limitations in the simpler and less expensive versions which only a greater elaboration and sophistication of added circuits can remedy.

The key principles in the modern synthesizer are first to combine several circuits for generating and processing electronic wave forms into compound units (these circuits are known as modules); second to link such modules so that one influences another by a system of voltage control. Instructions pass from point to point in the shape of steps of electronic pressure: that is to say, of voltage. It was the development of voltage control which allowed such compact and varied packaging; but voltage control is more autonomous than human control, and while it makes appliances cheaper and results easier, it also encourages mechanical routines which the more serious users of electronic circuitry go to great lengths to circumvent.

Much of the automatic control for music synthesizers is set up in sequencers, which are devices generating wave forms not for conversion into sound waves, but for transmission to other circuits as control signals. The wave form conditions the signals, but repetitively with each of its own recurrences. The more control is left to the sequencers, the swifter, but also the more autonomous, the processing; and it becomes a balance of advantages just how much to build in as blocks of instruction, and how much to reserve for selective manipulation. Very elaborate sequencers are more expensive, but allow for greater flexibility and human choice. Thus commercial synthesizers designed for economical production impose restrictions which custom-built systems in professional studios can very largely avoid. But always the central issue of electronic music remains: how far, and by what means direct or indirect, can the man communicate with the machine?

Knob-twisting and tape-splicing have great advantages; but the most recent approach to the perennial problem of control has now been carried very far indeed and shows no signs of slowing down. This is to synthesize music, not directly, but through instructions given to a digital computer, whose numerical calculations are then imparted by way of a digital-to-analogue converter. They are imparted as instructions to analogue circuits for synthesizing and processing wave forms, whose end product after amplification is acoustic vibration. Digital in this connection means operating by distinct items of information, whereas analogue means operating by continuous patterns of information. Numbers are digits, but wave forms are analogues. There are analogue computers as well as digital computers. But for computing instructions which cover, at least potentially, every parameter of any analysable sound, the digital method has the overall advantage.

At least 20,000 individual pulsations are required for each second of music resulting, if the information is to be adequately detailed and exact, and the acoustic output faithful and interesting. Not even the speediest computer can keep up with that except by drawing upon blocks of previously computed material stored in an ample memory space. It is possible with such assistance to achieve real-time synthesizing, by which the music can actually be heard emerging from the instructions at playing speed. The more assistance from previously computed material, the less immediate control of the synthesis. Progress is fantastic in this field, however, and digital techniques combined ever more intimately with synthesizing techniques are in the front line of development. There is, for example, the very advanced Allen computer organ, which relies on large scale integrated micro-circuits for conveying digitally encoded information in wave forms scanned and decoded as analogue pressure functions.

For electronic composition, on the other hand, as opposed to computer control of electronic performance, digital techniques afford the advantage of great accuracy; but they also raise problems of communication between composer and machine which are just as considerable as the opportunities are open-ended. The opportunities, like other computer potentialities, are in theory of unrestricted complexity. In practice, there has to be a balance between a versatility too complicated to control, and a supply of previously computed blocks of information already controlled. The more the composer can hear his emerging material as he goes along, the better the mutual feedback; but it is of the essence of digital computing that he has to prepare each set of instructions beforehand in language that the computer can accept.

And so we are brought back in this newest of electronic music to the oldest of artistic considerations: communication. There is this interface of man and machine, open-ended on the technical dimension, problematic on the human dimension. For how far can man and machine communicate? They are different in kind, and no improvement in systems can affect this difference. An electronic system can, on the one hand, be made to be more sensitively controlled, and it can, on the other hand, be got to give prompter and fuller information about the state of play, thus enabling the controller to introduce further instruction and receive further information. That is the interface, and very remarkable the results of such combined operations can be, both for analysing and for synthesizing acoustic compounds.

But any question as to which is servant and which is master has no real meaning. The entire exercise is man-made, including any apparatus for calculating statistical probabilities and in that way coming up with combinations to which, in a certain intermediate sense, the term random can be applied. There is nothing random about communication in the purposeful sense, however; and these combinations and others are chiefly useful to a composer in bringing to his attention, and rendering available to him, possibilities for sonority and manipulation which from their complexity would otherwise escape him. What he makes of them remains his own affair; and this applies to all the electronic possibilities and all the acoustic possibilities that ever there were.

Machinery always is the tool which extends the range of man's hands and man's will to further possibilities. It is something of a platitude how vastly machinery has served our convenience and increased our comfort, yet at how serious a hazard to our individuality. It is not so easy to be a person in your own right when the world around you is organized on a machine-sized scale. So much of the daily round for so many people involves mainly trivial responses, contributing to mass production in a mass society but not in themselves interesting or meaningful. But to lack a meaning leaves a man more desperate at heart than he may in the least suspect. He simply feels all wrong with things, and never contented with what does come his way. The anger, fully justified on this account, of which he does not suspect the cause, may exacerbate his practical disputes and grievances to the point at which concessions in money never can assuage them, since these concessions are standing in for but cannot satisfy the deeper need to find a meaning somewhere. Whatever brings meaning brings value. Music brings meaning.

MUSIC AS MEANING

Music brings meaning because music has meaning, if only in showing examples of order and purpose achieved from the emotionally indifferent properties of inanimate matter. What art has to show, man has brought about: such things can be; and this is to say the least of it encouraging. But there is a broader satisfaction in the work of art itself. We may hear, let us say, a symphony each least and greatest part of which relates to each other part by links and derivations and symmetries and contrasts of the loveliest inspiration, craftsmanship and felicity. We take it in with growing recognition; we return to it for fuller acquaintance; we assimilate it eventually with a comprehension almost equal and certainly parallel to the composer's.

It is also parallel to life. Explain it how we may, there is a correspondence although not an identity between the patterns of music and the feelings and intuitions which condition our ordinary living. Love and hate; hope and fear; courage and despair; conflict and resolution and eventual reconciliation if we can face up with enough hard-won awareness and acceptance to the somewhat exacting conditions of being mortal and human: such as these are the archetypal themes on which we play out our many personal variations. Music is not the same as these experiences, and does not directly represent them. But music can take us through some sort of an *as if* representation of our human states. Drama unfolds in us as we listen: not literally, still less verbally, but analogously. The music is the analogue to which our feelings and our intuitions line up.

And then indeed that deep and familiar satisfaction comes over us which great music in a fine performance brings. We ask no questions and we spin no theories, but we have no doubt about it that this is a valuable encounter. It is an encounter with something valid in ourselves which is also valid for other people. Such music is itself a specimen of reality which does add up, and which gathers beauty – shall we say – on Keats' famous principle that beauty is truth, truth beauty? The music is meaningful because the music is for real. Music is life-enhancing because music has to do with life. There are sensuous rewards, of course, and not confined to smooth sonorities but including harsh contrasts by which the complex nature of our living can find expression. But this, too, is for real. Life itself is bitter-sweet, and it is a poor music which paints it all sweet – or, for that matter, all bitter. The patterns through which music runs in parallel to life must needs be various, as indeed they are. It takes all sorts to make a world, and a good many sorts to make up the world of modern music.

Much of our modern music is explosive and fragmentary: so are our times, and it is well for our composers to have the courage of our times. Some of our music, again, is severely mathematical, as if in defence against disruptive hazards: these hazards all too obviously exist. Some of our music, on the contrary, seeks chance or aleatory escape-routes to liberation: escaping from the sheer pressure of conformity to collective standards is certainly a topical issue. On the darker side, there is a cult of psychodelic music for those whose way of escape is into hallucination. More constructively, there is much child-like exploration of the acoustic elements, as if in some needful longing to learn our beginnings afresh, and to play around with our new electronic potentialities. But play can be creative, as music can; and part of that creativeness may come from the very fact that music can be meaningful without having to be explained.

Electronic music draws human meaning from a region of physics far from the usual channels of our humane studies, and is perhaps all the more attractive to us on that account. But all music turns physical acoustics to human meaning. It is not the electronics nor the acoustics from which the meaning comes; it comes from musicians having put it there. Traditional instruments and idioms serve it as well as ever, and have been returning to good repute recently with the younger generation. Electronic techniques and idioms renew it without fundamentally changing it, since new matter is not on offer in this objective universe of ours, but only new manipulations; and we who do the manipulating change but little and slowly down the generations. Some of our electronic manipulations are new indeed; but this perhaps shows more in the manner than in the matter of performance.

It is new to be in command of such fantastic contrasts of rapidity, volume, timbre and pitch: none of them in principle unprecedented, but certainly unprecedented in such combinations and at such extremes. Again, it is new so to separate the physical effort of performance from its audible effect. Knobs and tapes do not require anything like that physical dexterity and energy which all traditional instruments in a measure require, so that music has always shared some of the bodily impulsiveness of dance. Your very muscles tingle as you caress an instrument which may feel like (and in the case the voice actually is) a part of yourself. There is what would now be called bio-feedback between you and the vibration of which you are both author and recipient. Indeed there is a partnership including (by empathy if not by activity) composer, performer and listener, none of whom can enter into the full experience without personally living through something at least of that experience: an active rather than a passive participation; for just sitting in a kind of sonorous showerbath may affect your mood but will do nothing for your personality. That is another aspect of the 'as if' behaviour. You have to live through the music as if it is your own. Both body and psyche have some say in that, and perhaps it is not ultimately meaningful to consider them apart.

Then what price a music of machines? There can be no music of machines. For whatever else it may or may not be, the psyche is not a machine, and whatever else a machine may or may not have got, it has not got a psyche. Psychological communication with machines or between machines is not possible. But some sort of communication with and between machines is possible. There can be music through machines. There can be this interface of man and machine, at which we communicate mutually although not psychologically. And music can come out of that communication. There need not perhaps be too much mystery about it. There is always something of this interface of mind and matter when we use traditional instruments. There has always been bio-feedback in that familiar relationship. It is only important to remember that whether traditionally or untraditionally, and whether through acoustic channels only or through electronic and acoustic channels combined, it is always the human being behind the interface who communicates.

PITCH NOTATION

Where in this book it is not intended to specify any particular octave, plain Roman capitals are used: as in the phrase, the key of C. Whenever a specific octave is intended, the letter is italicized.

The specific octave beginning on the 32-foot organ bottom C is notated *C„* to *B„*.

The next higher octave is notated *C,* to *B,*.

The next, *C* (bottom note of violoncello) to *B*.

The next, *c* (tenor C, bottom note of viola) to *b*.

The next, *c'* (middle C) to *b'*.

The next, *c"* to *b"*.

The next, *c'''* to *b'''*.

The next, to the top note of the piano (*c^v*), is notated *c^{iv}* to *b^v*.

The following is staff and letter notation, *c'* (middle C) to *c"*:

Chromatic notes are indicated by the usual suffixes; for example:

In equal temperament, B sharp has the same pitch as C natural, C sharp as D flat, etc., and it may be convenient to notate a chromatic scale upwards, as *c'*, *c' sharp*, *d'*, *d' sharp*, *e'*, *f'*, *f' sharp*, *g'*, *g' sharp*, *a'*, *a' sharp*, *b'*, *c"*; or downwards, as *c"*, *b'*, *b' flat*, *a'*, *a' flat*, *g'*, *g' flat*, *f'*, *e'*, *e' flat*, *d'*, *d' flat*, *c'*.

STAFF NOTATION

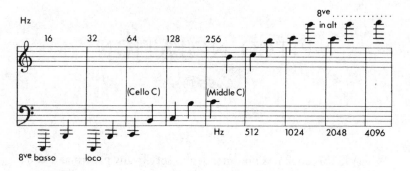

'HELMHOLTZ' NOTATION (AS USED IN THIS BOOK)

$$\begin{array}{ccccccccccccccccc} & & & & & & & & & & & & & & (c''' & b''') \\ C_{,,} & B_{,,} & C_{,} & B_{,} & C & B & c & b & c' & b' & c'' & b'' & c''' & b''' & c^{iv} & b^{iv} & c^v \\ & & & & & & & & (c^1 & b^1 & c^2 & b^2 & c^3 & b^3 & c^4 & b^4 & c^5) \end{array}$$

ENGLISH ORGAN-BUILDER'S NOTATION

CCCC BBBB CCC BBB CC BB C　B　c　b　c′　b′　c″　d″　c‴　d‴　c⁗

The notes of the harmonic series are not tempered, and can be notated only approximately as follows (the seventh, the thirteenth and the fourteenth coming out flatter and the eleventh coming out sharper than our scales require).

Fig. 28　First twenty-one harmonics of *C*

BOOK LIST

The following list shows a few selections made for various reasons, with no disparagement meant to other books from the extensive literature. Many of those mentioned have good bibliographies which can be followed up in any special directions desired. One good recommendation may in this manner be the gateway to a dozen others.

Bachmann, Walter, see Besseler.

Backus, John (1969) *The Acoustical Foundations of Music*, New York.

Baines, Anthony (1957; 3rd edn 1967) *Woodwind Instruments and their History*, London, (a classic study).

____ (ed.) (1961) *Musical Instruments through the Ages*, London.

____ (1966) *European and American Musical Instruments*, London.

____ (1976) *Brass Instruments*, London.

Barbour, J. Murray (1964) *Trumpets, Horns and Music*, Michigan.

Bartolozzi, Bruno (1967) *New Sounds for Woodwind*, tr. with additions by Reginald Smith Brindle, London (opened a new field; includes a disc recording).

Bate, Philip (1956) *The Oboe*, London.

____ (1966) *The Trumpet and Trombone*, London.

____ (1969) *The Flute*, London.

Benade, Arthur H. (1976) *Fundamentals of Musical Acoustics*, New York and London (a splendid reappraisal in depth).

Bessaraboff, Nicholas (1941) *Ancient Musical Instruments*, Boston.

Besseler, Heinrich, Schneider, Max and (since 1968) Bachmann, Walter (eds) (1961ff) *Musikgeschichte in Bildern*, Leipzig (a vast collection of pictures related to music: in progress).

Bevan, Clifford (1978) *The Tuba Family*, London.

Blades, James (1970; 2nd edn 1974) *Percussion Instruments and their History*, London.

Boyden, David D. (1965) *The History of Violin Playing from its Origins to 1761*, London (indispensable).

Boyle, Hugh, see Lloyd.

Brindle, R. Smith (1970) *Contemporary Percussion*, London (a composer's insight).

Carse, Adam (1939) *Musical Wind Instruments*, London (reprinted 1965, with introduction of great value by Himie Voxman, New York).

____ (1940; 2nd edn 1950) *The Orchestra in the XVIIIth Century*, Cambridge.

____ (1948) *The Orchestra from Beethoven to Berlioz*, Cambridge.

(All three are pioneering studies.)

Clutton, Cecil and Niland, Austin (1963; 2nd edn 1964) *The British Organ*, London.

Crane, Frederick (1972) *Extant Medieval Musical Instruments*, Iowa City (the true scholarly eye).

Critchley, M. and Henson, R. A. (1977) *Music and the Brain: Studies in the Neurology of Music*, Foreword by Sir Michael Tippet, Springfield, Ill. (important insights).

Dempster, Stuart (1979) *The Modern Trombone*, Berkeley.

Deutsch, Herbert A. (1970) *Synthesis: An introduction to the History, Theory and Practice of Electronic Music*, Port Washington, N.Y.

Donington, Robert (1963; New Version 1974) *The Interpretation of Early Music*, London (the New Version, revised and half as long again, is the definitive edition).

____ (1973) *A Performer's Guide to Baroque Music*, London.

____ (1982) *Baroque Music: Style and Performance, a Handbook*, London.

Epplesheim, Jurgen (1961) *Das Orchester in den Werken Jean-Baptiste Lullys*, Tutzing.

Fitzpatrick, Horace (1971) *The Horn and Horn-Playing . . . 1680 to 1830*, London.

Geiringer, Karl (1943; 3rd edn 1978) *Instruments in the History of Western Music*, tr. Bernard Miall, London (uneven, but a true musician's view).

Gregory, Robin (1961) *The Horn*, London.

____ (1973) *The Trombone*, London.

Griffiths, Paul (1979) *A Guide to Electronic Music*, London (especially lucid and musicianly).

Harrison, Frank and Rimmer, Joan (1964) *European Musical Instruments*, London.

Henson, R. A., see Critchley.

Hubbard, F. (1965) *Three Centuries of Harpsichord Making*, Cambridge, Mass. (an expert's vision).

Kinsky, Georg (1929) *Geschichte der Musik in Bildern*, Leipzig (captions unreliable but pictures many and valuable).

Langwill, Lyndesay G. (1965; 3rd edn 1975) *The Bassoon and Contrabassoon*, London.

Lloyd, Ll. S. and Boyle, Hugh (1963; 2nd edn 1978) *Intervals, Scales and Temperaments*, London (science and musicianship admirably combined).

Matthews, Max V. *et al.* (1969) *The Technology of Computer Music*, Cambridge, Mass. and London.

Mendel, Arthur (1978) 'Pitch in Western music since 1500: a re-examination', *Acta Musicologica*, Vol. L., Fasc. 1/11, pp. 1–93 (definitive).

Montagu, Jeremy (1976) *The World of Medieval and Renaissance Musical Instruments*, Newton Abbot, Devon.

_____ (1979) *The World of Baroque and Classical Musical Instruments*, Newton Abbot, Devon (both are general but have the real expert's excitement).

Morley-Pegge, R. (1960) *The French Horn*, London.

Munrow, David (1976) *Instruments in the Middle Ages and Renaissance*, London (the eagerness of a very fine and knowledgeable musician).

Nederveen, C. J. (1969) *Acoustical Aspects of Woodwind Instruments*, Amsterdam.

Niland, Austin, see Clutton.

Oram, Daphne (1972) *An Individual Note of Music: Sound and Electronics*, London (individual indeed).

Pincherle, Marc (1959) *Histoire illustrée de la musique*, Paris, tr. by Rollo Myers (1963) as *An Illustrated History of Music*, London (the pictures are valuable).

Read, Garder (1976) *Contemporary Instrumental Techniques*, New York.

Remnant, Mary (1978) *Musical Instruments of the West*, London.

Rendall, F. Geoffrey (1954; 2nd edn 1957) *The Clarinet*, London.

Ridley, E. A. K. (1974) *Wind Instruments of European Art Music*, London.

Rimmer, Joan, see Harrison.

Russell, Raymond (1960) *The Harpsichord and Clavichord*, Oxford.

Sachs, Curt (1940) *The History of Musical Instruments*, New York.

Schneider, Max, see Besseler.

Schott, Howard (1971) *Playing the Harpsichord*, London (glowing with musicianly insight).

Shuter-Dyson, Rosamund and Spender, Natasha (1980) 'Psychology of music', in *The New Grove Dictionary of Music and Musicians*, Vol. 15, pp. 388–427, London.

Smithers, Don. L. (1973) *The Music and History of the Baroque Trumpet before 1721*, London.

Spender, Natasha, see Shuter-Dyson.

Stubbins, W. H. (1965) *The Art of Clarinetistry: The Acoustical Mechanics of the Clarinet . . .*, Ann Arbor, Mich.

Taylor, Charles (1976) *Sounds of Music*, London (perceptively original).

_____ (1980) 'Sound' in *The New Grove Dictionary of Music and Musicians*, Vol. 17, pp. 545–63, London.

Tryhall, Gilbert (1973) *Principles and Practice of Electronic Music*, New York (unusually lucid; has disk recording).

Tyler, James (1980) *The Early Guitar*, Early Music Series 4, London.

Voxman, Himie, see Carse.

Williams, Peter (1966) *The European Organ 1450–1850*, London.

_____ (1980) *A New History of the Organ*, London (new and important).

Winternitz, Emanuel (1967; 2nd edn 1979) *Musical Instruments and their Symbolism in Western Art*, London (opened a new approach).

PS.: *The New Grove*, ed. Stanley Sadie, London, 1980 came too late for me to use in full, but see especially the articles on Acoustics, Hearing, Organ, Pitch, Psychology, Sound. (Indispensable and invaluable throughout.)

INDEX

Bold numbers for any particular instrument refer to the major entry, covering history, mechanism and playing technique.